Amicus Humoriae

Amicus Humoriae

An Anthology of Legal Humor

Compiled by

Robert M. Jarvis
Thomas E. Baker
Andrew J. McClurg

CAROLINA ACADEMIC PRESS
Durham, North Carolina

ISBN 0-89089-410-8
LCCN 2003112498

Carolina Academic Press
700 Kent Street
Durham, NC 27701
Telephone (919) 489-7486
Fax (919) 493-5668
www.cap-press.com

Printed in the United States of America

To "the junta," who never fail at being funny
—R.M.J.

To Thomas Athanasius, who always makes his father smile
—T.E.B.

To my mother, who taught me the value of laughter
—A.J.M.

Contents

III. Lawyers

IV. Judges

V. Legal Scholarship

VI. Bibliography

Foreword

Every so often, there appears in the pages of a law review an article or essay that is meant to be — and actually is — funny. Twenty-five of the best of these pieces are reprinted here. Because space limitations forced us to leave out many worthy candidates, we also have included a comprehensive bibliography. It is hoped that this approach will leave readers amused and informed.

A word should be said about our methodology. We excluded lawyer gaffes, jokes, poems, speeches, testimonials, and war stories; considered only previously-published materials, and then only if they appeared in a bar journal or law review; and gave preference to items appearing since Professor Ronald L. Brown's *Juris-Jocular: An Anthology of Modern American Legal Humor* (1989).

The original places of publication appear in the Acknowledgments. In resetting the works, we have taken the liberty of correcting obvious typographical errors.

Robert M. Jarvis
Thomas E. Baker
Andrew J. McClurg

Acknowledgments

Many people assisted us in the preparation of this book. Special recognition, however, is due to our research assistants: Todd E. Chelf, John P. Danos, Doug Giuliano, Michael Hirschkowitz, Norma Lorenzo, William J. Miller, Lindsey A. More, and Mary Trachian-Bradley. We also are grateful to the Publisher's staff, particularly Anna Kole, Kasia Krzysztoforska, and Jessie Strauss, and to Traci D. DeYorgi and Mixilinette Schultz, who provided invaluable early assistance.

Further thanks are due to the various rights holders who gave their permission to reprint the works that appear in this collection:

Anonymous, Regina v. Ojibway, 8 Criminal Law Quarterly 137–139 (1966) (authored by Stephen Breslin and Hart M. Pomerantz) (reprint permission granted by Canada Law Book Inc.)

Aside, *The Common Law Origins of the Infield Fly Rule*, 123 University of Pennsylvania Law Review 1474–1481 (1975) (authored by William S. Stevens)

Aside, *Don't Cry over Filled Milk: The Neglected Footnote Three to Carolene Products*, 136 University of Pennsylvania Law Review 1553–1566 (1988) (authored by Daniel P. Mazo)

Thomas E. Baker, *A Compendium of Clever and Amusing Law Review Writings: An Idiosyncratic Bibliography of Miscellany with in Kind Annotations Intended As a Humorous Diversion for the Gentle Reader*, 51 Drake Law Review 105–149 (2002)

C. Steven Bradford, *The Gettysburg Address as Written by Law Students Taking an Exam*, 86 Northwestern University Law Review 1094–1102 (1992)

Ronald L. Brown, *Rave Reviews: The Top Ten Law Journals of the 1990s*, 12 Legal Reference Services Quarterly 121–133 (1992) (reprint permission granted by The Haworth Press, Inc.)

Anthony D'Amato, *Minutes of the Faculty Meeting*, 1992 Brigham Young University Law Review 359–361

Wylie H. Davis, *That Balky Law Curriculum*, 21 Journal of Legal Education 300–303 (1969), originally published in the University of Georgia Advocate, May 27, 1968, at 6–7

Glen Freyer, *The Nebbish Letter*, 17 Nova Law Review 685–688 (1993)

David Eccles Hardy, *Great Cases in Utopian Law*, 6 Journal of Contemporary Law 227–230 (1979)

James L. Huffman, *Chicken Law in an Eggshell: Part III—A Dissenting Note*, 16 Environmental Law 761–773 (1986)

Robert M. Jarvis, *If Law Professors Had to Turn in Time Sheets*, 86 California Law Review 613–616 (1998)

Marianne M. Jennings, *Does Secured Transaction Mean I Have a Lien? Thoughts on Chattel Mortgages (What?) and Other Complexities of Article IX*, 17 Nova Law Review 689–704 (1993)

Erik M. Jensen, *A Call for a New Buffalo Law Scholarship*, 38 University of Kansas Law Review 433–437 (1990)

Maurice Kelman, *Is the Constitution Worth Legal Writing Credit?*, 44 Journal of Legal Education 267–272 (1994)

Ron Lansing, *Faculty Meetings: "A Quorum Plus Cramshaw"*, 17 Nova Law Review 817–823 (1993)

Paul A. LeBel and James E. Moliterno, *The Joe Isuzu Dean Search: A Guide to the Interpretation of Announcement Letters*, 39 Journal of Legal Education 265–267 (1989)

Jasper Bogus McClodd and Pepe Le Peu, *Legislative and Judicial Dynamism in Arkansas:* Poisson v. d'Avril, 22 Arkansas Law Review 724–740 (1969) (authored by Robert R. Wright, III)

Andrew J. McClurg, *Dear Employer...*, 47 Journal of Legal Education 267–269 (1997)

Andrew J. McClurg, *The World's Greatest Law Review Article*, 81 American Bar Association Journal 84–85 (October 1995)

Patrick M. McFadden, *Fundamental Principles of American Law*, 85 California Law Review 1749–1755 (1997)

Robert J. Morris, *The New (Legal) Devil's Dictionary*, 6 Journal of Contemporary Law 231–237 (1979)

William L. Prosser, *Needlemann on Mortgages*, 9 Journal of Legal Education 489–494 (1957)

Harold See, *Criteria for the Evaluation of Law School Examination Papers*, 38 Journal of Legal Education 361–362 (1988)

Gerald F. Uelmen, *Id.*, 1992 Brigham Young University Law Review 335–344

Charles Yablon, *Suing the Devil: A Guide for Practitioners*, 86 Virginia Law Review 103–115 (2000) (reprint permission granted through the Copyright Clearance Center)

I. Law Students

The Gettysburg Address as Written by Law Students Taking an Exam

C. Steven Bradford*

I. Introduction[1]

A Cameroonian proverb states that "[h]e who asks questions cannot avoid the answers,"[2] and, unfortunately, that proverb applies to law professors. At the end of each semester, law professors must endure the agony of creation that Mary Shelley's Dr. Frankenstein[3] had to experience only once in his life. We are horrified to see the monsters we have created, so different from what we intended. The joy of teaching is the constant challenge and interaction with students in the classroom; the agony of teaching is reading what some of those same students have written on their examinations.

Of course, not all law students' exams are bad. Some exam answers con-

* Associate Professor of Law, University of Nebraska College of Law. B.S. 1978, Utah State University; M.P.P. 1982, Harvard University; J.D. 1982, Harvard Law School.

Research for this article was funded in part by money I stole from my children's piggy banks. I wish to thank the many students who took my exams and made this article possible. My thanks also to my student research assistant, Debra Lepert, University of Nebraska College of Law class of 1992. She wants it made clear that she had nothing to do with the substantive content of this article, and that she was only in it for the money. I also would like to thank Richard Posner, Duncan Kennedy, Robert Bork, and Derrick Bell. They had nothing to do with this article, but I always wanted to see the four acknowleged in the same footnote. Finally, I would like to thank the articles editors of the *Northwestern University Law Review* for realizing that there is a place for humor in law reviews and for having the courage to act on that realization.

Of course, all blame for the contents of this article belongs to my parents, for raising me to be the sarcastic, cynical brat that I am.

1. This section heading is offered for the benefit of those readers who would otherwise have trouble locating the introduction.

2. Cameroonian Proverb, *reprinted in* RHODA T. TRIPP, THE INTERNATIONAL THESAURUS OF QUOTATIONS 316 (1970).

3. *See* MARY W. SHELLEY, FRANKENSTEIN (1818).

tain brilliant insights in spite of enormous time pressures. I learn much from grading such answers,[4] and I doubt that my experience is unique. A majority of exam answers are satisfactory, if not completely satisfying. These students provide no new insights, but at least demonstrate competent legal writing and an acceptable understanding of the subject matter of the course. Unfortunately, there are also those OTHER exams—the ones for which law professors earn most of their pay,[5] the ones that make grading exams such a miserable experience.[6] Those OTHER exams send law professors on early vacations and, eventually, to early retirement.[7] Those OTHER exams are often the ones indignant students bring into professors' offices the next semester, demanding to know why they did so poorly.

The grading process might be less frustrating if those OTHER exams were at least unique. Uniqueness is enjoyable, even the uniquely bad.[8] Who among us has not at some point sat transfixed by a horrid, yet entertaining, movie such as *The Attack of the Killer Tomatoes*?[9] Who among us has not turned to a friend while reading something and said, "You've got to read what this idiot said"? Who among us has not taken whipped cream and lotion and aggressively.... (Sorry, I got carried away).[10] Unfortunately, those OTHER exams are seldom original in any way. I don't know if a form book is available somewhere,[11] but students from different geographical, social, and racial backgrounds with varying interests and ideologies share common exam answer styles. Year after agonizing year, the same dreadful, torturous exam styles appear and reappear. At least ten[12] types of student answers are identifiable in those OTHER exams: (1) the Timeless; (2) the Empty; (3) the Waffler; (4) the Grammarian; (5) the Outliner; (6) the Repeater; (7) the Scholar; (8) the Avoider; (9) the Crit; and (10) the Footnoter. Each of these styles is different,

---

4. Or am I just saying that so the smart students don't get mad at me?

5. My neighbors argue that one who is required to work only six hours a week, 28 weeks a year, could not possibly earn his pay.

6. Grading exams is still not as miserable an experience as taking them or, as my wife will attest, being in a household with someone taking them. *See* MEG BRADFORD (*not* on file with the *Law Review*).

7. Contrary to popular belief, early retirement and tenure are different, although closely related, concepts.

8. *Cf.* Dan Quayle (Vice President of the United States).

9. "Tomato" is a politically incorrect term, but not, I believe, in the context in which the filmmakers used it. Vegetarians might disagree.

10. To my wife: This is a joke. There is no one else.

11. If so, it must be published by the same people who publish "canned" briefs of cases. The quality is similar.

12. There could be more than ten, but I ran out of fingers and I wrote this with my shoes on.

although some particularly inept students are capable of writing answers fitting three or more categories.

To illustrate these recurring styles, let me pose a simple hypothetical exam question. Suppose that an exam question asked law students to write the opening line of Abraham Lincoln's Gettysburg Address. The actual opening line of the Gettysburg Address is: "Four score and seven years ago our fathers brought forth, upon this continent, a new nation, conceived in liberty, and dedicated to the proposition that all men are created equal."[13]

Excellent students would recite these lines flawlessly. Most other students would capture the essence of Lincoln's message. However, a simple recitation of this sentence would be too difficult for some students.[14] What follow are examples of how this question would be answered on the OTHER exams. WARNING: THOSE WITH A WEAK STOMACH SHOULD READ NO FURTHER. READING THESE ANSWERS COULD BE HAZARDOUS TO YOUR HEALTH.

II. The Bottom Ten

A. *The Timeless*

"Four...(Nearly out of time)...score...(Time almost out)...and...(Out of time. Exam was too long!)."

The Timeless student never has enough time to finish the exam. When I began my teaching career and read answers like this, I assumed I was not providing enough time for students to answer the questions. I gradually shortened my questions and gave the students more time to answer, and the number of Timeless students decreased. However, no matter how simple the question, and no matter how much time I give students to answer it, there are

---

13. There are several different versions of Lincoln's Address. *See* 2 William B. Barton, The Life of Abraham Lincoln 485–93 (1925) (giving nine different versions). Apparently, not a single reporter brought his tape recorder to the speech. The opening sentence quoted in the text is consistent with most of these versions.

14. The point is not that law exam answers should consist only of recitation. The point in using the Gettysburg Address example is to illustrate the structure of poor answers independent of particular questions. If the reader wants to deal with the general issue of what law exams should test and what a good answer should look like, the reader can become a writer and write his or her own article. This is my article and so, like most legal authors, I can assume and ignore whatever I want.

always Timeless students who simply do not finish.[15] These are probably the same people who always brought home unfinished and uncolored pictures from kindergarten.[16] One wonders what these students do with their time. Are they using some of the time I give them to work on some other professor's take-home question? Or perhaps they have a thriving mail-order business. After they graduate from law school (if they do), many of these students become judges.[17]

B. The Empty

"............"

Many law professors have searched bluebooks in vain[18] for missing answers to questions. Some students never answer all of the questions. There are several explanations for such behavior. Some Empty students are Timeless students who did not even have time to indicate that they were out of time. Other Empty students strategically decided that it would be more detrimental to their overall grade to show their ignorance on the particular question than simply not to answer and hope for mercy from the grader. "The surest way to conceal from others the limits of one's own knowledge is by not overstepping them."[19] The ultimate Empty answer is the No-show—the student who, although registered for the class, does not appear for the exam. It is difficult to understand the decision process of the No-show. How could one's position possibly be worse taking the exam than receiving the automatic failure which results from not appearing?[20]

---

15. Therefore, I have once again lengthened my questions and shortened the time period. If there are always going to be Timeless students, I don't want them to be lonely. Also, less time means fewer bluebooks. Giving more time to accommodate Timeless students also gives more time to those students who write encyclopedias instead of exam answers.

16. I have a child who did this. The teachers explained that she spent the time learning to socialize with other children. You'd think that law students would already know how to socialize.

17. *Cf.* your favorite overdue, long-expected opinion.

18. This should not be confused with "vein," which is a small blood vessel in the arm which many law professors would like to cut open after reading bluebooks.

19. GIACOMO LEOPARDI, PENSIERI 135 (W.S. Di Piero trans., 1981) (¶ LXXXVI).

20. Lest I receive dozens of letters from the law and economics types out there, I should explain that this is a rhetorical question. I'm one of you. I *know* the answer; it's just too boring to discuss.

C. *The Waffler*

"Approximately two to six score years ago (more or less), our fathers (some lower courts say it was our grandfathers) brought forth, somewhere in the world, a new nation, country, or some other enterprise, which according to some people was conceived in liberty, and dedicated to the proposition that all, most, or some men (and men might mean 'women' in some contexts) are created equal, or maybe not. This may not be exactly right. It's something like that, but I could be wrong."

The Waffler *is* dreadfully afraid of taking a position, perhaps realizing that a definite position one way or the other could be completely wrong. The Waffler therefore takes all positions, and is always partially right. Of course, the Waffler is also always partially wrong. Many Wafflers later in life write legal treatises.[21] Others become politicians.

D. *The Grammarian*

"For score seven ago, our fathers bring new nashun; conceited in library. dedicate the to preposition that all man are equl."

The Grammarian is the student who managed to escape elementary school, junior high, high school, and college without learning the slightest thing about grammar, spelling, punctuation, or writing. The Grammarian's work product is often used as an example of the decline of the American educational system. Given the pressures of an exam, almost everyone makes mistakes like this; what sets apart the Grammarians is the constant, repetitive nature of their errors.[22] Grammarians pay the highest salaries to legal secretaries, because, for the Grammarian, brief-writing and memo-writing are necessarily team enterprises. Many Grammarians who are unable to find legal jobs become public school teachers.[23]

---

21. "The majority view is.... The minority view is.... The view of two really stupid people living in Idaho is...."

22. Notice how the focus on constant, repetitive errors cleverly allows me to avoid attacks from people who would point out the errors in my own writing. Isn't law review writing fun?

23. My grandfather was a public school teacher; my grandmother was a public school teacher; my wife was a public school teacher; some of my best friends are public school teachers. I almost removed this line, but then I realized that they've all made insulting jokes about lawyers. So there!

E. The Outliner

"Gettysburg Address-
-87 years ago
-our fathers
-on this continent
-a new nation
-liberty
-all men equal."

The Outliner never learned to write a complete sentence (or perhaps Outliners skipped school the day their teachers discussed verbs or conjunctions). Some of the other categories of students can become Outliners with hard work. For example, many Timeless students through careful time management can become Outliners. Grammarians can also become Outliners, because outlining eliminates the need to construct sentences properly.[24] I have always wondered if George Bush was an Outliner when he was an undergraduate at Yale.[25]

F. The Repeater

"The question is to restate the Gettysburg Address as spoken by Lincoln. As I understand the issue, my task is to write the Address in a close approximation to what Lincoln actually said. I shall proceed on the assumption that this is what you mean...."

The Repeater is better at restating the question than answering it. Repeaters spend four or five bluebook pages restating the facts without adding any legal analysis whatsoever. They then spend another three or four pages restating the issues the question asked them to discuss. The actual answer seldom takes more than a page. Repeaters often lapse into Timelessness. After the long, ritual restating of the question, they run out of time and argue that the exam was too long. It is obvious from the Repeater's answer that he or she can read;

---

24. This sentence is an illustration of the advantage of being an Outliner. Does the adverb "properly" belong at the end of the sentence, immediately before the preposition, immediately after the preposition, or in a suburb outside of Cleveland? An Outliner would not have to deal with this issue. He would write the sentence as follows:

Grammarians = Outliners
-No need
-Proper sentences.

25. Speaking of George Bush, are there really 1000 points of light, or only 999 or even 998? Has anyone really counted? The media have been incredibly trusting on an item that spearheads Bush's carefully crafted domestic policy.

it is less obvious whether the Repeater has the slightest understanding of the subject matter the question was testing. Repeaters make very good mediators and psychiatrists.

G. *The Scholar*

> "Abraham Lincoln was born on February 12, 1809 in a log cabin near Hodgenville, Kentucky. His parents were Thomas Lincoln and Nancy Hanks. When Lincoln was seven years old, his family moved to Indiana....In 1834, Lincoln was elected to the Illinois House of Representatives and, in 1836, Lincoln obtained a license to practice law....Lincoln was elected President in 1860, defeating Stephen A. Douglas, John C. Breckinridge, and John Bell....Lincoln's Gettysburg Address was a 268-word speech given at the dedication of the national cemetery at Gettysburg. It followed a two-hour oration by Edward Everett...."

Pardon the ellipses, but a faithful reproduction of the Scholar's answer would fill several pages and destroy many more trees.[26] The Scholar suffers from a surplus of knowledge and an inability to organize that knowledge with any sense of priority. The Scholar knows too much, is not sure what is most important, and is therefore determined to transfer all of that knowledge to the bluebook. The Scholar is worried that leaving out a single detail might be interpreted by the professor as ignorance. The correct response is usually hidden somewhere in the Scholar's answer; finding that answer is like sifting through sugar to locate salt. Courts created page limits to deal with Scholars; Scholars created footnotes and appendices to deal with page limits. Never get into a conversation with a Scholar at a party; it (the conversation, not the party) never ends. Many Scholars become law professors.[27]

H. *The Avoider*

> "The opening line of Lincoln's address at Gettysburg is reminiscent in both rhythm and effect of Marc Antony's famous oration in the play *Julius Caesar:* Friends, Romans, countrymen, lend me your ears; I come to bury Caesar, not to praise him. The evil that men do lives after them; The good is oft interred with their bones; So let it be with Caesar."[28]

---

26. Why is the environmental movement putting so much of the blame for the destruction of the world's forests on logging companies and Brazilian farmers, instead of where it rightfully belongs — the law reviews?

27. Law professors, of course, are extremely fun at parties. Or, at least we would be if someone would invite us.

28. WILLIAM SHAKESPEARE, JULIUS CAESAR act 3, sc. 2.

The Avoider is a font of knowledge; unfortunately, none of that knowledge is relevant. In other words, the Avoider is an uninformed Scholar.[29] Lacking an answer to the question, the Avoider answers some other, unrelated question. The Avoider hopes that the grader will credit the general knowledge in the answer enough to assign a passing grade, even though the Avoider has no specific knowledge of the issue raised by the question. Avoiders often enter politics after graduation.

I. The Crit

"This question conceals several illegitimate assumptions. The question as framed assumes the legitimacy of Zionistic, capitalistic oppression; it glorifies the meta-hierarchy represented by the imperialistic, capitalistic warmonger Lincoln. In any event, the meaning of the question is indeterminate. It fails to identify the particular Lincoln who was the speaker; a reader from another culture might believe this to be a reference to some other Lincoln. Further, what do you mean by the 'opening' of the Address? At what point does the 'opening' end and the ending open? One's sense of opening is culturally derived and therefore indeterminate."[30]

The Crit follows the old adage: "If you don't know the answer, question the question." The Crit is thus a very special class of Avoider. The Crit is freed from the need to acquire any substantive knowledge,[31] since so much is culturally derived and indeterminate. In this sense, Critical analysis really is liberating. It liberates the Crit from having to study. Most Crits become corporate lawyers when they graduate; capitalism pays much better wages than Marxism.

J. The Footnoter

"As you said in class on April 1 at 2:10 p.m., the Gettysburg Address was a speech by Abraham Lincoln to dedicate the national cemetery at Gettysburg. As stated on p. 1401, fn. 17b, of the casebook, the Address begins with the

---

29. "Uninformed Scholar" is probably an oxymoron, like "military intelligence," "legal writing," or "distinguished professor."

30. I must admit that, as a non-Crit, I can't do justice to the Crit style. Most Crit writing is much more opaque than the example in the text. I was careful to include some of the Crit buzzwords: imperialistic, oppression, hierarchy, and the modifier "meta." At best, however, this is still only a meta-Crit answer.

31. "Hee is a foole that has nothing of philosophy in Him But not so much as hee who has nothing else but philosophy in Him." SAMUEL BUTLER, PROSE OBSERVATIONS 259 (Hugh De Quehen ed., 1979). Samuel Butler's main failing was that hee didn't know howe to spelle.

words 'Four score and seven years ago.' The full Gettysburg Address appears in Vol. 2, pp. 485–493 of Barton, *The Life of Abraham Lincoln....*"

The Footnoter has an inbred fear of being wrong and therefore refuses to say anything without providing direct authority for the proposition. The Footnoter fails to realize that "an ounce of a man's own wit...[is] worth a ton of other people's."[32] On law exams, which are often purposely indeterminate, the Footnoter leaves most of the important issues undiscussed, because there is nothing to cite. The Footnoter, like the Scholar, is frustrating to the grader, because the Footnoter clearly has some knowledge of the subject being examined. Unfortunately, that knowledge is hard to find amidst the tangential citations and cross references. The Footnoter has taken law review style[33] to heart. If that is how famous law professors and lawyers communicate, the Footnoter thinks, that must be the way to earn an "A." After graduating from law school, many Footnoters become tax lawyers or accountants.

III. Conclusion[34]

I am sure that more than these ten examples of bad exam styles could be given, and that I could insult even more people in both text and footnotes if I thought about it longer. Unfortunately,[35] I can't stand to think about such exam answers for very long—I wake up in the middle of the night screaming.[36] Readers who have other examples should burn them; I do not want to see them. Once a semester is often enough to deal with such things.

Having picked on law students for most of this article, let me turn now to those who write and grade the exams—the law professors.[37] Law professors are entitled to no great credit for being able to write exams that produce answers of the sort discussed above. As Charles Caleb Colton wrote, "[T]he greatest fool may ask more than the wisest man can answer."[38] We law professors

---

32. LAURENCE STERNE, TRISTRAM SHANDY 133 (Modern Library ed., 1928) (citing his father). How did Laurence Sterne weigh wit? Is this what my wife means when she says I have a big head?

33. I hesitate to use the word "style" in connection with law review writing.

34. Yes, the end is finally approaching.

35. Or fortunately, depending on one's opinion of this article.

36. Only two other things have ever had this effect on me: (1) the Rule Against Perpetuities, and (2) the thought of my children growing up to be just like me.

37. I will spend much less time criticizing law professors than I did criticizing law students. That is because I am a law professor and I am no longer a law student. It is therefore obvious to me that there is less fault to find in law professors.

38. CHARLES C. COLTON, 1 LACON 152 (1829) (¶ CCCXXII).

might be more humble (and less willing to write smart-ass,[39] sarcastic articles like this) if we had to reread the exam answers that we wrote as students in law school, particularly those from courses we now teach. We may remember our brilliance as students, but those who graded our exams probably had a substantially different view.[40] Finally, a retort[41] for those students who wish to defend themselves against the onslaughts in this article: " 'Tis not every question that deserves an answer."[42]

---

39. Some people might find the word "smart-ass" inappropriate in law review discourse, but why should I care what the anal-retentives think?

40. Professor Loss, please do not dig out my old Securities Regulation exam. I will wash your car, cook your meals, do anything that you ask if you spare me the humiliation of having to reread what I wrote on that exam. And please do not let my students see it. They think I know what I'm doing. (O.K., I admit it. Not all of them think that.)

41. Do students who fail Torts have to take Retorts?

42. Thomas Fuller, Gnomologia ¶ 5094 (1732). Note the last of a series of obscure quotations. It's amazing how four or five quotation books and a good research assistant can cover for my lack of education.

That Balky Law Curriculum*

Wylie H. Davis**

Like the course of the common law, curricular change in American law
schools has been typically slow and timid. The "core" subjects, for example,
offered at the Harvard Law School in 1876 were Real Property, Contracts,
Torts, Criminal Law and Procedure, Evidence, and Equity. In this aspect, things
are about the same in 1968. The Harvard Law Faculty recently eliminated all
required courses after the first year.

Again like the common law, our national curricular trend over the last hundred years — while supposedly wise and reasoned — has lagged behind a pervasive and explosive revolution in the American way of life. But new strong
forces are at work in both legal education and the administration of justice.
Most of our law schools are said to be in a state of ferment; certainly they are
generating some heady goings-on, and the matter of what to do about curricular structure and content is a constant preoccupation of law faculties,
bench and bar, professional organizations, and even, lest we forget, law students. (A few brave faculties, in fact, are now adding students to their curriculum committees; and I view this as a good move as well as a shrewd one.)

Of course, these winds of change blow up much division and controversy. I
have seen law teachers, who have no peers in nitpickery, verge on purple
apoplexy in debate over the curriculum. The whole academic business is fraught
with vested interests, gored oxen, ground axes, pet peeves, visionary schemes,
and intractable inertia. Not infrequently, the controversial curriculum issues will
be resolved by compromises and trade-offs that really satisfy nobody. A few
schools, however, can afford the chaotic luxury of letting professors offer whatever they enjoy, if it's remotely related to law. Since no one can define "law," this
sort of franchise has few, if any, limits. A professor I know at another law school
applied this year for a year's sabbatical leave and foundation grant (to support
field research) in order to work up a new seminar entitled "Sex et Lex."

* Reprinted with permission of *The Georgia Advocate* from its issue of May 27, 1968.
** Professor of Law, University of Georgia School of Law.

This interdisciplinary enrichment of law curricula and social-science research method naturally attract scholars who dislike the musty restrictions of law-book research. And so offerings like Law and Technological Change (dubbed "Fission, Fusion, and Flux" at one school) and Legal Aspects of the Vietnamese War will continue to proliferate, usually without the slightest objection or even interest by professorial colleagues whose sole concern is to squat protectively on their own established courses like brooder hens. (The eggs, I might add, are often infertile.) The one-wordly trend, in fact, is irreversible. Several American law schools now offer Soviet Law, International Commercial Transactions, and Comparative Law in many approaches and variants. A few others offer courses or seminars on Red Chinese Law and Mandarin Metaphysics.

Many pressures nudge our thinking about modern law curricula, and at times one or another will predominate. For years some practitioners and some teachers (most in both groups have glanced at the fray disinterestedly) have quarreled with one another about "practicality" versus "theory" in the law schools. Aside from the fact that the theoretician often proves to be the most practical man around—as Einstein demonstrated—and the educated realist must often be as pointedly eggheaded as any academician, there is an inherent obstacle to curricular "balance" between theory and practice: Most law teachers, and the best of those who aspire to teach, have generally had brief experience in law practice, or none; and it is a lamentable but firm fact that experienced, mature lawyers usually make poor teachers, even in the "practical" procedure and evidence courses. More and more law schools, however, including the University of Georgia, are at least gnawing on this problem with such incisors as legal aid, trial practice, and the encouragement of pregraduation, summer employment of law students by practitioners.

Other forces are equally influential. A stunted curriculum, like a mediocre faculty or physical plant, may be dictated by anemic funds. No law school can concoct a sophisticated curriculum without generous backing for the recruitment of excellent teachers and students, and the support of research. The University of Georgia's posture in this respect, albeit a threshold one, is now more favorable than that of most American law schools. Another influence, and one that goes about as far as money to explain the wide spectrum of American law curricula, is the innovative compulsion of superior law faculties. I have already alluded to some of our orbital offerings around the country, and even the first-year "basic" courses are by no means immune from such disturbing tinkering—disturbing, that is, to the first-year professor who has intoned the same stuff for twenty years or more and isn't going to let curricular rock 'n roll upset his golf game, or even put him out of work, if he can help it. Some years ago a young law teacher had the effrontery to propose in the *Journal of Legal Education* a merger of Contracts and Torts. Presumably he would have called it "Contorts," but in any event he made this silly suggestion in cavalier disregard of the palpable fact that a contortionist would have to be hired to teach it.

Probably most law professors today, and certainly most law students, would agree that the usual third-year program in legal education is sterile and uninspiring—in short, a big bore. Various nostrums for this condition have been urged. One professor in the May, 1968, *Journal of Legal Education* suggests, among other adjustments, trying the English system of outside examiners: "…the teacher of a course does not himself prepare the questions or grade the examinations." This might indeed add an element of excitement; and all law professors, I'm sure, would applaud such a change on other grounds as well. Personally, I am skeptical about the efficacy of anything less than dancing girls as a gimmick for relieving the ennui of third-year law students. We need more than gimmicks for this thorny problem. One radical solution is a two-year course to graduation. This has been seriously proposed by a prominent Harvard law teacher (Prof. David Cavers), and not—in my opinion—without merit.

I believe, however, that the best solution to this problem is two-fold: (1) To encourage and offer ample opportunity for subject-matter specialization in both the second and third years—a "tracking" approach; and (2) to replace all of our customary third-year offerings, and some in the second year, with problem-oriented, multi-subject offerings that emphasize library and empirical research, practical internship, and legal writing. Such a program would be expensive, as well as unpalatable to many established professors. But those who raise the money and pay the bills might bear in mind the possibility that legal education, as presently pursued, is the least expensive of all professional education in terms of student-teacher ratios, relatively modest hardware requirements, and auxiliary services.

Alumni and students of the University of Georgia School of Law will be glad to know that Dean Cowen has recently constituted a special committee to examine the School's curriculum and make recommendations. Personally, I make no claim to insightful genius; but all of us on occasion get flashes that are fresh and promising. One such idea has been blinking at me of late, and I intend to press it upon the special curriculum committee. In a nutshell, my proposal is to abolish all of our existing offerings and to substitute therefor a single course: Mule Law I through XXIX. All segments would be required and a single (very thick) casebook, supplemented by dynamic mimeographed problems, would be used for the entire three years. I will, of course, edit and publish the casebook. The following small sample of cases (efficiently collected by Editor Jerry Blackstock) will demonstrate the vast legal range of such an offering:

United States v. Mittry Bros. Const. Co., 4 F.Supp. 216 (D. Idaho 1933) (claim for purchase price of mules and horses furnished by materialman was not covered by government contractor's bond); United States v. Mattlock, 26 F.Cas. 1208 (D. Ore.1872) (word "cattle," as used in the Indian Intercourse Act of 1834, included mules); Atlantic Coast Line R.R. v. Carroll Mercantile Co., 206 Ala. 320, 89 So. 509 (1921) (disposition of mules to buck was judicially noticed); Jones v. State, 10 Ala.App. 152, 65 So. 411 (1914) (crime to sell or exchange mules knowing them to be diseased and with intent to defraud); Alaska Lumber Co. v. Spurlin, 183 Ark. 576, 37 S.W.2d 82 (1931) (mules will occasionally walk or run away); Terry v. Little, 179 Ark. 954, 18 S.W.2d 916 (1929) (mules do not drive themselves; it is necessary for someone to control their work); Taylor v. State, 44 Ga. 263 (1871) (under the Georgia Code "horse" stealing includes a mule or ass, and both sexes thereof, without regard to any artificial alternations); McLamb & Co. v. Lambertson, 4 Ga.App. 553, 62 S.E. 107 (1908) (word "horse" is generic and includes mules and asses, but term "mare" does not describe a female mule); Miller v. Kelly Coal Co., 239 Ill. 626, 88 N.E. 196 (1909) (where master furnishing mule to servant knew of the animal's vicious disposition and servant was kicked by the mule, master was liable); Toledo, W. & W. Ry. v. Cole, 50 Ill. 184 (1869) (railroads have a duty to erect and maintain fences sufficient to prevent mules from getting on the tracks); Winbigler v. Cliff, 102 Kan. 858, 172 Pac. 537 (1918) (operation of a horse and mule market in a residential district was a public nuisance); McElveen v. Goings, 116 La. 977, 41 So. 229 (1906) (being within the term "work horses" as used in a constitutional exemption provision, mules are not subject to seizure by a creditor); Meredith v. Kidd, 147 So. 539 (La.App.1933) (in suit for death of mules struck by an auto, trial court properly excluded testimony about expense and time required to obtain a new pair of mules); Sparks v. Brown, 46 Mo.App. 529 (1891) (a mouse is a small rodent quadruped; it follows that a mouse-colored mule is one whose color is that of a mouse); Commonwealth v. Davidson, 4 Pa.Dist. 172 (1894) (reward for apprehension of horse thief does not apply to apprehension of a mule thief); Goldsmith v. State, 38 Tenn. (1 Head) 154 (1858) (crime of horseracing included running of a mule race); Allison v. Brookshire, 38 Tex. 199 (1873) (mules exempt under statute exempting two horses for each family); State v.

Gould, 26 W.Va. 258 (1885) (cruelly beating a mule is within statutory prohibition of cruelly beating a domestic animal).

This bold vehicle would explore every legal "subject" from Administrative Law to Zoning, from Corporate Reorganization to Lunar Law. It would be tightly integrated, and as an incidental advantage it would give fitting recognition to a noble animal. For every law professor, moreover, who fancies himself to be a latter-day Socrates in his classroom method, this curriculum would offer new potential. About three years ago I put the following Contracts case to a Chicago-type student:

> Davis: Mr. Hohfeld, suppose A makes an agreement with B to sell the latter a brace of mules, Nellie and Kelly, for $100 per animal. Unknown to either party at the time of contracting, Kelly has just died of a coronary. Upon discovery of this fact, is B, the buyer, legally excused from the contract on the rationale that a mutual, *material* mistake of fact excuses both parties?
>
> Hohfeld: Why sure, Fess Baby. Kelly's death was material because it prevented B from using the mules for breeding purposes.

Obviously, the adoption of my proposal would put us a horse up on every other law school in the country.

Is the Constitution Worth Legal Writing Credit?

*Maurice Kelman**

Recently discovered in the archives of the College of William and Mary, America's first law school, is an unsigned, undated memorandum addressed to George Wythe, America's first law professor. Handwriting analysis identifies the author as Abigail Sedgewick-Pinsky, thought to be America's first legal writing instructor.

Although the document is inexplicit on the point, the reader gathers that Ms. Sedgewick-Pinsky was helping Professor Wythe and the college administration decide whether to grant independent study credit to James Madison of Virginia and Gouverneur Morris of Pennsylvania for their accomplishments as drafters of the Constitution and, in Madison's case, the Bill of Rights. Both men served on the Constitutional Convention's Committee of Style, which formulated the final text. Madison, the preeminent Framer, said of his colleague's contribution: "The finish given to the style and arrangement of the Constitution fairly belongs to the pen of Mr. Morris." Professor Wythe himself had been selected as one of Virginia's representatives to the Philadelphia convention but dropped out because of his wife's illness. Later, as a delegate to his state's ratification convention, Wythe championed the Constitution against the likes of Patrick Henry.

What follows, minus an introductory paragraph complaining of overwork and a poor salary, is Abigail Sedgewick-Pinsky's full memorandum. I have taken the liberty of inserting footnotes that relate her comments to later interpretations by the Supreme Court and to modern literature on the subject of drafting.

---

* Maurice Kelman is Professor of Law at Wayne State University.

Memorandum

To: Professor George Wythe

1. The Preamble

Let's begin at the beginning. The Preamble uses the expression, "We the People." This is fatuous. Who else are "We" if not the people? The periwigs? The quill pens? Paul Revere's silverware?[1] In any case, why is there a preamble at all? It lacks operative force of its own,[2] and phrases such as "establish Justice," "insure domestic Tranquility," and "secure the Blessings of Liberty to ourselves and our Posterity" don't clarify anything in the main text. They are just prattle—blah, blah, blah.[3]

2. Legalisms

Legalistic words and phrases should be replaced with natural every-day language. The Framers have done surprisingly well in this regard, although they don't quite deserve an A. I've spotted a handful of stuffy lawyer expressions: "thereof" (Art. I, §§2, 4, 8, Art. IV, §§1, 2, and Art. V), "therein" (Art. IV, §2), "herein" (Art. I, §1), "whatsoever" (Art. I, §8, cl. 17), "before mentioned" (Art. VI, cl. 3), "to all Intents and Purposes" (Art. V), "any Thing...to the Contrary notwisthstanding" (Art. VI, cl. 2).

3. Metaphors

Poetic expression enjoys an honored place in literature, but it doesn't belong in a legal instrument.[4] A prohibition of double jeopardy is fine by me, but why does Mr. Madison's Seventh Amendment[5] say "twice put

---

1. Actually "the people," a term found not only in the Preamble but in the First, Second, Fourth, Ninth, Tenth, and Seventeenth Amendments, is not altogether free from ambiguity. See United States v. Verdugo-Urquidez, 494 U.S. 259 (1990) (5–4 split over whether a Mexican national whose homes in Mexicali and San Felipe were searched without warrant by American DEA agents is one of "the people" protected by the Fourth Amendment).

2. Jacobson v. Massachusetts, 197 U.S. 11, 22 (1905).

3. "Most general purpose clauses wind up as pious incantations of little practical value because what little information they contain is usually inferable from the working text." Reed Dickerson, The Fundamentals of Legal Drafting, 2d. ed., 286 (Boston, 1986).

4. "Metaphors in law are to be narrowly watched, for starting as devices to liberate thought, they end often by enslaving it." Berkey v. Third Ave. Ry., 155 N.E. 58, 61 (N.Y. 1926) (Cardozo, J.).

5. The Madisonian Bill of Rights contained twelve amendments. When all but the first two were ratified in 1791, proposed Amendment VII mutatis mutandis became the Fifth Amendment.

in jeopardy of life or limb"? Will this phraseology make the provision inapplicable to an accused who faces neither hanging nor amputation of a hand?⁶ And what about the due process guarantee in the same amendment? It extends to "life, liberty, or property." Is this supposed to be a figurative way of saying that the government shall not inflict any <u>grievous losses</u> on citizens without fair procedure?⁷

4. Euphemisms

Law should be plainspoken. Just as there is no need for metaphorical flourish, likewise euphemism is to be avoided. I particularly applaud Art. I, §8, cl. 11, for telling it like it is. It doesn't talk about entering "hostilties" or launching "police actions" or undertaking "peacekeeping missions." It bluntly says "To declare War." On the other hand, "three fifths of all other Persons" (Art. I, §2, cl. 3) and "such Persons as any of the States now existing shall think proper to admit" (Art. I, §9, cl. 1) sacrifice clarity for delicacy. Messrs. Madison and Morris should simply have said "foreigners."⁸

5. Superfluous Words

A pet peeve of mine is the redundanccy that afflicts so much legal writing. Lawyers are rarely content with one word when they can toss in a synonym or two. They don't say "void," they say "null and void." They don't say "will," they say "will and testament."⁹ Such verbosity might be tolerated as an irritating but harmless vice were it not for the judicial fancy that every word in a legal instrument serves a function and nothing is to be discounted as verbal fat.¹⁰ That is why students who pass my legal writing course do not fill their papers with paired syn-

---

6. No, the Court recognized "life or limb" as a synecdoche. *Ex parte* Lange, 85 U.S. (18 Wall.) 163, 170 (1874).

7. See Meachum v. Fano, 427 U.S. 215, 224 (1976) ("We reject at the outset the notion that *any* grievous loss visited upon a person by the State is sufficient to invoke the procedural protections of the Due Process Clause."). Unlike "life or limb," the phrase "life, liberty, or property" is no bigger than the sum of its parts. Board of Regents v. Roth, 408 U.S. 564 (1972).

8. Ms. Sedgewick-Pinsky here illustrates her own point by mistaking the elliptical reference to slavery.

9. "The draftsman should avoid combinations of words or expressions having the same meaning." Dickerson, *supra* note 3, at 207.

10. E.g., Nixon v. United States, 113 S. Ct. 732, 737 (1993) (rejecting a contention that the word "sole" in the Art. I, §3, cl. 6 commitment to the Senate of "the sole Power to try all Impeachments" is "a mere 'cosmetic edit' added by the Committee of Style").

onyms. I consider Madison and Morris the worst offenders I have ever encountered in this category. There is hardly a sentence in their Constitution, starting with the Preamble ("ordain and establish"), that does not contain a doublet. Whenever a single word would have done the job nicely, they opted for prolixity.[11] *It would be too tedious to list all the needlessly wordy formulations, so here is just a sampler: "Necessary and Proper," "by and with," "Advice and Consent," "Aid and Comfort," "Speech or Debate," "Privileges and Immunities," "Full Faith and Credit," "cruel and unusual," "preserve, protect, and defend."*

The writers reached a nadir in the provisions dealing with impeachment of recreant government officials. The offender, once removed, cannot again "hold and enjoy" a federal office of "honor, Trust or Profit" and is "liable and subject" to criminal prosecution. And what are the grounds for impeachment besides treason and bribery? Why, "other high Crimes and Misdemeanors" (as if misdemeanors aren't already crimes).[12] *By the way, is "high" intended to modify "Misdemeanors" as well as "Crimes"?*[13]

6. Mean What You Say

A cardinal principle of hermeneutics is that words mean what they say, not what the speaker hoped but failed to articulate. Clumsy drafting is not rectified by the author's later protestations of a different intent. I fear the Framers blundered badly when composing that part of Art. III, §2 which gives the federal courts authority over "Controversies...between a State and Citizens of another State." Doesn't the wording plainly suggest that a private litigant who happens, let's say, to be a citizen of New York can bring a federal lawsuit against the State of Virginia? I was too busy grading legal writing exercises to pay much attention to the ratification debates, but I do recall some of the Antifederalist crowd kvetching about how Article III strips away the historic right of every state not to be sued without its consent. I also remember Mr. Hamilton's effort at damage control. He claimed there was no basis for alarm because it was never the Framers' purpose to abolish sover-

---

11. In point of fact the Committee of Style spared Art. I, § 10 from a Contracts Clause that would have spoken of laws "altering or impairing" the obligation of contracts instead of simply "impairing." Charles Warren, The Making of the Constitution 556 (Boston, 1928).

12. Not necessarily. See Raoul Berger, Impeachment: The Constitutional Problems 159–65 (Cambridge, Mass., 1973).

13. See *id.* at 161–62 n.178.

eign immunity: that simply was not, as he put it, "in the plan of the convention."[14] *That's all well and good (oops, a doublet), but the Constitution as written is what Article VI declares to be "the supreme Law of the Land," not Mr. Alexander Hamilton's here's-what-we-should-have-saids.*[15] *Were I a federal judge I would let the textual chips fall where they may: I'd let that 'bocker sue the knickers off old Virginny.*[16]

7. Same Words/Same Meaning

I always caution my students that when they use the same word in various places in a legal document, they should expect that the word will be given a uniform construction.[17] *One can only hope that the drafters were mindful of this precept when they referred to state legislatures in Art. I, §4 and again in Art. V, and to citizens of the several states in both Art. III and Art. IV, and when they spoke of law in Art. I, §§ 9, 10, as well as in Mr. Madison's Third and Seventh Amendments.*[18]

---

14. The Federalist No. 81, ed. Clinton Rossiter, 487 (New York, 1961).

15. "[T]he worst person to construe [an instrument] is the person who is responsible for its drafting. He is very much disposed to confuse what he intended to do with the effect of the language which in fact has been employed." Hilder v. Dexter, 1902 App. Cas. 474, 477 (Lord Halsbury).

16. A Supreme Court majority, comprising two Framers and two Ratifiers but seeing things the same way as Ms. Sedgewick-Pinsky, read Art. III, § 2 literally. Chisholm v. Georgia, 2 U.S. (2 Dall.) 419 (1793). The decision triggered a curative amendment, the Eleventh, which was also a sorry piece of drafting. See Hans v. Louisiana, 134 U.S. 1 (1890); Monaco v. Mississippi, 292 U.S. 313 (1934).

17. Ms. Sedgewick-Pinsky's admonition is overstated.

>   Undoubtedly, there is a natural presumption that identical words used in different parts of the same act are intended to have the same meaning.... But the presumption is not rigid and readily yields whenever there is such variation in the connection in which the words are used as reasonably to warrant the conclusion that they were employed in different parts of the act with different intent.

Atlantic Cleaners & Dyers, Inc. v. United States, 286 U.S. 427, 433 (1932).

18. That is to say, the First and Fifth Amendments. See *supra* note 5. Actually, the three words instanced by Ms. Sedgewick-Pinsky have variable meanings in the Constitution. "Legislature" includes the lawmaking role of gubernatorial vetoes for purposes of setting the times, places, and manner of congressional elections, Smiley v. Holm, 285 U.S. 355 (1932), but not when it comes to ratifying constitutional amendments, Hawke v. Smith, 253 U.S. 221 (1920). Corporations are not "citizens" within the coverage of the interstate privileges and immunities clause, Paul v. Virginia, 75 U.S. (8 Wall.) 168 (1869), but are citizens within the grant of diversity-of-citizenship jurisdiction to federal courts. Marshall v. Baltimore & O.R.R., 57 U.S. (16 How.) 314 (1854). The bar against ex post facto "laws" refers only to statutes, Ross v. Oregon, 227 U.S. 150, 161 (1913), whereas due process of "law" reaches governmental action of every kind—legislative, judicial, executive, administrative. Monroe v. Pape, 365 U.S. 167 (1961); Shelley v. Kraemer, 334 U.S. 1 (1948).

8. Overspecification

The interpretive maxim expressio unius est exclusio alterius *(the statement of one thing implies the exclusion of other things) is familiar to us — or should I say Us the People? It cautions good drafters against using overly specific or, if I may coin a word, underinclusive language when wider coverage is desired. In Art. I, § 8, cl. 8 we find the phrases "Authors and Inventors" and "their respective Writings and Discoveries." There are geniuses who are neither writers nor inventors but whose creations surely merit inclusion in any federal copyright system. Doesn't the Constitution's ill-advised phraseology run the risk of* expressio unius *construction?[19]*

The same concern applies to the Art. II, § 2 definition of the President as "Commander in Chief of the Army and Navy of the United States" and to the Art. I, § 8, cl. 14 grant of power to Congress "to make Rules for the Government and Regulation of the land and naval Forces." It is important to bear in mind that a constitution is intended to endure for ages to come and, consequently, to be adapted to the various crises of human affairs.[20] I have read somewhere about gigantic hot air balloons being flown in Europe. Suppose the day comes when American leaders decide that such contraptions should be incorporated into the armed services. It's regrettable that the authors of the Philadelphia document were not prescient enough to say "land, naval, and balloon forces" and "Commander in Chief of the Army, Navy, and Balloons of the United States."[21]

---

19. Happily the Court has resisted that temptation. See Burrow-Giles Lithographic v. Sarony, 111 U.S. 53 (1884) (photographs can be copyrighted); Diamond v. Chakrabarty, 447 U.S. 303 (1980) (genetically engineered life forms are patentable).

20. Here we encounter another shameless piece of plagiarism by the venerated John Marshall. See McCulloch v. Maryland, 17 U.S. (4 Wheat.) 316, 415 (1819). Compare the Chief Justice's ripoff of Alexander Hamilton in the same opinion. *Id.* at 421.

21. Ms. Sedgewick-Pinsky overlooked a more important example of overspecification — the Fourth Amendment prohibition of unreasonable searches and seizures of "persons, houses, papers, and effects." The phrase has been stretched to include conversations. Katz v. United States, 389 U.S. 347 (1967), *overruling* Olmstead v. United States, 277 U.S. 438 (1928). The justices also voyaged into "penumbras, formed by emanations" from the Fourth Amendment to discover a generalized right of privacy. Griswold v. Connecticut, 381 U.S. 479, 484 (1965). Yet on occasion the Court has reverted to text-parsing, as in Oliver v. United States, 466 U.S. 170 (1984) (open fields around a private residence are neither "houses" nor "effects" and therefore are not covered by the Fourth Amendment).

9. Vagueness

If overspecificity is the Scylla of legal drafting, excessive vagueness is the Charybdis. I fear that Messrs. Madison and Morris have come to grief on the latter's rocky shoals. Some of the vital provisions of their document are couched in terms so uncertain that women and men[22] can only guess at the meaning. What, after all, constitutes the "general Welfare of the United States," interstate and foreign "Commerce," the "Privileges and Immunities of Citizens in the several States," or "a Republican Form of Government"? Who can say with confidence what is encompassed in "the freedom of speech, or of the press" or when punishment is "cruel and unusual"?

I have not forgotten it is a <u>constitution</u> I am critiquing.[23] I know very well that flexibility rather than rigidity is a virtue in an organic law, but able draftspersons can achieve a prudent measure of fuzziness without lapsing into gibberish. For all the guidance Mr. Madison furnishes with his Due Process Clause he might as well have written "nor shall any person be deprived of mimsy without the borogoves of law" or "deprived of momraths without outgrabe."[24] If the judges of the Supreme Court should ever assert a power to annul laws for conflict with the Constitution—a point, incidentally, about which Mr. Madison and Company could have been more explicit[25]—the danger arises, a clear and present danger I might say, that the vacuous phrases of the Constitution and in particular the Bill of Rights will tempt judges to repackage their private values and policy preferences as the Law of the Land.[26]

---

22. Ms. Sedgewick-Pinsky was not only America's first legal writing instructor but a protofeminist. She did not, however, take issue with the Framers' use of the masculine pronoun in references to the President. ("He shall hold his Office during the Term of four Years." Art. II, § 1, cl. 1.)

23. See *supra* note 20.

24. A task for literary detectives: Find out whether Rev. Charles Lutwidge Dodgson or one of his Oxford contemporaries had access to the files of William and Mary.

25. But see Marbury v. Madison, 5 U.S. (1 Cranch) 137 (1803). Nowhere in his most celebrated opinion did John Marshall fault the Framers for leaving the awesome power of judicial review to inference and syllogistic reconstruction.

26. See generally Robert H. Bork, The Tempting of America (New York, 1990). One can easily imagine Ms. Sedgewick-Pinsky's reaction to Gouverneur Morris's boast to a friend: "That instrument [the Constitution] was written by the fingers which write this letter. Having rejected redundant and equivocal terms, I believed it to be as clear as our language would permit." Letter to Thomas Pickering, Dec. 22, 1814, *quoted in* Warren, *supra* note 11, at 687.

10. Conclusion

Naturally, the pending matter will not be decided by a mere legal writing instructor. I direct your attention, however, to our academic regulations, which clearly state that only students in their senior year are eligible for work-study credit.

A postscript: The foregoing memorandum must have been submitted to George Wythe shortly before he resigned his professorship in September 1789. No record is extant showing that the College of William and Mary actually gave scholastic credit to the two distinguished Framers, nor is it known whether Ms. Sedgewick-Pinsky's trashing of the Constitution had anything to do with Wythe's abrupt exit from the halls of academia. "The exact cause of Wythe's dissatisfaction cannot be determined from the contemporary documents that have survived," writes a biographer, but "the situation must have indeed been unpleasant."[27]

---

27. Imogene E. Brown, American Aristides: A Biography of George Wythe 222 (Rutherford, N.J., 1981).

Needlemann on Mortgages

William L. Prosser

In the law of California, the distinction between a mortgage and a deed of trust is, I am told, a matter of great intricacy, and its consequences are sometimes peculiarly perplexing to lawyers, and even more to students of the law. As their ramifications are explored at the Law School of the University of California at Berkeley, in the course on Security Transactions given by Professor Stefan A. Riesenfeld, they are reported to lead to mental anguish in an extreme degree. At the end of the course stands an examination, which, I am informed, is looked upon by the class with much the same unfavorable eye with which the prophet Mahomet looked upon marriage. It will be recalled that he likened it to an ordeal, wherein a man putteth his hand into a sack containing a thousand asps and one eel, and it is by the favor of Allah alone that he may draw forth the eel. The fact that law school generations have taken the course, and the examination, and have lived to tell the tale is, of course, considered quite immaterial.

Especially harrowing to the soul of the California student is the fact that there is no textbook to which he may resort for solace and aid. The student view of the profound and learned *Hornbook on Mortgages,* written by Professor George E. Osborne, of Stanford, is that it is an excellent book, and doubtless sufficient and satisfactory for Stanford, but that it signally fails to come to grips with many of the highly complex problems discovered by Professor Riesenfeld in the California law. There is no other short text. This is an aching void and the cause of infinite student woe.

On a dull Sunday afternoon, when the usual dismal January rain was drizzling down on Berkeley, two of the student assistants behind the library desk, with nothing else to do, decided that it was time that this void should be filled. The thought was father to the deed. They proceeded to prepare and to insert in the card catalogue of the Law School library a card reading as follows:

Dean and Professor of Law, University of California, Berkeley.

```
294r        Needlemann, Sol H.  1910–
N76
1956        California Law of Mortgages

            West Publishing Co., St. Paul, Minn., 1956
            —126 pages
            1.  Current Law
            2.  Mortgages and Deeds of Trust—
                Distinguished and Explained
```

In addition to this the name of *Needlemann on Mortgages* was inserted in the "flip card" index, designed for quick location of books expected to be used frequently. A second card was prepared for the library desk, indicating that on this particular rainy Sunday, the book had been called for and taken out by some person unidentified, whose name was signed on the back. All that remained was to mention to two or three members of Professor Riesenfeld's class, selected as those most likely to disseminate news, that the library had acquired *Needlemann on Mortgages* and that it was the complete answer to all prayers.

Wildfire spread. In a day or two, word was around the school that manna had descended from heaven. The library desk was stormed. The book was, unhappily, out. The desk card was produced. The signature on the back of it was utterly illegible. It began with something like an A or an O, which might equally be a B, a D, a Q, an R, or an N. In the middle of it there was a tall letter, possibly a b, an f, an l, a d, or an uncrossed t. It ended, in all probability, with an n or an m, which might, perhaps, be a double s. The name might have been Anderson, Androsian, Oberlin or Ostermann. It might, with almost equal probability, have been Doublecross or Qrxfvmcn. It is, perhaps, not surprising that presently dark forebodings were voiced that the Russians might be at work. It was even suggested that the book might have been taken out by Needlemann.

For several days, the siege of the library desk continued; but the book was not returned. A diligent search of all of the offices of the faculty, beginning, of course, with that of the dean, failed to discover it. Suspicion grew that some hound in human form, seeking an unfair advantage in the competition for grades, had purloined the book, deliberately leaving behind him a specimen of his examination book handwriting which even Osborn—meaning, of course, *Osborn on Questioned Documents*—could not decipher. Appeals to the desk men to do something at once drew forth only grim mutterings that for this, someone's head would roll in the basket; and demands that another copy of the book be ordered forthwith received the answer that this had, of course, been done. There was, however, some unaccountable delay in St. Paul, and no book came.

At a meeting of the second-year class, the class president made an earnest and impassioned appeal to the unknown individual who had the book to play fair with his classmates and return it at once. This proved to be entirely futile. Professor Riesenfeld was approached by some of the class and asked where to obtain a copy of *Needlemann on Mortgages*. He made confusion worse confounded by asserting categorically that there was no such book—a statement obviously incredible in the face of the card in the catalogue. He would, he said, know. "The only book on the California law of mortgages," he declared, "is the one I am writing." Rumor, which is rife, has it that he then retired to his office and spent $16.75 on long distance telephone calls in an effort to track down this sudden and mysterious competitor. This, however, has not been verified. However it may be, student perplexity was in no way diminished when Professor Riesenfeld, in a subsequent class hour, referred in an offhand manner to *Needlemann on Mortgages* as containing an excellent discussion of a minor point into which he had no time to go.

With all of the magnificent resources of the Law School broken down and lying prostrate at their feet, the indefatigable student body, with a persistence worthy of the fine traditions of the school, sought elsewhere. The San Francisco County Law Library turned out not to have the book, nor did the Alameda County Law Library in Oakland. Calls were made to the law schools of Hastings and Stanford, but these excellent and worthy institutions proved, once again, to be broken reeds. A careful and exhaustive search of Martindale-Hubbell, ranging through all the cities and towns of California, found no lawyer named Needlemann. The identity of the learned author remained shrouded in mystery and silence.

Again, rumor, emanating from the library desk, supplied a clue. It was suggested that this Needlemann must be none other than the well-known Father Needlemann, until recently a professor of the Law School of Loyola University in Los Angeles, who two or three years ago had left his position and the state. Los Angeles is a large city more than four hundred miles to the southward, concerning which any report, of whatever character, tends to be received in Berkeley with implicit belief. The telephone to Los Angeles produced, however, no enlightenment. Neither at Loyola, nor at the University of Southern California, nor at our sister school of the University of Southern California at Los Angeles, had any one ever heard of Father Needlemann or of *Needlemann on Mortgages*.

One member of the class discovered that the West Publishing Company had an office in San Francisco. He journeyed to that city, expending fifty cents on bridge tolls and as much more for parking, only to be told that the Company had published no such book and was confident that it had been published by no one else. This student, I am informed, feels himself aggrieved. He considers that he has a cause of action against the University of California, under the doctrine of *respondeat superior,* for his dollar and the value, if any, of his wasted time. This cause of action is believed to sound in deceit. As to whether he has also a cause of action for the intentional infliction of severe mental distress by extreme and outrageous conduct, see Prosser, *Insult and Outrage,* 44 CALIF.L.REV. 40 (1956).[1]

Meanwhile, vaulting ambition soared in the hearts of the conspirators behind the desk. They discussed plans of a student forum, at which some one with a thick Teutonic accent should appear to impersonate Needlemann, and deliver an utterly incomprehensible lecture on the law of mortgages. These were the best laid plans of mice. They came crashing to the earth when suddenly, one rainy morning, unfounded rumor stalked the corridors that Assistant Dean William N. Keeler had become interested in the matter and was about to make a personal investigation to discover what had become of *Needlemann on Mortgages.* Dean Keeler is a mild and gentle man, but he is reliably reported to have defeated his weight in mountain lions in single combat. Faced with this dire inquisition, the morale of the culprits disintegrated like a haystack in a hurricane. They came forward and confessed. Consternation and righteous indignation reigned in the class on Security Transactions. No one, however, was lynched. I am told that this was only because it was felt that the dean would not like it. The dean is familiarly known to the student body as Wild Bill, and there is a legend that when aroused to fury, he spits chemically pure sulphuric acid. It is also understood that somewhere in the law school of the University of Minnesota, there is the skin of a rattlesnake which he strangled with his bare hands.

Thus, there is lost to California, to legal scholarship, and to posterity, a masterpiece, unique of its kind and of ineffable value to the world. Before the curtain descends on the little drama, I should like to add, for the benefit of future historians, a few words about the distinguished legal scholar whose great work has perished in this distressing manner in the halls of our Law School.

Sol Humperdinck Needlemann[2] was born on April 1, 1910, in the city of Pilsen. As his name indicates, he was the descendant of a long line of English

---

1. Adv't.

2. Not under any circumstances to be confused with Professor Kurt H. Nadelmann of New York University, to whom humble apologies are due for the coincidence of the similarity in names. I am informed by the students in question that "needlemann" had no other connotation than that of "needling" their fellows.

tailors. The founder of the continental branch of the family was kidnapped while travelling in Prussia and was impressed into the regiment of giant grenadiers maintained by Friedrich Wilhelm I. During the Seven Years War, while in the invading army of Friedrich II, he was wounded while retreating after the battle of Prague and remained behind to settle in Pilsen, where he became a brewer. His beer, which is named after the town, is still manufactured by the family. It is, of course, a household word both in Germany and in the United States.

The future author was educated originally to be a rabbi. Even during his childish years, he displayed remarkable talents—among them, an unusual skill at the game of chess. At the age of four, he defeated his father, no mean player; and at fourteen, he had become a grandmaster of the game. His greatest single feat was at the tournament at Bad Order in 1928, when he finished first over a field of the twenty-four best players in the world, including Capablanca, Lasker, Alekhine, Nimzovitch, Bogoljubov, Moussorgsky, Prokofieff, Shostakovich, Borodin, Rimski, and Korsakov. His 32 4-move draw with Lasker, lasting more than sixteen hours, is still renowned as the only master tournament game which was finished in solitude and total darkness—after the spectators and the referee had gone home and the janitor had turned out the lights. This one game completely demolished Schinken's move in the Eier line in the Bratwurst variation of the Queen's Gambit Declined, which never has been played in any master tournament since.

In 1930, an event occurred which profoundly affected the future career of this young genius. While he was swimming in the River Main, he was saved from drowning by the Archbishop of Worms, who, at the time, was descending the river in a flatboat on his way from Kulmbach to Würzburg. The pious prelate jumped overboard, pulled the youth ashore, expertly administered artificial resuscitation, and conferred his benediction.

This rescue had three natural and inevitable consequences in young Needlemann's life. One was his immediate conversion to the Catholic faith. The second was a determination to study law. The third was a burning desire to come to California.

There followed years of study, during which this double master of chess and law amassed a record of university degrees believed to be unequaled in the entire history of legal education. No known compilation of all of them exists, but included in the list were doctorates from Heidelberg, Göttingen, Tübingen, Jena, Magdeburg, Breslau, Berlin, Vienna, Aarhus, Padua, Bologna, Milan, Paris, Louvain, Salamanca, Barcelona, Oxford, Cambridge, Edinburgh, Mexico, Lima, Chicago, the University of Kansas City, the St. Paul College of

Law, Stanford, and, of course, Yale. Included also was a degree of Doctor of Legal Hermeneutics from the University of Omsk, earned during a brief interval while Needlemann was a prisoner in Siberia. The suggestion of Russian influence is, thus, not entirely without foundation, although so far as I have been able to discover, it never led to a congressional investigation.

From the beginning, and as a product of his career as a chess master, Needlemann was fascinated by the law of mortgages. The marked similarity between the positional problems arising, for example, after the twelfth move in the Tchigorin defense to the Ruy Lopez and the problems arising in the law of subrogation will be readily apparent to any student of both subjects. Needlemann's first contribution to legal scholarship was his noted article on circuity of lien, which appeared in the *Ausgewählte Beiträge zum Vergleichenden Pfandrecht*, published in 1933 under the auspices of the University of Bologna, in company with articles by such other distinguished legal scholars as Reulbach, Overall, Pfiester, Brown, Kling, Schulte, Hofmann, Sheckard, Steinfeldt, Tinker, Evers, and Chance.

Having attained an enviable international reputation Needlemann achieved in 1947 the ambition of his life and came to California. He became a professor of law at Loyola, giving courses in Comparative Law and Security Transactions. His first accomplishment within the state was the completion of an exhaustive sociological and economic survey, conducted with a grant in aid from the Uplift Foundation, of the mortgage situation in Los Angeles. This survey finally and conclusively demonstrated that a mortgagor is invariably a person who needs to borrow money; and on this basis, it has become the foundation stone for many economics textbooks since.

Although Needlemann never had taken holy orders, his plump, beaming personality soon won for him the affectionate student nickname of Father Needlemann. Anyone who has had the singular good fortune to attend a symposium[3] held by the genial Father Donovan at the meetings of the Association of American Law Schools will undoubtedly remember Needlemann as a jolly, rotund, broad, expansive, fair-haired individual with a slight, but attractive, Swedish accent, bubbling over with new discoveries in the law of his beloved mortgages, gesturing dramatically with a cluster of hors d'oeuvres in one hand and a glass in the other, and enthusiastically sharing the refreshments with all comers.

---

3. "*Symposium.* In ancient Greece, a drinking together, usually following the banquet proper, with music, singing, and conversation; hence, a banquet or social gathering at which there is free interchange of ideas." WEBSTER'S COLLEGIATE DICTIONARY 1011 (5th ed. 1945).

His departure from Loyola in 1953 was not, as has been so unkindly suggested in San Francisco, due to a violent dislike for Los Angeles and the feeling that human endurance could stand no more. He loved the place, and especially he loved Loyola. He left only to write his book, which was to be, and was, the *magnum opus* of his life. He retired to a little cattle ranch in northwestern Mexico, on the outskirts of Aguardiente, where he labored for three years to untangle the California law of mortgages and deeds of trusts. He needed no library and no cases, because he had memorized them all. He finally completed the book, which was at once accepted for publication by West.

Before it was published, he was called to his ultimate reward. Without warning, Sol Humperdinck Needlemann suddenly died, of a surfeit. At this distance, there is no available information as to a surfeit of what. Professor Riesenfeld thinks that it may have been a surfeit of rolling options. Be that as it may, it was a happy death. His great work was done.

Thus perished, in the flower of his achievement, this remarkable genius, this distinguished legal scholar, this author of a lost masterpiece. The tradition, I might even say the legend, remains behind him as an enduring monument to the things that are done in the state of California.

As to what became of the book, no one knows.

Criteria for the Evaluation of Law School Examination Papers

Harold See*

"Do you want me to pass out the report cards, Ma'am? Or empty a few waste baskets? Wash your car?"

> Peppermint Patty
> *Peanuts,* June 5, 1984
> Charles Schulz

It is a generally accepted proposition that grades should be determined in a systematic manner based on individual performance. It is hardly more controversial that the criteria by which student performance is judged should be known in advance by the students. Economic analysis of law teaches us that if students behave rationally, their performances will reflect the criteria by which they understand their performances will be evaluated. Analysis of a set of examination papers should reveal the criteria those students believed were to be applied to them. Weighted frequency of occurrence obviously determines the respective weights students believe are assigned to those criteria. And, if the system is to be *fair,* the weights will determine how professors should grade the examinations.

After careful analysis extending over several years, I developed the following criteria as being most consistent with student expectations and thus most fair:

Criteria	Point Values
1. A restatement of the question asked	10 pts.
2. Use of colorful ink	7½ pts.
3. Illegible handwriting	12 pts.
4. Clever comments	2 pts. each
5. Big words (proper use optional)	1 pt. per word
6. Misspellings	1 pt. each
7. Misspelling of names and other key words that appear correctly spelled in the examination question	3 pts. each

---

* Harold See is Professor of Law, University of Alabama.

8. Half truths about the law	10 pts. each
9. Just-plain-dead-wrong law	5 pts. each
10. Accurate knowledge	1 pt.
11. Legal analysis	½ pt.
12. Analysis of an issue that may be relevant in another course	10 pts.
13. Assumptions contrary to the facts given	8 pts. each
14. Arbitrary references to case names, section numbers, Supreme Court justices...	2 pts. each
15. Arbitrary inclusion of legal terminology	3 pts. per use
16. Simplification of the problem by assuming away the issue	7 pts. per issue
17. Stating that an analysis of the problem needs to be "made by the court"	8 pts. per issue
18. Skipping a question	8 pts.
19. Skipping a question without putting the question number in the examination book	12 pts.
20. Verbatim reproduction of a standard outline of the course	"B+" for the course
21. Verbatim reproduction of a standard outline of the course including typographical errors	"A" for the course
22. The word "TIME" at the end of the examination book	15 pts.
23. The words "I enjoyed the class" at the end of the examination book	Add one letter grade to score

The results of the inquiry clearly indicate that to evaluate student performance fairly—that is, to evaluate performance in a manner consistent with student expectations—many of us will have to change the criteria we have been applying.

II. Law Professors

Minutes of the Faculty Meeting*

*Anthony D'Amato***

The regular meeting of the Faculty was called to order on Tuesday, September 17, 1991, at 4:10 p.m., in Room 223.

A motion was made to approve the minutes of the previous meeting of the Faculty. A point of order was raised to the effect that the minutes of the preceding meeting could not be found. An amendment was then offered to the main motion to approve the minutes of the preceding meeting irrespective of what they contained. There was a general heated discussion as to whether this was constitutional. At 6:24 p.m., a document was found. While it was not the minutes of the preceding meeting, it was in fact the hours of the preceding meeting. A substitute motion was then offered to approve the hours of the preceding meeting. The motion carried.

A motion was introduced by the Student Petitions Committee to approve the transfer of James Johnson for his third year to the Mahareshi Law School so that he could be with his significant other. The motion carried.

The Student Petitions Committee then moved that the Faculty approve the transfer of Laura Lawson for her third year to the Mahareshi Law School so that she could be with her significant other, whose transfer to Mahareshi Law School had recently been approved by the Faculty. The motion carried.

The Dean asked the Faculty whether it wished to consider a consideration of adding Section 6.17 to the Rules of the Law School. He pointed out that the Faculty had three choices: first, to consider Section 6.17, second, to consider considering Section 6.17, and third, to disapprove Section 6.17 and then proceed to reconsider its disapproval. A general debate followed on the proper procedure to take with respect to Section 6.17. A motion was made to disapprove Section 6.17; it carried. Then a motion was made to reconsider the disapproval of Section 6.17. A substitute motion was made to postpone the reconsideration. The substitute motion was tabled and the main motion carried.

A question was raised as to whether Section 6.17 now stood as approved or disapproved. The Dean said that, because of the parliamentary intricacy of the preceding motions, he did not know the status of Section 6.17. Then a question was raised as to the content of Section 6.17. The Dean said he was unaware of its content, and asked whether any faculty member knew what was in Section 6.17. There was general silence.

The Dean then called for the report of the Building Committee. The Faculty was told that construction on the new wing of the Law School was proceeding at a rapid pace. The Committee cited as evidence the fact that, since its last report, the new structure had grown considerably. However, one faculty member presented an alternative explanation. He said that the structure had not in fact grown, but rather that everyone had become smaller. There was general debate. The Faculty was unable to resolve which of the two competing theories was correct. A motion was introduced to table the report of the Building Committee. The motion carried.

The Dean then reported on the fund-raising efforts for the new wing. He said that there was good news and bad news. The good news was that the Building Campaign Fund had reached midpoint. The bad news was that the Building Campaign Fund still had halfway to go. A hat was passed around the table. The Dean urged all professors to contribute 50% of their last month's salary. A total of $2.16 was collected.

The Curriculum Committee reported upon the advisability of holding classes on Saturdays. There was a brief debate. It was pointed out that students on Mondays tended to forget the previous week's work, undoubtedly because of the long two-day weekend. A motion was made to add Saturday classes to the Law School schedule. A substitute motion was made to add Sunday classes as well, because it was in the spirit of the main motion. The substitute motion was defeated. Then there was debate that the main motion was rendered inconsistent by the defeat of the substitute motion. However, the main motion carried.

Dinner was then served, consisting of corn chips and water. The total bill was $2.16.

A motion was introduced to substitute potato chips for corn chips at the next faculty meeting. A vote was taken. The Faculty was evenly divided. The Dean then offered to cast a tie-breaking vote. The hypothetical question was raised that if the Dean were to cast a tie-breaking vote, what would he vote for? The Dean replied that he would vote for corn chips. A substitute motion was introduced to disempower the Dean from casting tie-breaking votes. The Dean ruled the motion out of order. The Dean's ruling was followed by a general food fight.

A faculty member demanded to see a verified copy of the original motion regarding potato chips. However, the original motion had become a paper airplane and had last been seen flying out the window.

The Dean asked whether there was any old business. The Associate Dean moved to reconsider the earlier action of the Faculty that either approved or disapproved Section 6.17. The Associate Dean moved that, although no one knew what Section 6.17 contained, whatever it contained should only be given retroactive effect and should be denied precedential effect. A question was raised by a faculty member whether there was any power to deny precedential effect to a given action by the Faculty. Arguments were heard on all sides. In the middle of the night, the question was raised whether denying precedential effect to a faculty action would itself have precedential effect. Debate continued throughout the night on this aspect of the question. A substitute motion was introduced the following morning that if the main motion regarding Section 6.17 was denied precedential effect, then the amended motion to deny precedential effect itself be denied precedential effect. A motion was made at 10:30 a.m. The motion carried. Unfortunately, your loyal Secretary was too tired to notice what it was that carried.

Finally, under the heading of "New Business," the Law School's faculty representative to the General University Committee gave a report on the state of the University. She reported that the University has been declared bankrupt and all its buildings and assets are being auctioned off. A motion was made to conceal the fact that the Law School is part of the University. The motion carried unanimously.

A motion was made to adjourn. The motion was tabled until the next regularly scheduled faculty meeting.

Respectfully submitted,

Tony D'Amato

Tony D'Amato, Secretary.

If Law Professors Had to Turn in Time Sheets[*]

Robert M. Jarvis[**]

Since January, the members of the East Overshoe State Law School faculty have been required to keep a daily log of their professional activities. The following time sheet was submitted on April 19 by Professor Quentin T. Pomerantz.

10:45 a.m.	Arrived promptly at my office. Observed Physical Plant Department delivering new furniture to Professor Gold's office. Noticed my desk and chairs are looking shabby. Made mental note to discuss with Professor Gold my sudden doubts regarding his pending application for tenure.
10:45–11:00 a.m.	Listened to voice mail messages. Had twelve from students worried about my upcoming exam. Made mental note to get unlisted phone number.
11:00–11:05 a.m.	Remembered it was "Doughnut Tuesday" in the faculty lounge. Went to faculty lounge intending to take a dozen (or so) home but discovered all doughnuts had been eaten. Made mental note to send e-mail to faculty secretaries reminding them doughnuts are for faculty members only.
11:05–11:45 a.m.	Got into lengthy discussion with Professors Green and Johnson over lack of scholarly production by law school faculty. Discovered we all agree half the faculty is loafing, should be fired, and should have their salaries redistributed to the half that is working. Got into heated disagreement over which half is which. Started to leave

* Copyright © 1998 California Law Review, Inc.
** Professor of Law, Nova Southeastern University.

but stayed to referee fistfight between Professors Green and Johnson. Had Professor Johnson ahead on points until Professor Green's KO. Made mental note to sit as far away as possible from Professor Green at future faculty meetings.

11:45–2:00 p.m.   Went to faculty club for lunch. Dined with Professor Stone from the Business School. Discovered we both agree half the University faculty is loafing, should be fired, and should have their salaries redistributed to the half that is working. Got into fistfight with Professor Stone over which half is which. Made mental note to avoid eating at faculty club for next few weeks.

2:00–2:30 p.m.   Prepared for class by looking for Teacher's Manual. Eventually remembered casebook does not have a Teacher's Manual. Made mental note to select different casebook next term.

2:30–4:00 p.m.   Taught Criminal Law class. Topic (according to casebook) was "Appeals." Discussed at length the appeal I am working on. Also discussed fact that if argument goes badly, this semester's grades will be delayed 3 to 5 years. Students seemed agitated. Made mental note not to discuss my personal life in class.

4:00–4:25 p.m.   Went to mailroom to check my mail. Also checked colleagues' mail. Noticed Visiting Professor Stanza receives lots of interesting lingerie catalogs. Made mental note to invite Professor Stanza out for a drink.

4:25–4:45 p.m.   While reading my mail, came across invitation to be keynote speaker at symposium in my primary field of research. Conference to be held next February 17–20 in Iceland. All expenses to be paid by sponsor. Also received form letter announcing Honolulu Bar Association will be holding *Recent Developments in Hawaiian Native Culture Law* CLE program February 17–20. Cost for me to attend about $14,000. Made mental note to discuss with law school's business manager my newly-acquired interest in Hawaiian Native Culture Law.

4:45–5:15 p.m.	Continued reading my mail. Saw new issue of *Eleemosynary Law Review* (top journal in my field) had arrived. Carefully checked all footnotes in all articles to see if my book had been cited. Made mental note to cancel my subscription to *ELR* in light of its recent decline in scholarship standards.
5:15–6:00 p.m.	Met Dean for drink at local watering hole. Suggested my class load be reduced in light of my unusual productivity during past year. Dean suggested instead my paycheck be reduced in light of my unusual proclivities during past year. Decided to take my offer off the table. Made mental note to check with other faculty members to see if they agree Dean seems unusually hostile these days.
6:00–8:00 p.m.	Attended law school alumni reception. Sampled various offerings from the bar. Explained (somewhat incoherently) to current and former students my single-handed defense of their right to date faculty during last month's debate on proposed Code of Faculty Ethics. Before I could finish, shown door by two rather large waiters. Made mental note not to drink at these sorts of functions in the future.
8:00–10:00 p.m.	Returned to my office. Re-read latest draft of my law review article *Charitable Giving in Boston, 1820–1860: A Case Study in Early Altruism*. Realized article is complete gibberish. Made mental note to fire research assistant who wrote it.
10:00–10:30 p.m.	Watched *Gilligan's Island* re-run on TV in faculty lounge. Still can't figure out how Professor is able to build a radio out of Gilligan's hat and two coconuts but can't get castaways off the island. Made mental note to apply for sabbatical to explore issue more fully.
10:30–10:45 p.m.	Returned to my office. Again read over latest draft of law review article. Still complete gibberish. Decided to change title to *Deconstructing the Shifting Paradigm: A Modernist, Post-Feminist Critique of the Spice Girls and Their Role in Post-Post-Industrial Society (With Apolo-*

gies to Hegel). Sent article to *Harvard Law Review.* Acceptance seems likely. Made mental note not to fire research assistant.

10:45–11:00 p.m.   Finished reading newspaper begun at breakfast. Noticed New York Yankees have given $22 million contract to hitter with lifetime batting average of .177. Left law school to find all-night sporting goods store. Made mental note to ask clerk for location of nearest all-night batting cage.

Total Hours Worked: 13 (includes time spent dodging angry students in parking lot)

Faculty Meetings:
"A Quorum Plus Cramshaw"

Ron Lansing[*]

WHEN THE SIGN PAINTER put "BEATRICE CRAMSHAW, HEAD FACULTY SECRETARY" on her office door, she told him to add "MISS" before her name. When he painted "MS." before her name, she told him to "change it at once." The sign painter complained to the Dean that she was "a crotchety ol' pisshead." The Dean was sympathetic but asked him to "please do whatever she says."

She had not always been *Miss*. For three years in the early 1940s, she was *Mrs. Cramshaw*. But when she was widowed by the war, she wanted it to be known that she was "available" even though she kept her dead soldier's last name out of respect. At 64 years of age, that was no longer her reason for being *Miss*; she was no longer "available." But she had always been known as *Miss Cramshaw* and "that was that." Besides, she found no liking for the "modern *Ms.* nonsense."

As Head Faculty Secretary, Miss Cramshaw always rendered extremely detailed minutes of monthly faculty meetings. Each dean had always told her that she need not be so elaborate, that all she needed to record were the votes and the actions taken and very brief recitals of announcements; discussion comments and her personal observations were unnecessary.

But Miss Cramshaw was not to be denied her way of reporting minutes. She had always faithfully recorded as much of the happenings as her aging hands would allow. Faculty meetings were, after all, her once a month opportunity to share and hobnob at the top. Those meetings were not open to anyone; only those who served could be there; it was an honor to be included. Her detailed recordings were a way of demonstrating her indispensable service to those meetings.

She held no use for modern word processing machines, calling them "lazy, televised nonsense." She succumbed to photocopying only when the increasing size of the faculty taxed the platen in her Smith-Corona to the point that it could no longer squeeze more carbons and onion skins.

---

[*] RON LANSING, SKYLARKS & LECTERNS: A LAW SCHOOL CHARTER 28 (1983). Reprinted with permission of Ron Lansing.

In a day of dwindling workload, she took even more tender care with the preservation of detailed faculty minutes. Recording the words that were said was more accurate for her than summarizing meanings; meanings, after all, have to be understood; words do not.

And so it was that the Minutes of the September Faculty Meeting of the Welden Hall Law School of Litchfield College appeared like this:

The Dean called the meeting to order at 12:12 p.m.

Professor Gerald Meigert suggested the absence of a quorum.

The Dean stated that he would wait a few more minutes.

Professor Conrad Kayell admonished that the meeting was already "ten minutes" late in getting started. [Twelve minutes, exactly.]

Professor Joseph Laurence III urged that the meeting get started, that his Admissions Committee had important matters on the agenda.

The Dean suggested that the meeting could maybe get started with some announcements while awaiting stragglers.

Professor Meigert agreed that that would be all right as long as no votes were cast or actions taken.

Professor Kayell wondered why mature people couldn't get to meetings on time.

Instructor Romain Johnson inquired about what the quorum rule was.

The Dean ventured that it was two-thirds of the faculty.

Professor Laurence asked where the quorum rule was written.

The Dean and Registrar Roger Willowby could not find it stated in the Faculty By-Laws or Rules of Procedure.

Professor Meigert said that a two-thirds quorum rule had always been observed in his fifteen years at the law school.

Professor Kayell could not remember how far back the two-thirds quorum rule had been observed. [No one bothered to ask the Head Faculty Secretary.]

Professor Laurence emphasized that if the quorum rule was nowhere spelled out in legislation, then it could not be imposed.

Professor Meigert advised, in no uncertain terms, that a roomful of lawyers trained in the common law system need not be reminded that not all rules are written, that some develop by observed practice.

Associate Professor Brock Webster noted that, as far as observed practice was concerned, there have probably been many faculty meetings in which business has been transacted without a quorum simply because no one had ever bothered to raise the issue. Therefore, "what custom may have given in terms of a two-thirds quorum regard, custom can take away by disregard."

The Dean stated that there were important matters to be taken up on the agenda and that he would really like to get along with the meeting.

Professor Meigert reminded that there was no meeting "to get along" that there was no quorum.

Assistant Professor Alicia Smith stated that quorums should never be set so high as two-thirds, that two-thirds is an impossible demand, and that it brings business to "a crunching halt." She stated that the principle of a quorum is "largely an anachronism," that quorums are usually set in other organizations at one-third or even as low as ten percent.

Professor Meigert asserted that this was not some "other organization" and that "we need no custom outside of our own."

The Dean asked if the meeting could please proceed insofar as there were eighteen faculty present which ought to be enough to do the meager amount of business on the agenda.

Professor Kayell then elaborated on the historical reasons for a quorum. He said that it was originally a democratic principle that arose at a time when the means of notifying members of meetings was difficult because of the absence of telephone and delays in postal service; in other words, quorum was not designed to assure enough attendance to do business, but was rather designed to insure the opportunity to attend; if a quorum of members showed up, then it was assumed that fair notification had been accomplished.

Associate Professor Webster then noted that modernly the ease of communicating meeting notices by advance technologies, satisfied the democratic principle, and that, therefore, quorums were no longer necessary.

Professor Kayell wondered why, if *some* people could make it to meetings on time, why *all* people couldn't. He expressed particular concern with the repeated absences of Professor Casey Doe.

Associate Professor Webster continued by adding that quorums were a vital democratic principle in representative bodies, such as the U.S. Senate, where members represented constituencies; but quorums had no place in faculty meetings where faculty members represented no voters and were not by their absence disenfranchising innocent people but were only voluntarily relinquishing their own rights.

Professor Meigert reminded again that "all this may be well and good" but the insistence on quorums in these faculty meetings was nevertheless the custom and the law "no matter what the reasons."

The Dean asked that the faculty move along to the agenda.

Assistant Professor Smith moved that the quorum rule, if there was one, be abolished.

Instructor Johnson seconded.

Professor Meigert declared that the motion was out of order because a motion to change the Faculty Rules of Procedure required a ten day advance notice.

Professor Laurence reminded Professor Meigert that the motion did not change the written Rules because the Rules did not expressly provide for a quorum.

Professor Meigert reminded Professor Laurence that a quorum, although unwritten, was a part of the Rules by virtue of custom.

Associate Professor Webster observed that "we've been over this ground before."

Professor Paul Pender then said that the motion was out of order for another reason: If there was no quorum, then, without a quorum, there was no official meeting from which this motion or any motion could be made.

Assistant Professor Smith asked if a quorum included the two voting student representatives, because if it did, then there was a two-thirds attendance. She computed that there were 28 full-time faculty members (including the Dean and the Librarian and the four writing instructors), and that only 18 were present, for a total of 64 percent present. But if the two student representatives were counted, then there would be 20 out of 30 present, or 67 percent, the necessary two-thirds quorum.

The Dean asked for a clarification vote on the question.

Are the two voting student body representatives considered part of the faculty for quorum purposes? The vote was fifteen (15) "YES" and two (2) "NO" and three (3) abstaining.

Professor Kayell wondered why people come to faculty meetings if they're simply going to abstain from voting.

Assistant Professor John Santori rose to a point of personal privilege to explain why he had abstained. He said that he thought it was all "b___ s___" [!!!], that he couldn't care less about quorums, that the whole meeting was taking valuable time from his task force study for the State Tax Commission.

Registrar Willowby asked for permission to speak, and, then, noted that the two student representative had voted "yes" in the last vote, and that it might be improper for someone to vote on a vote that would allow them to vote.

Professor Laurence corrected the Registrar by pointing out that the vote did not concern the students' right to vote; it concerned their status in the quorum.

The Registrar thanked Professor Laurence for that clarification but then noted that his point was still well taken. Furthermore, he thought that this might be a good time to raise again his frequently made point that staff should also be given a vote in faculty meetings if students are given such a vote.

One of the student representatives said something. [I could not hear because everyone was talking at once.]

Professor Meigert interjected by observing that the Registrar's noted inequity simply means that neither students nor staff should be allowed to vote.

Professor Paul Pender observed that staff vote or student vote in faculty meetings was not the question at hand. The question at hand is: Should students be allowed to vote on whether they are to be included in a quorum? He expressed the hope that the discussion would be precise in its focus on that specific question.

Professor Meigert argued that no one, student or faculty, should ever be allowed an official vote if there was no official quorum. A vote without a quorum is not official, and any non-quorum vote that effectively declared a quorum was a form of "bootstrapping" and against logic and Robert's Rules of Order. [The rest of it I simply could not hear.]

The Dean expressed again that "as good gentlemen all," he hoped the quorum issue could be put behind and the rest of the agenda entertained.

Assistant Professor Smith corrected the Dean and admonished him that the faculty was composed of "good gentle*persons*."

The Dean apologized by saying that he intended no offense and that he meant the word "gentlemen" as a "generic and neutral" term.

A student representative said something to the effect that she was offended. [I could not hear her because everyone was talking at the same time without being recognized by the chair!!!]

Professor Meigert said that the meeting, if there was a meeting, was getting far afield.

The Dean declared that a quorum existed and that the first item on the agenda, Approval of Minutes, should be taken up.

Assistant Professor Smith objected, saying that her motion was on the floor and had not been acted on. The Dean was in doubt and so he asked the Faculty Secretary to read any pending motions.

[I read the pending motion: "Moved that the quorum rule, if there is one, be abolished."]

The Dean apologized [again] to Assistant Professor Smith for inadvertently ignoring the motion.

Professor Meigert repeated that the motion was out of order for lack of the ten day notice and urged the Dean to so rule.

The Dean asked for advice and discussion from the faculty.

Professor Laurence urged the Dean to make a ruling, any ruling; "any command will do."

Eventually, Associate Professor Webster moved to table the motion.

Professor Laurence seconded.

Instructor Johnson attempted to argue against the tabling.

Professor Laurence admonished Instructor Johnson that a motion to table was not debatable.

The vote to table was taken and it passed: thirteen (13) "YES"; five (5) "NO"; two (2) abstaining. Assistant Professor Smith, Instructor Johnson, Librarian Neirjensky, and the two (2) student representatives opposed.

The Dean ruled that the motion to table had passed.

Librarian Neirjensky pointed out that the motion did not pass because it required a two-thirds vote for passage.

Professor Meigert said it only required a majority vote.

Librarian Neirjensky begged to differ and said that any nondebateable motion to kill debate required a two-thirds vote.

Professor Laurence said that it did not make any difference because 13 "ayes" out of *18 voting* is over 70 percent.

Librarian Neirjensky urged that 13 "ayes" out of *20 present* is less than two-thirds.

[Professor Meigert then admonished the Librarian in words this Secretary refuses to report.]

The Dean asked if anyone knew a way out of this parliamentary tangle.

At that moment, Associate Professors William Wright and Harold Thompson entered the meeting, and upon being informed and advised, promptly voted in favor of tabling the motion.

Professor Kayell asked them why they could not get to meetings on time, pointing out that the meeting was supposed to have started "30 minutes" ago. [34 minutes exactly.]

The Dean asked if it would now be all right to get to the first item on the agenda. Hearing no objection, the Dean asked for approval of the minutes of the last meeting.

Librarian Neirjensky indicated that he had not been receiving copies of the faculty minutes. [Which was wrong!] The Head Faculty Secretary carefully pointed out that I give all faculty members and staff complete copies of the minutes within three days after each meeting, that only once in 27 years had there ever been any deviation from that procedure and that was when I had to attend Judge Fortner's funeral in 1966. If anyone did not receive a copy of the minutes, it was more likely the product of their own misplacing rather than a neglect on my part.

The Librarian said that he did not mean to imply any neglect of duty and that he was sorry he mentioned it.

Professor Windom Trabeau said that, as a visitor here, he had no objection to the content of the minutes but wondered whether the minutes had to be so detailed. He thought it was "remarkable" and said he had "never seen such complete minutes before in any law school or organization." [I thank the professor for his kindness.]

Assistant Professor Smith also expressed concern about the detailed minutes and wondered if the Dean was imposing that kind of slavish commitment on the staff in other areas.

The Dean said that he could assure Professor Smith that "the detail was entirely the product of the Head Faculty Secretary's own devotion." [And this is true.]

Professor Santori felt that the detail often invaded the inner sanctum of the faculty and divulged privacies that the rest of the law school community ought not be privy to.

Professor Kayell defended the minutes and stated that they had been this way for "25 years" [27 really] and that the careful attention of the Head Faculty Secretary to such detail had often proved to be a welcome source of law school history; that whatever cost of duplication was involved, it was certainly worth the price; that he hoped the Secretary would take his remarks as a vote of confidence. [She does.]

There being no further discussion, the minutes were approved. [As they always have been approved for 27 years.]

The Dean expressed the hope that the meeting could proceed to the next item on the agenda....

The Joe Isuzu Dean Search: A Guide to the Interpretation of Announcement Letters

*Paul A. LeBel and James E. Moliterno**

Each year, law faculties receive numerous announcements of searches to replace retiring administrators. Those that are forwarded to our faculty are taped to the side of the refrigerator in the faculty lounge. Like nursery school drawings—the only other category of items that are routinely taped to refrigerators—the contents of these announcements fall into a familiar pattern, but they might not always present a completely accurate picture. The following example of an announcement letter and its interpretation is presented as a public service to faculty members faced with the task of deciding whether to update a resumé and get a friend to make a nomination.

The Letter	The Interpretation
Dear Dean X:	This letter is addressed to someone with a demonstrated history of the poor judgment involved in taking a job like this, so maybe we'll get an application from the addressee. The Madison Avenue equivalent is the cigarette ad targeted at those who already enjoy smoking.
Dean Y has recently decided to fulfill his longstanding ambition to return to full-time teaching and scholarship, and plans to return to a position on	Y hasn't written a word other than memos to faculty in the last fifteen years, and his students think that "Cancelled" is the last word in the

---

* Paul A. LeBel is Professor of Law, College of William and Mary. James E. Moliterno is Assistant Professor of Law, College of William and Mary.

the faculty at the beginning of the next academic year.

Accordingly, the ABC School of Law is pleased to announce a nationwide search for a dean who can fill the position so ably held by Dean Y.

ABC is a law school that has undergone considerable changes during the ten years of Dean Y's innovative leadership.

Enrollment has risen by nearly fifty percent, as the school has attempted to make legal education available to a wider segment of the state's population.

The law school enjoys a close relationship with its loyal body of alumni, many of whom are engaged in practice within a short distance from the school.

Maintaining good relations with the state and local bar associations has also been an important part of the law school's contribution to the profession.

Located in the center of the state capitol, the law school is housed in a building that was recently added to the state's historic preservation register.

course title, but he hasn't managed to land another dean job yet.

Having finally gotten rid of Y, we now have a chance to get someone who has some clue about how this business works.

Correcting the mistakes of Y will be the main task of the new dean, and we've had enough of this innovation nonsense—the best ideas are our ideas, and the new dean had better understand that.

The only way we've stayed afloat is to admit every warm body who can come up with the tuition.

Because every decision is certain to displease at least some segment of the constituency, a good third of your time will be spent dealing with phone calls from alumni.

After a few years of bar luncheons and dinners, you'll be qualified to publish a comparative guide to the preparation of chicken in every Ramada and Holiday Inn in the state.

Making sure that there are enough pails to catch the leaking water will occupy more of your time than faculty development and curriculum reform combined.

Expansion of the physical facilities in a cost-effective yet aesthetically pleasing manner that is architecturally consistent with the existing structure is one of the highest priority goals of the law school community.

A blend of the talents of Frank Lloyd Wright, Henry Kissinger, and Donald Trump wouldn't be able to pull this one off.

Applications, nominations and recommendations should be sent to Professor F.G.H., Department of Sociology, chair of the Dean Search Committee.

There are so many inside candidates for this job that the law faculty can't even run the search.

The Search Committee will make every effort to maintain the confidentiality of applications.

We realize that one of the few things that would be more embarrassing than getting this job is applying for it and not getting it, so your secret is safe with us.

Dear Employer...

Andrew J. McClurg[*]

Never is my opinion so highly valued by my students as when they are seeking letters of recommendation for employment.

Usually I welcome the opportunity to perform this service. When the students who come calling are earnest persons of high moral character who have aced every course they took with me, I am pleased to help them along in their careers. Below that stratum is a large group of less-than-stellar students who have a strong work ethic and a competent grasp of the law; while my praise for these students may be less effusive, I willingly write letters of recommendation for them.

And then there are students like Harold Weenicker...

---

[*] Andrew J. McClurg is Professor of Law, University of Arkansas at Little Rock. Harold Weenicker is not a real law student—or even a real person.

Brickyard □
School of Law   *Laying Legal Foundations for More Than a Century*

September 15, 1996

Ms. Laura Keenbeam
Managing Partner
Keenbeam, Broadbaum & Finch, P.A.
600 Capital Suite Plaza
Chicago, Illinois 60611

    Re: Job Application of Harold Weenicker

Dear Ms. Keenbeam:

Harold Weenicker, a former student of mine, is applying for a position with your firm and has asked me to write a letter of recommendation on his behalf.

During his law school career, Mr. Weenicker was enrolled in several of my courses, most of which he completed. In those that he did, he always showed up for the final exam, usually on time. While his grades were somewhat less than spectacular (in the C to C- range), his essay answers were always very creative. In fact, Harold informs me that his Torts exam is actually being considered for publication in a Gothic short story anthology.

Mr. Weenicker truly distinguished himself in Constitutional Law. In a class of more than one hundred students, he talked the most.

Mr. Weenicker is assertive and capable of strongly defending his positions, as he demonstrated during a spirited discussion of *Martin v. Hunter's Lessee*. I was particularly impressed by his ability to jab and circle to his left. However, Harold can also be a pleasure to be around, particularly when he is taking his medication.

It is my understanding that a major portion of your firm's practice is in the area of criminal defense. Thus, Mr. Weenicker's two felony convictions may actually prove to be an asset, given his real-world experience with the rules of criminal procedure. The same goes for your domestic relations practice. Harold's recent divorce, which you may have read about in the papers, would seem to make him a natural fit.

Reviewing Mr. Weenicker's résumé, one cannot help but be impressed by the variety of extracurricular activities he participated in while in law school. Truthfully, I did not know our law school even had a chapter of Students for a Law-Free Society until Harold successfully campaigned for the presidency of the organization.

Mr. Weenicker's strong commitment to social justice is reflected in his reliable participation in our Habitat for Humanity projects, where he never failed to bring the beer. And certainly his recognition in *Who's Who Among College Students in Natchez, Mississippi*, and his listing in the *American Directory of Mortal Kombat Players* warrant praise.

In short, I can state with confidence that a decision to hire Mr. Weenicker could possibly turn out not badly.

I would be happy to provide any additional information you may require regarding Harold Weenicker, but will be tied up for the next six months, so you may wish to contact someone else. I understand that his supervisor in the Witness Protection Program speaks highly of him.

Sincerely,

Joseph P. Bugler

Joseph P. Bugler
Professor of Law

P.S. Frankly, I believe Mr. Weenicker's role in the recent incident leading to our dean's early retirement and the closing of the law school for two weeks has been exaggerated.

III. Lawyers

The Nebbish Letter

*Glen Freyer**

Franklin Nebbish
43 Twill Drive
Gabardine, FL 57889

April 1, 1993

Mr. Ignatious Linkletter III, Jr.
Hiring Partner
Lockhart, Linkletter, Lanier and Cabbage
Washington, D.C. 20005

Dear Mr. Linkletter:

As a twenty-second year associate, I'd like to take this opportunity to answer some commonly asked questions about my resume in anticipation of our interview a month from next Thursday.

With regards to leaving my current firm, I assure you it is not for any dissatisfaction with the quality of my work. Rather, I had been hired specifically to do bankruptcy work, but between the time I was interviewed and the time I came on board, the bankruptcy section split off and formed its own firm. You can understand how upset I was when I learned of this three years later, though it now explains why the senior partner always crossed out "debtor" and "creditor" on all my pleadings.

This is not to say that I wish to be pigeon-holed as a bankruptcy lawyer. I have always sought to avoid such classifications, and if my former employers agree on anything, it is that I defy classification. I only entered bankruptcy law to flee a bloody depressing, though otherwise thriving, practice in divorce law. Being divorced three times myself, I saw divorce law as a unique opportunity

---

* © 1993 Glen Freyer. Glen Freyer is a full-time Trial Attorney with the United States Department of Justice, Environment and Natural Resources Division, and a perpetual wannabe.

65

to apply personal experience to my daily job and no doubt would have made partner at Miller, Miller-Davis, but for the threat of a paternity suit, which, I might add, was never filed.

During the four year gap immediately preceding my work as a divorce attorney (or "legal counselor to the maritally challenged" as I prefer) I was not so much unemployed as a sole practitioner without any clients. I am reasonably confident my old boss would give me a favorable recommendation. (Get it?) (Ha-ha.) Contrary to my mother's lamentations (we are still very close), my decision to take a paralegal job before returning to full legal duties was not an act of desperation, nor even, in my mind, a step down the law firm ladder. Instead, it was a once-in-a-lifetime, grab-it-while-you-can chance to bolster my *Bluebook* skills which had grown rusty in twenty years of unchecked application. I believe that "retooling," if you will, makes me a better candidate. (Ha-ha. I'm still chuckling over that last one. I *was* the boss. Ha-ha-ha.)

For the one year prior to that, I filled in for Rusty the Bailiff on *The People's Court*. That experience honed my appreciation of small claims court and its attendant procedures. I also became close personal friends with Judge Wapner who is a brilliant jurist and the kind of guy who would show you his Victoria's Secret catalogue if you asked. I believe the Judge would give me a favorable recommendation. He can be reached through his agent.

However, my real practical experience came in four years at the white collar civil litigation firm of Harry, Wendt and Browndum, during which time I was eighth chair on a major federal tax case. No one ever told me what the case was about, but I believe one of the issues I researched actually may have been incorporated into a footnote in a trial brief which would have been filed had the parties not reached a last minute settlement. While I believe I would have made partner with this firm as well, a restraining order, erroneously placed upon me by my second wife, required me to move out of the northern half of the country.

Many prospective employers have asked why, before Harry, Wendt, I did not stay on as corporate counsel to one of the largest frozen food giants in the country (you know who I mean). Frankly, while many aspire to pseudoretirement as in-house counsel, I feared losing the formidable legal skills I had amassed. Contrary to local accounts, it was not because of the fated button mushroom incident which I believe the press blew way out of proportion (no indictments actually resulted).

Previously, I was a public defender in the inner city of Terre Haute. Although

I had never practiced criminal law before, my clients all seemed to like me. References can be obtained by writing the prison directly. I might add that I received an award and honorary dinner that year from the Terre Haute District Attorney's Office, though I was never told exactly what for.

When one of my former clients was released and went on to become the Dean of a major metropolitan law school in Montana (accreditation expected in late 1996, but will not be announced until 1997 to coincide with the Crown's return of Hong Kong to the Chinese), I became a legal writing instructor. It was then that I learned how law school exams are graded. As with magicians, sadly I am sworn to secrecy. All I can say is it's actually pretty funny.

In the publish or perish frenzy of legal academia, I wrote an article, subsequently published in the New England Journal of Medicine, entitled *Streptococcus: a Legal Analysis*. The article was cited by the Supreme Court in a string cite for the proposition that every word in a statute must be read to have some meaning, even if the meaning doesn't make any sense.

Before these two jobs, I was managing partner in my father's law firm for eight days before a trustee took it over in receivership. Many policies implemented during my short tenure, including that all associates use law books sometime during the calendar year, have remained in effect.

Prior to that, there's not much to tell. Oh, sure, there was my police record and disbarment, but they are triflings in a career that has spanned two, almost consecutive decades. I was only keeping the hookah pipe for a friend and still maintain that the state exceeded its police powers when it shackled me to a tree until I stopped whining. But those days of doing drugs, tracks up and down your arms, so shit-faced you can hardly see, crying "F*** the police" are long gone. I will sorely miss the late eighties. Also with regard to my tattoo, it is the scales of justice. I know the top looks like a cross-bow where it peeks out over my collar, but it is the scales, and a most tasteful rendition at that. I assure you I was blind drunk when I got it, but then you know how wild Claims Court Clerks can be when you get two or three of them together in one room.

As a final point, I note that some prospective employers have felt compelled to ask why I attended seven different law schools, to which I respond that I shop for education no less thoroughly than I shop for a toaster. Some have asked why I would shop seven places for a toaster, to which I have no response, but I can get one by Thursday if you're really interested. With six years of law school under my belt, I can't help but feel that I am a more competent attorney for the experience. I can also recite large portions of *Palsgraf* verbatim which is a real crowd pleaser at children's parties.

I am not an apologist for my career choices. I feel it is important to say that right at the beginning of this letter. (In rereading this letter I note that I did not say it right at the beginning, but I assure you I was thinking it the entire time.) The point is, my career is the career of every lawyer, the career every lawyer lusts after, the career every lawyer would choose if he were not so afraid of being considered a slacker, a loser, a dolt. I am not unwilling to climb the law firm ladder or to play the game. I have years of untapped ass-kissing left in me and the perspective of life's ups-and-downs to appreciate just how important that is. Post hoc, ergo propter hoc. That's what I always say, although usually after I've been drinking when its meaning is more clear.

Circumstances beyond my control have prevented me from attaining many of the prizes my peers believe are the sine qua non of a career in justice, but who could argue with my record? Nay, who? (I would be writing *my own* recommendation. Ha.)

I look forward to meeting you and your fellow partners to discuss your partnership track and how profits are shared. Such frank talks always get me extremely excited as I'm sure they do you. If you have any questions after reading over my resume, please contact me and I will gladly address them further or to your satisfaction, whichever comes first. If after all this you are still unsure, I will consider springing for lunch, though I warn you, it may cause me to seriously question your commitment to any future business collaboration. Thank you way, way ahead in advance.

                                        Sincerely,

                                        Franklin Nebbish

enc: resume
         naked photos of your wife
FN/fn

Does Secured Transaction Mean I Have a Lien? Thoughts on Chattel Mortgages (What?) and Other Complexities of Article IX

*Marianne M. Jennings**

Table of Contents

* Marianne M. Jennings is a professor of legal and ethical studies in business at Arizona State University, which is a fancy way of saying she is essentially unemployable in the private sector. She tried her best at the practice of law, beginning with criminal defense work at the federal level (i.e. bank robbers who have the courtesy to commit crimes on video tape). She lost every case but did successfully place a few of the tapes on *America's Funniest Videos*. Having lost every case and her self-esteem, she turned to a medium in which results are not expected: the halls of academe. She has done remarkably well.

Marianne wishes to thank some people for helping her with this article, but none of them were willing to have her/his name associated with it. Her law student, David Gass, when approached about a line of credit replied, "Please, I'm trying to get a job here."

69

I. Introduction

Article IX[1] of the UCC[2] is called Secured Transactions;[3] Sales of Accounts and Chattel Paper.[4] The title alone tells you you're in big trouble because: a) no one ever uses the term "secured transaction;"[5] b) the term chattel paper has never been used in real life by anyone who continues to hold a job;[6] and, c) no one sells accounts anymore.[7] Therefore, you have a title that reflects a law for things that are out of use, out of work, and out of date.[8]

But beyond the title of Article IX,[9] there are other complexities. My theory is that no one really understands Article IX[10] and that's why most of us are still

---

1. That's "9" for those of you who forget your Ms, Cs, Vs, Xs, Ls and haven't watched the credits to a movie in so long that your recollection remains unrefreshed by the only mode of modern communication that continues to use roman numerals (i.e., movie copyright dates; it's Hollywood kids—the land of Axel Rose, Woody Allen, Pee Wee Herman, Madonna and other such shining examples who make us glad that we don't use roman numerals if these folks are evidence of what will happen to you if you do) apart from the UCC folks and people who do the outlines for law review articles. Just let them try to outline this article. I'm doing my subject heads in the metric system. By the way, I have it on good authority (albeit non-Bluebook authority because I didn't get his first name) that Hollywood is considering a switch to the metric system.

2. That would be Uniform Commercial Code for those of you who opted out of rigor for years two and three of law school or who have been practicing personal injury law for seventeen years and forgotten that there are statutes.

3. Should this be a colon or a comma? Far be it for me to correct a UCC-typo.

4. Has anyone ever seen a piece of chattel paper? If so, is it stamped "Chattel Paper" with one of those stamps like we have for "Copy" or "Paid," or for non-personal injury lawyers and their bills "Past Due"?

5. In fact, business people would be either a) drummed out of their rotary club or b) sent to work for the RTC (that's Resolution Trust Corporation for the three lawyers who have escaped unscathed from the savings and loan crisis) if they used this term. Business people say things like, "I have a lien on his inventory" or "His eyeballs are mortgaged to me," or more correctly, "His chattels are mine!"

6. In fairness to the authors of the UCC, no one has yet come forward to confess to authorship (and if their *Miranda* warnings are given, they'll never own up to writing those sections on priorities. *See, e.g.,* UCC §§ 9-301, 9-302, 9-308 (1992) (chattel paper is defined in § 9-105(b)).

7. What with no economy and all, there doesn't seem to be much interest in buying "Accounts Payable." There are no more "Accounts Receivable" only "Past Dues."

8. This same description could apply to members of Congress and we're still tolerating them, so why do I pick on Article IX? Elaboration will arrive. That's lay language for the Bluebook's *see infra* 9-83 and accompanying text. Thankfully, the short title is Uniform Commercial Code—Secured Transactions. Also should the—be a: ? *See supra* note 3.

9. That's "Article 9 liters" in metric.

10. Describe the last time someone could explain to you why a purchase money security interest in consumer goods is perfected automatically, but the perfection doesn't count if someone buys the secured property (i.e., chattel). *See* UCC § 9-307(2) (1992). In fact, describe the last time someone could explain to you the automatic perfection of a pur-

operating with the 1972[11] version of Article IX, and why car titles and liens are handled through a different set of rules altogether.[12] In fact, my students go out of their way to tell me that they would not accept a six-figure salary if the job involved any sort of work with Article IX or saying the word "chattel."[13]

Article IX has become one of those areas of law completely dependent on forms, devoid of any real comprehension and capable of disasters of biblical proportions in the event the forms were lost.[14] Additionally, we just don't have enough charts for Article IX. In fact, no one has been able to reduce all the complexities of Article IX to chart form.[15]

---

chase money security interest in consumer goods. In fact, describe the last time someone could explain to you what a purchase money security interest (PMSI) is. Better yet, name a human being who talks about Article IX and has a social life.

11. Oh, sure, there were amendments in 1977. These amendments made Article IX applicable to uncertificated securities. When was the last time someone was able to explain what uncertificated securities are? Better yet, when was the last time you saw an uncertificated security? *See* UCC § 9-103(b). Now there is currently an Article IX study committee. These people are in high demand for judicial appointments and wakes. The committee's charge is to decide whether Article IX needs revision. The committee was formed in 1990 and last seen in 1991. Police are still investigating, but it is believed they disappeared leaving only a single chattel as a clue, somewhere around § 9-301. *See* WILLIAM H. BURKE, ET AL., INTERIM REPORT ON THE ACTIVITIES OF THE ARTICLE 9 STUDY COMMITTEE (1991).

12. Otherwise, we run the risk of having our cars referred to as chattels. Okay, the Mercury Bobcat, Plymouth Volare and Pacer (formerly of American Motors) deserve to be called chattels, but it's a tragedy to label a Lexus a chattel.

13. I have no documented proof that they would turn down a six-figure salary to avoid secured transactions. But, what I can offer as circumstantial proof is the fact that their preliminary question to interviewers is: "This job doesn't involve PMSIs does it?" Hence, this self-screening device precludes obtaining documentation of the six-figure claim. Preclusion by self-screening devices is rare among lawyers seeking employment. I offer this example as evidence of the trauma inflicted upon students who have taken a course on UCC Article IX. Also, I think preclusion by self-screening is an exception to the general priority rules under Article IX. *See* UCC §§ 9-301 to -316 (1992).

14. Actually, I've also described bankruptcy, negotiable instruments, discovery and ERISA. But, with the exception of bankruptcy, there are no chattels in the other areas. A disaster of biblical proportion would include having the counter help (i.e., filing officer per § 9-407) out sick, thus leaving lawyers unattended as they attempt to file financing statements. We would need a new priority under § 9-319 (which does not exist) for the authority to give creditors whose lawyers tried to file financing statements without counter help priority over unsecured creditors. We could punish the lawyers by instituting a future ban on them ever having a consumer PMSI.

15. Even negotiable instruments (i.e., Articles III and IV; "Articles 3 kilos and 4 meters" in metric) have been reduced to charts. One of the most famous appears in White & Summers. JAMES J. WHITE & ROBERT S. SUMMERS, UNIFORM COMMERCIAL CODE 581 (1982). It's that chart with → ← ↑ ↓ going so many different ways it makes you think it would have been easier to try for that Ph.D. in Biochemical Calculus and Engineering and forget the law.

My follow-up to my theory on no one understanding Article IX is that no one has ever read Article IX.[16] We could motivate change (in reading habits and perhaps Article IX itself) by including pictures. We might even be able to get students to accept six-figure salaries that involve work with financing statements. Also, I believe we have burdened the counter help at recording offices for too long. A final theory I have is that the counter help are the only ones capable of executing Article IX requirements. This ability stems from never being forced to read Article IX.[17]

5K. (That's Metric for "II.") Creating a Security Interest (That's a Lien for Article IX Neophytes)

For folks who practice law and dabble in Article IX,[18] creating a security interest is easy. You buy a security agreement form from the local form place,[19] fill it out,[20] and you've got a security interest. However, Article IX creates all sorts of form nuances. For example, on the security agreement, you have to describe the collateral in which you are creating the security interest. Many people would just like to write "Vern's inventory" in the blank space following the instructions, "List collateral here."[21]

But Article IX requirements on security agreements are a little bit fussier

---

16. I exaggerate. There was that one guy who read it and now operates a ferry near Squim, Washington, wears two mismatched L.L. Bean boots and hasn't spoken since the 1977 version except to mutter, "How can field warehousing constitute perfection?"

17. They have never even touched the Gilbert's Outline on Article IX. Their comprehension is so extensive you can witness lawyers actually holding creditors' chattels while standing at the counter asking, "Can I file this?" The counter help tenderly refuse to accept their salt water aquaria and javelins and explain that possession and filing need not be done simultaneously under Article IX. One or the other will work for perfection. *See* UCC §9-302 (1992) *infra* notes 44–64.

18. These would be the folks who got tired of running ferries in towns with populations of 50, all of whom had their own boats.

19. Run by the folks who used to be counter help at the financing statement filing places, but got tired of helping lawyers create perfected security interests for free and decided to make some money, while avoiding one-on-one daily contact with lawyers. A desire, I might add, often expressed by 99% of the American public.

20. The form is a chart, really. Those counter folks label all the boxes so you know exactly what to do. You must avoid law school to be able to draft forms with such clarity.

21. The form also has in parentheses: "Put down the stuff you want a lien on." These counter people clearly understand the level of intellectual comprehension and cognitive reasoning skills their lawyer customers possess.

and certainly more formal than say, "Mr. Green Jean's livestock."[22] You must "reasonably identify"[23] your collateral. Actually, "Vern's Inventory" might work if Article IX didn't throw in confusing issues about what Vern's inventory could become.[24] For example, collateral that started as inventory can turn into proceeds, accounts, or in the case of farm inventory, can actually multiply.[25] In *Cargill, Inc. v. Perlich*,[26] Shipshewana State Bank[27] took a security interest in "the hogs on Perlich's farm together with the young, product and produce thereof."[28] As it turns out, hogs are purchased, fattened, and turned into bacon

---

22. Mr. Green Jeans was Captain Kangaroo's friend. I don't know either of their first names in spite of the Bluebook's fifteenth edition requirement that all cited folks now have first names.

23. Section 9-110 includes this language. When I was in law school, we were required to memorize the titles and numbers of the UCC sections. Our professor assured us that these section numbers would be a means of speaking shorthand and such shorthand would be expected in the practice of law. I memorized them all and moved to Arizona where our statute numbers for the UCC didn't match the code sections until 1984. Further, the first time I went to court, I began using my long-fought-for shorthand. The judge stopped, looked at me over the top of his glasses and said, "I have no idea what you're talking about. And if you say PMSI one more time I'm citing you for contempt."

24. Vern's inventory is not made up of chameleons. It's just that Vern could sell that original inventory. Unless, of course, Vern just has inventory to impress his friends with statements such as, "My inventory is high this month." Indeed, without any sales, Vern's inventory is bound to remain high. I learned this while seeking my undergraduate finance degree. But, we never knew Article IX existed. In fact I don't think any business folks know or care about Article IX. It's those trustees in bankruptcy who get all worked up about it.

25. Clarification: The inventory reproduces; it is not a mathematical function. The farm collateral is not sitting around doing multiplication tables. Well, they could be (*see* Mr. Green Jeans, *supra* note 22), but you can't get a security interest in multiplication tables or math ability. If you could, there would be many defaults and sales come SAT time each semester.

26. 418 N.E.2d 274 (Ind. Ct. App. 1981).

27. Shipshewana is a small town near Squim, but as far as I have been able to determine, it's ferryless.

28. *Cargill*, 418 N.E.2d at 277.

over a six-month period.[29] Hogs were coming and going and Perlich didn't pay his loan back to the bank. The bank wanted the hogs.[30] Perlich said they weren't the same hogs that existed when the security agreement was executed and "young,"[31] product[32] and produce"[33] wasn't a good enough description to cover new hogs.[34] But the Indiana court, drawing on its vast farm trivia experience, held the clause was sufficient to cover after-acquired hogs. So the bank lucked out with whole hog coverage, so to speak.

We thus learn from the hogs and develop our first chart.

---

29. Article IX and litigation on it are full of farm trivia like this. For example, the definition of "farm products" under §9-109(3) says farm products applies to crops or livestock in their unmanufactured states and lists ginned-cotton, wool-clip, maple syrup, milk and eggs as examples. UCC §9-109(3) (1992). When do eggs become manufactured and what form do they take when they are manufactured? [*See generally* Roger I. Abrams, *Law and the Chicken: An Eggs-agerated Curriculum Proposal,* 17 NOVA L. REV. 771 (1993) (for a dissertation regarding law and chickens).]. The comments to §9-109 offer this clarification:

> [W]hat is and what is not a manufacturing operation is not determined by this Article. At one end of the scale some processes are so closely connected with farming—such as pasteurizing milk or boiling sap to produce maple syrup or maple sugar—that they would not rank as manufacturing. On the other hand an extensive canning operation would be manufacturing. This line is one for the courts to draw.

UCC §9-109 cmt. 4. I think if we leave it to the courts, we should soon have a ruling that canned eggs are inventory and not farm products. Other farm trivia: Hailstorms destroy cotton crops, and hence collateral (when it is the cotton) and hence security interests and hence the farmer growing the crop and hence the bank carrying the farmer, cotton and hail. Valley Nat'l Bank v. Cotton Growers Hail Ins., Inc., 747 P.2d 1225 (Ariz. Ct. App. 1987).

It's just plain nifty to realize that one can purchase hail insurance, isn't it? Ultimate farm trivia: You can have a floating lien on cheese. This floating lien cheese (or is it floating cheese lien?) doesn't sound like the type of cheese you'd want on your sandwich, but it does give you Article IX priority. Masson Cheese Corp. v. Valley Lea Dairies, Inc., 411 N.E.2d 716 (Ind. Ct. App. 1980).

30. One has to wonder what the bank officer's "To Do" list looked like:
  – Review new FASB guidelines;
  – Prepare loan data for HUD;
  – Repossess Perlich's hogs.

31. This would be baby hogs. Or it could be hogs in their mid-twenties.

32. This would be pork, bacon, pork rinds and other high cholesterol foods denounced by everyone but, nonetheless, purchased and eaten by everyone as evidenced by Perlich's high hog turnover (unlike Vern).

33. I don't think we really want to know what this is. Hog produce has little appeal even in the most charitable vision.

34. Whether young or old. For other cases hog-tied under Article IX, see FDIC v. Bowles Livestock Comm'n Co., 937 F. Supp. 1350 (D. Neb. 1990) and Farmers State Bank & Trust Co. v. Mikesell, 554 N.E.2d 900 (Ohio 1988).

CHART 1
Making Sure You Have a Security Interest

1. Buy a form (preferably a security interest form).
2. Fill in the blanks (seek help from filing clerks or counter help if you get confused).
3. When describing the collateral, be sure to explain what it can turn into, and include what it makes, for example: Ivor's Chickens; Ivor's Chickens' eggs; Ivor's frozen chicken parts; McNuggets (Chicken); Ivor's canned eggs; Ivor's omelettes (canned).
4. There is no need to take hogs to be filed.

Keep in mind there are exceptions to the requirement that you need a security agreement (form) to create a security agreement. This is the Article IX version of "Possession is nine tenths of the law."[35] If you got the collateral, you got priority.[36]

My favorite means of possession under Article IX is field warehousing. Initially students wonder how a creditor is able to get fields into a warehouse and how inventory is done.[37] But under this type of possession the creditor sends an agent to camp out[38] at the debtor's place to watch over the collateral.[39] Usually the buyer can't touch the collateral or anything it turns into unless the agent says it's okay. You don't need too much in the way of paperwork when the creditor's agent is sitting on the collateral with a .44 Magnum.[40] It's just lovely to have this Article IX exception for a security device that was last used in the days of Dillinger.

---

35. We learned this as toddlers when we grabbed a Pound-a-Peg hammer from another child and yelled, "Mine." This was the Article IX equivalent of an automatically perfected consumer PMSI. We immediately had priority. Of course we did not learn of our Article IX priority until our adult years. It's best this way due to anticipated problems with juvenile delinquency induced by early exposure to chattels and being pounded by hammers.

36. This line was adapted from Al Pacino in THE GODFATHER II (MCMLXXIV).

37. However, by this point in the semester, they are more than willing to accept it as yet another bit of Article IX farm trivia.

38. Well, he's just there during business hours. What with the farm, field and stream focus, I did not want to mislead you and have you convinced that Article IX is a haven for the *Hee Haw* crowd.

39. Preferably a trustworthy agent, i.e., non-lawyer agent.

40. This Article IX principle was adapted from Marlon Brando and James Caan in THE GODFATHER (MCMLXXII), or is it Mario Puzo's *The Godfather?* Or is it Don Corleone and Sonny (Santino) Corleone?

10K. (That's Metric for "III.")
Why a Security Interest is Never Enough
and Article IX Places So Much Pressure
on Creditors for Perfection

The drafters of Article IX were a compulsive lot. Having collateral is not good enough for a creditor. Creditors need to obtain perfection if they expect to have any real rights in the collateral. Once you reach perfection,[41] you win out over those slothful secured parties and the derelict unsecured parties whose lack of personal drive relegates them to positions beneath the perfected.[42]

The first way to perfect your security interest is by possession. Possession is IX tenths of Article IX. Again, the gun and guard have equal weight with filing papers. The only trick is to get the collateral in your possession before the other secured parties pull some alternative means of perfection.[43]

Those alternative means of perfection include the ever-popular filing of a financing statement.[44] The filing of the financing statement is mental gymnastics. First, you have to figure out what your collateral is.[45] Collateral is divided into several Article IX categories. Collateral can be inventory, consumer goods,[46] fixtures,[47] farm products,[48] chattel paper,[49] equip-

---

41. Inserting a religious tone here, once you reach perfection, you should probably be transferred to the next life and priority and foreclosure on Article IX security interests may no longer be one of your high priorities, so to speak.

42. In fairness to both secured and unsecured parties, I should note that their lack of ambition may be attributable to the fact that they looked at §§ 9-302 to -305 of the Uniform Commercial Code and decided they would rather risk Chapter 7 bankruptcy than read about Article IX perfection. *See* UCC §§ 9-302 to -305 (1992). These unsecured and secured creditors are no worse off than students who reject six-figure salaries rather than say "PMSI." *See supra* note 14.

43. A gun will also come in handy here. You might also try some farm products and animal heads in their beds to convince them to allow you to take possession. *See* GODFATHER I, *supra* note XL.

44. No one who expects to get anything filed uses this term. The correct term is UCC-1. Try telling the counter person that you would like to file a financing statement and they will respond, "Fresh out of law school, eh?"

45. As we know from *supra* notes 31–34, this may be intriguing for items such as hog produce.

46. These are goods of consumers. The Bluebook people made me do this footnote.

47. Goods affixed to real property or some law students in the student lounge.

48. We've been down this road *supra*. Let's not go hogwild.

49. This would be paper covering chattels. From the same family as wallpaper. Actually chattel paper is commercial paper or negotiable instruments. Now, wouldn't it make more sense to use the same term here as we use in Articles III and IV? Also, wouldn't it

ment,[50] accounts[51] and general intangibles.[52] The best part about collateral under Article IX is that the answer is never the same. A computer in the hands of IBM is inventory. A computer in the hands of H & R Block is equipment. A computer in the hands of a law student is a consumer good that is not paid for.[53] A computer in the hands of a farmer should be covered by hail insurance.

The ever-changing quality of collateral contributes to the ever-fluctuating process of filing a UCC-1. There are two places to file a financing statement to reach perfection. One is local and one is central. No state should be without these government offices: the Local Recorder and the Secretary of Central.[54] The basic thrust of the filing location is that some UCC-1s are filed with land records and other UCC-1s are filed with all the other business stuff[55] with the Secretary of State.

Here's the real problem. If you file in the wrong place, it's as if you didn't file at all. So, Chart 2 is designed to show you where to file the UCC-1s according to the types of collateral and also to demonstrate how, by creating confusion about collateral, the drafters of Article IX were able to double filing revenues in all states.

---

make more sense to use a term that some functioning human being with an income has used in the twentieth century (that's XXth century)? If you say to a debtor, "I'll need to have your chattel paper as collateral," he will respond by saying either: a) "Fresh out of law school, eh?," or b) "I'm calling the vice squad."

50. The real definition for this is found in UCC § 9-109(2) (1992).

51. This would be where you pledge your accounts receivable as collateral. It tends to hurt the cash flow, but not as much as not selling inventory. See Vern in *supra* note 24.

52. Surprisingly, hog produce is not a general intangible. "General intangibles" sounds like something you would pledge when all you have for collateral is a Pacer and an eight-track cassette player. The term seems to connote "no documented value." Actually, § 9-106 defines general intangibles as anything other than the stuff listed before that is not chattel paper, but includes payment for the use or hire of a vessel. UCC § 9-106 (1992). It's a good thing sailors' wages are classified as general intangibles. For those keeping score, farmers and sailors score big under Article IX.

53. But the creditor could take an additional interest in a general intangible, like have the student's pledge of a stream of six-figure earnings that will come once he or she learns to say UCC-1.

54. Actually, UCC § 9-401 (1992) has three possible alternatives which states could adopt for filing and a note to remind legislators to select only one of the three alternatives. I believe this reminder supports my theory that no one understands Article IX because the drafters even had to explain that the sections proposed were different rules for filing. Otherwise, states probably would have adopted all three and then faced the priority problems later. See *infra* notes 56–64.

55. An imprecise term that includes limited partnerships, d/b/as, a/k/as, tradenames, corporations and other business paraphernalia.

CHART 2

Proper Filing Locations for Financing Statements* According to Collateral Type[56]

Collateral	Place of Filing	
	Central	Local
Consumer Goods	✓	✓
Fixtures	✓	✓
Inventory	✓	✓
Equipment	✓	✓
Chattel Paper	✓	✓
Farm Products	✓	✓
Accounts	✓	✓
General Intangibles	✓	✓

*UCC-1 for non-law students

In addition, Article IX has other means of perfection.[57] As near as I've been able to figure, two of these means of perfection involve time limits of twenty-one days[58] and four months,[59] and apply to both chattel paper[60] and tractors moved out of state.[61] With that limited scope, I believe we could garner sup-

---

56. Sitting in a field warehouse with a .44 Magnum is looking good, eh?

57. These other means are studied in law school and ignored by everyone else except in cases where Don Corleone is involved.

58. *See* UCC 9-304(4) (1992). You have 21 days to find the negotiable instrument or chattel paper used as collateral. Is this really a problem? Don't most creditors want to see collateral first? Except, of course, in the case of general intangibles which, as we know, are largely air.

59. *Id.* § 9-103(3). If the debtor trots out of state with your collateral, you have four months to figure out that he has gone and refile in the state where he has gone to (at both the Secretary of Central and Local Records).

60. Interestingly, § 9-304 switches back to terms like instruments and negotiable documents, largely ignoring chattel paper. I'm all for it, of course. *Id.* § 9-304.

61. In Exchange Bank v. Jarrett, 588 P.2d 1006 (Mont. 1979), Daniel F. Holland (Holland), a Florida contractor (from Kissimmee), borrowed money from the Exchange Bank of Osceola (Osceola) and gave Osceola a security interest in his tractor-scraper. Osceola filed a financing statement in Florida (with counter help, of course). Holland then took his tractor-scraper collateral to Montana. (I don't know the difference between a tractor and a tractor-scraper but the court uses the terms interchangeably and does not indulge in farm trivia enlightenment.) Holland then sold his tractor-scraper to Spencer Jarrett without Osceola's permission and proceeded to default on the Osceola loan. (Osceola and Kissimmee have Squim potential.) The bank filed its UCC-1 in Montana after the sale to Jarrett, but before four months had expired. The bank was able to keep the tractor-scraper. No bank should be without one. Jarrett was last seen wandering the streets of Kissimmee in search of Holland muttering phrases such as, "Perfection without filing?"

port for just ignoring these exceptions altogether. In fact, as the counter help will tell you, "Hey, no filing, no perfection."[62]

26K. ("IV.")
The Marathon of Article IX—
Priority of Parties

Just the order of Article IX is a clue as to how much trouble you're in if you try to figure out the priorities of creditors in the same collateral.[63] Part 3 of Article IX covers the order of priorities and precedes Part 4 on filing, which tells you how to get priority. I believe most people get lost in priorities because right in the first section of Part 3, there is a discussion of lien creditors.[64] Most secured parties thought they had a lien when they filed their UCC-1, and hence believed they were lien creditors until the priority issue arose. Confused and concerned about their priority, you find them traipsing back to the counter help (filing officer) and asking, "You know when I filed that UCC-1 thing, well, did that give me a lien or not?"[65]

Once the identity crisis is over (through the realization that Article IX does not give you a lien), you are free to proceed to a real discussion of priorities. It will be the first discussion of Article IX priorities ever held. Courts exercise the greatest judicial restraint in Article IX cases on priorities. That restraint involves never really deciding on priorities but finding some flaw in the pa-

---

62. Jarrett has obviously not spoken with the counter help.

63. This is the UCC's charitable description of debtors who pledge 30 bottlecaps as collateral for five creditors who are owed $12 million in the aggregate. Just a twist to the right or left (no pun intended) and it would be fraud. Under Article IX it translates into fun and games in bankruptcy court as the trustee tries to decide whether to just give the creditors a pro rata share of the bottlecaps or actually be forced to read Article IX and decide who has priority and give them all to that creditor. Counting bottle caps is more fun than reading about priorities under Article IX. In fact, chewing bottlecaps is more fun than reading about priorities under Article IX.

64. UCC § 9-301(3) (1992) defines a lien creditor as a "creditor who has acquired a lien on the property involved by attachment, levy or the like...." This definition doesn't help because security agreements are brought about by "attachment" too. See UCC § 9-203 (1992). Go figure. In addition, any statute that offers a definition that includes terms as vague as "and the like" gives the appearance that the drafters didn't know what was going on either. *But see* my theory *passim* on no one understands Article IX.

65. To which the counter help will respond, "Hey, we're just here to tell lawyers what to do. We don't do windows and we don't read statutes, especially not Article IX."

perwork to get rid of all the parties but one. Hence, no priority issues.[66] In fact, I have yet to discover another theory on Article IX.

All those rules for filing in different places[67] exist to help courts narrow down the parties to avoid priority conflicts. For example, suppose a consumer buys a tractor for use in his vegetable garden which sometimes produces sufficient yield for sales. Where does John Deere, the seller/creditor file? Or does John Deere have a PMSI in consumer goods hence eliminating the need to file? Either way the court has a nice out and can avoid deciding between John Deere and the seed company that took a security interest in the tractor as well.[68]

Now, even the best courts are occasionally unable to nitpick their way out of Article IX priorities. At some point we have the showdown at the OK Corral.[69] Priorities under Article IX are covered in sixteen sections, not counting the rules on filing. Those sixteen sections can be reduced to two charts.

---

66. *See, e.g.,* National Cash Register Co. v. Firestone & Co., 191 N.E.2d 471, 472 (Mass. 1963) ("All contents of the luncheonette including equipment such as: booths and tables; stand and counter, tables; chairs; booths; steam tables; salad unit; potato peeler; U.S. Slicer; range; case; fryer; compressor; bobtail; milk dispenser; silex; 100 class air conditioner; signs; pastry case; mixer; dishes; silverware; tables; hot fudge; ? Haven Ex.; 2 door stationwagon 1957 Ford A57R107215....'" was held to include a cash register hence defeating a second security interest in the cash register). If you are going to list hot fudge, wouldn't you include a cash register? By eliminating the cash register, the court found security interests in different collateral, didn't have to delve into priorities, avoided making reversible error, didn't make a higher court spit at them because an Article IX priorities case was dumped on them, and got to go home early. Also, judges have offices near the counter where UCC-1s are filed. They can turn to the counter help at anytime to solicit errors. In short, appellate courts have the Article IX pros as consultants.

67. *See supra* notes 44–53 and Chart 2.

68. One has to wonder about tractor collateral for a couple of envelopes of pumpkin seeds. One also has to wonder about consumers using tractors in 9 X 12 gardens. But, as we know, Article IX is into priority conflicts and not reality.

69. This is not to imply that all showdowns involve farm products or equipment. Although a filing (UCC-1) on the "OK Corral" would not include hot fudge or cash registers.

CHART 3*
Article Priority Rules**

General Rules Parties Perfected vs. Perfected	Priority Rule First to Perfect
Exceptions to the General Rule:	
PMSI in inventory (later) vs. Perfected	PMSI in inventory (Perfects before delivery/notifies perfected party)
PMSI in equipment vs. Perfected	PMSI in equipment if perfected within 10 days of delivery
Fixtures vs. Perfected	Fixtures if perfected within 10 days of annexation

* Source: UCC § 9-312 (1992). When you read it you won't believe how great this chart is.
** Assuming the court finds no errors in your paperwork. If such error is present, you lose all your standing. Priority rules don't apply.

If you have a situation that doesn't fit into Chart 3 and it's not a buyer situation (see Chart 4), you should consult Beulah the Palm Reader.[70] She has an inside track on who will have priority in your Article IX bottlecaps. Now, if you have a buyer situation, say a buyer who has purchased a Garfield suction cup doll with thirty-two perfected Article IX security interests, you will want to know if the buyer will get to keep Garfield.

Before proceeding to Chart 4, you will need to determine if the Garfield buyer was a buyer in the ordinary course of business.[71] If he bought Garfield at a Garfield store, he's a buyer in the ordinary course of business. If he bought Garfield from a member of the Hell's Angels outside Pierre's Lucky-7 Bar, he is not a buyer in the ordinary course of business.[72] Chart 4 shows what happens to Garfield, his buyer and the creditors of the Hell's Angels.

---

70. No Bluebook cite. *But see* seedy motels.
71. Defined in UCC § 1-201(9) (1992).
72. He is probably also lucky to be alive.

CHART 4

> [a] UCC-1 filed; correct as to form; description = "All store's inventory of Garfield suction-cup dolls and their cash register."
>
> [b] Also applies to Garfield dolls without suction cups. See section 9-307 which makes it clear Article IX priority rules are not respecters of suction cups.
>
> [c] Assumes he is able to leave Pierre's.
>
> [d] There is a minority view that Don Corleone wins regardless of the presence of a UCC-1.
>
> [e] But don't ever call them this.

Now, there is one variation in this buyer exception. So we are moving into exceptions to the exceptions to Article IX priorities. This exception to the exception says that automatically perfected PMSIs in consumer goods[73] aren't good against buyers who don't know about them even if they're not buyers in the ordinary course of business. So Don Corleone could lose even with automatic perfection, but without filing. This is a nice exception because it allows debtors to sell their refrigerators, stairmasters and clappers to their neighbors, pocket the money and leave the creditor with no collateral.[74]

37K. ("V." in Roman Numerals)
The Olympics of Article IX

To be certain you've conquered the charts and intricacies of Article IX, and assuming after having read this and Article IX, you are not sitting naked in a tower with a high-powered rifle,[75] take the following brain fryer[76] and choose the correct answer.

Fogel purchased a TV set for $900 from Hamilton Appliance Store. Hamilton took a promissory not signed by Fogel and a security interest for

---

73. The UCC provides for automatic perfection of the creditor's interest in consumer goods with no filing required. UCC § 9-302(1)(d) (1992). But they neglect to mention this automatic perfection doesn't work against buyers. That's a pretty important omission, eh?

74. Except when Don Corleone is creditor. This is an exception to the exception to the exception. If you do sell the Don's collateral to your neighbor, large men with no necks and hairy thumbs will visit both of you. This exception applies even if your neighbor is a bona fide purchaser who had no knowledge of the PMSI and has never seen one of the Godfather movies. See id. § 1-201(19).

75. Or a .44 Magnum.

76. This is not one of Ivor's products. See supra Chart 1.

the $800 balance due on the set. It was Hamilton's policy not to file a financing statement until the purchaser defaulted. Fogel obtained a loan of $500 from Reliable Finance which took and recorded a security interest in the set. A month later Fogel defaulted on several loans outstanding and one of his creditors, Harp, obtained a judgment against Fogel which was properly recorded. After making several payments, Fogel defaulted on a payment due to Hamilton, who then recorded a financing statement subsequent to Reliable's filing and the entry of the Harp judgment. Subsequently, at a garage sale, Fogel sold the set for $300 to Mobray. Which of the parties has the priority claim to the set?[77]

Answer Choices:
- A. Beulah, the palmreader.
- B. Determine why anyone would give Fogel credit.
- C. Ask the counter people if Hamilton had any errors in his UCC-1 and avoid priority problems.
- D. Mobray, but only in the Pacific Time Zone; Answer is Harp, EST.
- E. Does anyone have a lien here?
- F. Was any chattel paper involved? Is the TV a chattel?
- G. Garfield
- H. Hamilton
- I. Harp
- J. Reliable

The correct answer is "H," Hamilton.[78] Hamilton had an automatically perfected PMSI which did not require filing.[79] Reliable's interest was not a PMSI, but was perfected by filing *after* Hamilton's perfection. The judgment of Harp was not perfected (i.e., recorded)[80] until *after both* Hamilton and Reliable perfected. Mobray is not a buyer in the ordinary course of business.[81] But with a non-filed but perfected PMSI in the television consumer good, Mobray would fall into the exception to the exception to the exception and get to keep the TV. However, that ruthless Hamilton filed a financing statement[82] after Reliable and Harp did their filing but before Mobray did his buying. This conduct gives us an exception to the exception to the exception to the exception

---

77. This problem appears courtesy of the AICPA from its Business Law Examination for CPA certification. It would explain why so many accountants are in litigation today over their audits. In their zeal to conquer Article IX, they lost their audit skills as well as rational thought processes.

78. For many students this is the last choice. It even follows Beulah.

79. *See* UCC § 9-302 (1989).

80. Different counter help but the same paper work theories.

81. He should be ashamed of himself. He is also a frequent patron of Pierre's Lucky-7 Bar and has two Garfield suction dolls in his Pacer.

82. UCC-1 and by all counter help accounts, it was one of the finest they've seen.

which is if you file on a PMSI in consumer goods, you can win big time even over buyers. This gives us some good advice on Article IX and a final chart.

CHART 5
Rules for Surviving Article IX

1. Always file to perfect (UCC-1) even when they (drafters of Article IX)[83] tell you, "No problem."
2. Never try to figure out collateral or where to file. Just file everywhere.
3. Rely on counter help.
4. Never read Article IX.
5. Put errors in paperwork to avoid priority conflicts.
6. Keep Beulah's card.[84]

---

83. Not identified by name because no one has 'fessed up.
84. I have it on good authority she's earning six-figures off PMSI creditors alone. She's considering a branch office for buyers not in the ordinary course of business.

The New (Legal)
Devil's Dictionary

Robert J. Morris*

Ambrose Bierce (1842–1914?) was one of America's great and cynical humorists. He began writing devilish definitions for a weekly newspaper in 1881 and these became a book entitled *The Cynic's Word Book* in 1906—the predecessor in interest to what we know as *The Devil's Dictionary*.

Unfortunately Mr. Bierce did not live to see the great advances in American jurisprudence which have beset, nay plagued, the latter half of the twentieth century. Thus in this particularly crucial and arcane area his *Dictionary* is notably deficient, for the redress of which condition the following seventy odd definitions are most humbly offered.

It is earnestly hoped by this author that this present addendum may work to the end that the name of Bierce might take its richly deserved place on the jurist's bookshelf along with the likes of Prosser, Corbin, and Crater. For whatever edition of the original *Devil's Dictionary* you may possess, the following is offered as a pocket part (q.v.).

Alienation, n. Use of the Socratic method (q.v.). In property law, the making of enemies, especially of one's family, in land swindles, mine saltings, horse-trading and will-making.

Appeal, n. In law, a Ptolemaic faith born of a Newtonian hope in the bosom of a Galilean fool living in a Euclidean universe.

Assignment, n. In contracts, an action whereby A, the assignor, transfers to B, the assignee, certain rights or obligations. If A transfers equally to both B and C, the latter take equally, each being a half-assignee.

Bankruptcy, n. The light at the end of the tunnel. A second chance at incompetence and fraud. A reprieve from justice which ought to place the debtor in jail if you, but not if me.

---

* J.D. Candidate 1980, University of Utah College of Law.

Black Letter Law, n. Concrete, solid law, embodying such substantive and tangible concepts as title, corporation, justice, implication, and truth, not to mention the intent of the legislature.

Bright Line, n. A legal sign seen as through a glass darkly on a listing ship about to capsize in its own vortex.

Citation, n. Decoy; an exercise wherein law review writers make "creative bibliography" via footnotes which take the reader's eye off the ball. Often abbreviated "cite," which is said to be for sore eyes, but is in fact a cause of sore eyes. A speeding ticket is a citation, as is an honorary doctorate — proving that cops-and-robbers is not a game confined solely to academe.

Code, n. Encrypted language which must first be decoded before it can be understood. Some codes, such as the United States Code, have never been decoded or understood and thus are relegated to that arcane library which contains Egyptian heiroglyphics, scriptural exegesis, and most television scripts.

Commerce Clause, n. In constitutional law, the universal solvent. The true Christmas Saint who brings goodies to all, to be distinguished from Santa Claus, who merely brings them if you've been good.

> Hitch your wagon to a star
> Makes no difference who you are
> Total power's yours because
> You've a friend in the Commerce Clause.
>   *Gert Pakalolo*

Commercial Paper, n. Fodder; paper in forms which can be traded or pledged for value, sold outright, or given as gifts. Legal pads, notebook fillers, toilet tissue, newsprint, purloined research papers, old tests, and canned briefs are commercial paper.

Con Law, n. The law of cons, and sometimes of ex-cons, all of whom receive greater protection thereby than the rest of us. To be distinguished from "con game," which occurs in plea bargaining and rate increases for public utilities and other monopolies.

Concurring, adj. Dissenting.

Contracts Clause, n. In constitutional law, a great black hole, once a quasar but now relegated to the realm of the Privileges and Immunities Clause.

Conviction, n. (1) If you're a crook, the law's way of telling you to slow down. (2) Something you believe with all your heart, might, mind, and strength—for the purpose of this litigation, anyway.

Criminal Lawyer, n. A grammatical redundancy, like "tiny infant" or "sweet sugar."

Cure, v. To ripen or season, as a ham or a default. It takes about four months in a smokehouse and a thousand dollars worth of sugar to cure a default.

Distinguish, v. (1) To bestow the title of Juris Doctor and thus to outfit in a three-piece suit. (2) To explain crucial differences between apparently similar cases—such as differences in typeface, the names of judges and their spellings, uses of commas, and paragraphing. Some opinions, like some judges, are never distinguished.

Due Process, n. Equal protection.

Equal Protection, n. Due process.

[NOTE: The two definitions immediately preceding have been condensed from the law review articles and legal treatises of 5,000 eminent jurists, whose scholarly perspicacity has greatly advanced legal knowledge throughout the known world, if not within our holy religion.]

Equity, n. From *Equus,* the horse. A system of getting around the law at full gallop wherein one horse's arse gets from another that which he couldn't get by due process of law (q.v.).

Execute, v. To carry out, as certain miscreants are carried out to the guillotine.

Fee, n. Absolute ownership, as of your property by your lawyer.

Fiction, n. A kernel of truth in an otherwise usual legal opinion.

Going Public, v. ph. Streaking or flashing past the front door of the S.E.C.

Headnotes, n. Graffiti. Interstitial material composed between a full house and a royal flush upon a wall of separation to aid in one's briefs.

Hornbook, n. A scholarly legal treatise which poses one of the few true existential dilemmas left to us since Vietnam, to wit, whether to believe what *it* says is the law or what the *professor* says is the law—the two usually being mutually exclusive.

Immaterial, adj. Substanceless, ghostlike, ephemeral; descriptive of the quality of work usually done at the state capitol or by Congress, as well as the quality of service rendered by public commissions.

Inalienable Rights, n. pl. Those rights which the Army takes from you during basic training and gives back to you one by one as privileges.

Incompetent, adj. Tenured.

Incorporation, n. In constitutional law, magic, sleight-of-hand, whereby the nine-man prestidigitator chooses a number between 1 and 10 and changes it into a 14; in business law, a gathering of eagles about an incorporeal carcass for the purpose of skinning the body politic and getting immunity for themselves.

Indian, n. Living proof that constitutionally mandated racial discrimination is alive and well in the United States, if not in Tucson.

Indigent, n. A poor person, often of a minority, always recognizable because he or she is the one who usually goes directly to jail, does not pass Go, but does collect $200, in welfare.

Infamous Crime Against Nature, n. Total abstention from good wine, imported liquor, Colombian coffee, and fine cigars.

Infant, n. Child, Little Devil, liability, vandal. The living proof of one's own folly, libido, mortality, and rapidly approaching death.

Irrelevant, adj. A characterization I apply to some interest of yours about which I don't want to talk or am ignorant of.

Jargon, n. A Greek mythical hero, a golden god, who got fleeced.

> "When trying all the whys and whats
> Or simply lying on our cots
> Our minds are full of blanks and blots,"
> Quoth Jargon and the astronauts.
>
> *Porfiro Wong*

J.D., Lat. Juris Doctor, an academic degree conferred for the purpose of authorizing its recipient to doctor the law, as well as heel himself.

Journal of Contemporary Law, n. Successor in interest to Slick Comix. A most serious and scholarly treasury (a fact proved by its publishing this Dictionary), containing things both old and new, but mostly obscure.

Judge, n. Ringmaster. v. To toss a coin.

Judicial Review, n. A song-and-dance routine; mummery. Often spelled "revue" and accompanied by a smorgasbord. A process of immense cost-benefit value to the public in that it combines author and critic in the same judge. To be compared with "law revue" which does not depend on talent.

Jury, n. Twelve or fewer average dupes, a full jury still being somewhat less than a full deck. Jurypersons are often referred to as "peers," but you and I know that we have no peers. If it were so, all of them would, like the poor defendant, likewise be presumed guilty and would be his accomplices in crime. Lucky for us the Constitution does not mandate twelve jurors, else our follies would be paraded before more witnesses than absolutely necessary.

Justice, n. (1) A judge (q.v.) raised to a higher power; (2) mirage.

Law Review, n. Warranty; validation of the law school experience and one's boggling investment there, if not one's very existential meaning in an indifferent, duty-risk universe. Job security and anonymity rolled into one.

Life, Liberty, and the Pursuit of Happiness, n. ph. A cheap cigar, a can of warm beer, and thou.

Lis Pendens, Lat. The sword of Damocles. Constructive notice, which means about as much as constructive pregnancy.

Lives, Fortunes, Sacred Honor, n. pl. A trinity which once made its fleeting appearance upon this continent, but then disappeared again, giving rise to the speculation that God is a leftist and Dred Scott his vicar.

Meander Line, n. From water law, descriptive of the train of thought of a typical law review comment, court opinion, or law school Socratic discussion.

Mr., Ms., n. An honorific appelation used in direct address. When used in law classes to simulate respect and formality, a prostitution of the honorific.

Mortgage, n. A Faustian transaction with the home-buyer in the role of the good doctor.

National Debt, n. The only aggregate sum of money greater than your student loan, the United States and you owing a living to somebody or other.

Negligence, n. Bread and butter.

Of the People, By the People, For the People, prep. ph. An exercise in being prepositioned by a whore.

Oil and Gas, n. pl. Cause and effect in a Mexican dinner.

On all Fours, adj. ph. Descriptive of one's bodily position during an interview with the dean, senior partner, or judge. In case law, a precedent whose headnote (q.v.) numbers match.

Outline, n. A capsule summary in writing, or skeletal diagram, of a law school course, any relation of which to that which will be tested on the final exam being purely coincidental.

Per os, Per anum, Lat. Inscription often seen on the shingle of a dentist and a proctologist who are in the same office, if not cahoots.

Pocket part, n. The best part — coming after the IRS part and the alimony part, on the way to the bank.

Pollution, n. A brooding omnipresence in the sky.

Privilege Against Self-Incrimination, n. Free admission of guilt in open court, when exercised; the bearing of testimony; the irrebuttable presumption of guilt. Automatic conviction on a hanging tree.

Quasi, adj. A meaningless particulate which no one knows the pronounciation of and which is always hyphenated in English words like quasi-contract and quasi-judicial. No one knows the origin of the word, if word it be, but many within our holy religion, as well as scholars at Notre Dame, claim that continued usage of the word gives one a hunchback, a theory which certainly rings a bell.

Rational Basis, n. Our guess.

Ratio Decidendi, Lat. About 9 to 1.

Redemption, n. When a miscreant Note meets its Maker.

Resume, n. A capsule summary in writing of your incompetence, if not irrelevance and immateriality. Unjust enrichment for the printer, and impediment for you. The only publication you will probably ever get.

Reversion, n. Backsliding to your old pre-law school ways, including a sense of humor, the milk of human kindness, values other than money, and never saying, "Sue the bastards," or "estoppel."

Risk-Creating Conduct, n. Trial, especially to the court.

Rules of Construction, n. pl. Statutory rape.

Self-Dealing, n. The capitalist shuffle, played by the board of directors, who are real cards that ought to be dealt with.

Seriatim, Lat. A rank of heavenly beings a little lower than the chubs.

Separation of Powers, n. ph. The exercising of the awesome power of government only on odd or even days, most days at the capitol or Congress being odd, by a totalitarian government. The placing of the separate bureaucracies to which you must repair to get a driver's license in as widely disparate locations as possible so as to maximize inconvenience to the taxpayer. Cutting the legislators off from all contact with the people so as not to allow facts to impinge upon their judgment.

Sic Utere Tuo Ut Alienum Non Laedas, Lat. The two aliens growing in this womb are not ladies.

Socratic Method, n. The soybean extender of law school, stretching what would otherwise be a one-year course at most into a three-year curricular nightmare high in cholesterol. Spoon-fed textured vegetable protein.

> A teacher whose method Socratic
> Proved bilious, inane, and erratic
> Did his homework one day
> Reading Plato, they say,
> And then stored his technique in the attic.
>
> *Clem Aleksandreyevitch,*
> "The Lawyer's Chapbook"

Sovereign State, n. Federal vassal.

Stream of Commerce, n. River of blood; flood of litigation.

Strict Scrutiny, n. Voyerism of a suspect class.

Sua Sponte, Lat. The Portuguese navigator who discovered Blackacre and claimed it for his prints.

Supreme Law of the Land, n. ph. Decisions handed down by OPEC, GM, AT&T, ITT, IBM, and USS.

Trademark, n. Prepuce tattoo.

Treaty, n. In Russian, the other half of "trick or."

Trier of Fact, n. Believer in fiction (q.v.); at times, the judge, the jury, the wife, or the mother-in-law.

Uncle Sam, n. Your rich uncle from whom, however, you will never inherit because at present he is without a will.

Widget, n. A silver new nothing with a handle. Widgets can be purchased only in lots of 1 million and are manufactured only by defendants.

Id.*

*Gerald F. Uelmen***

A great tradition of the American bar is under increasing attack. The tradition I refer to is name-calling. From the earliest inception of our profession, lawyers have been masters in the art of invective. We are frequently retained because our inarticulate clients need our voices to hurl epithets at their enemies. The greatest lawyers of the age were noted for their skill, dexterity and wit in insulting their opponents, as well as the judges who ruled against them.

Consider the argument of Cicero, the Roman orator who tried murder cases before the birth of Christ. In one of his trials, he turned to the prosecutor and said:

> Now Erucius, please do not take offence about what I am going to say next. I assure you I shall not be saying it just in order to be unpleasant, but because you need the reminder. Even if fortune has not given you the advantage of knowing for certain who your father was, which would have given you a better idea of how a father feels towards his children, at any rate nature has endowed you with your fair share of human feelings.[1]

Or consider the reaction of Rufus Choate, the greatest lawyer in Boston during an era which included Daniel Webster, as he summed up an adverse ruling by Chief Justice Shaw: "That judge is...a fool, — he can't put two ideas together...he's bigoted as the devil!"[2]

Clarence Darrow's denunciation of Harry Orchard, the prime witness in

---

* This article may simply be cited "*Id.*," followed by a page number which need not relate to any of the page numbers in this article. No reference to the author or this law journal is necessary. We will get all the glory we need in the *Guiness Book of World Records*, where this article will be enshrined as the most frequently cited law review article ever written.

** Dean and Professor of Law, Santa Clara University School of Law. B.A., 1962, Loyola Marymount University; J.D. 1965, LL.M., 1966, Georgetown University Law Center. Dean Uelmen is the co-author of two widely-acclaimed collections of legal humor: DISORDERLY CONDUCT (W.W. Norton Co., N.Y. 1987) and SUPREME FOLLY (W.W. Norton Co., N.Y. 1990). *See* Widely, *Book Review*, 62 BEST BUYS THIS WEEK AT PRICE CLUB 2 (1990).

1. MARCUS T. CICERO, MURDER TRIALS 52 (Michael Grant trans., Penguin Books 1975).
2. CLAUDE M. FUESS, RUFUS CHOATE: THE WIZARD OF THE LAW 176 (Archon Books 1970).

the Haywood murder trial, sets a standard to which all lawyers should aspire:

> He is unique in history. If he is not the biggest murderer who ever lived, he
> is the biggest liar, at least, who ever lived.... Why, gentlemen, if Harry Or-
> chard were George Washington, who had come into a court of justice with
> his great name behind him, and if he was impeached and contradicted by as
> many as Harry Orchard has been, George Washington would go out of it
> disgraced, and counted the Ananias of the age.[3]

Now I will be the first to admit that the level of invective among lawyers
has declined in quality in recent years. Consider the lawyer who turned to his
opponent during a deposition, and said: "You are an obnoxious little twit.
Keep your mouth shut."[4]

Or consider the lawyer whose pithy response to an obnoxious letter concluded: "****[5] you. Strong letter to follow."[6] But this decline in the erudition
of our discourse should inspire a summons to greater heights of malediction.
Instead, we are hearing bar presidents and judicial committees bemoaning the
decline of "civility" in our profession. Recently, the Committee on Civility of
the Seventh Circuit released an interim report which placed the blame for declining civility right where it obviously belongs—in the lap of the law
schools.[7] Just as the remedy for lawyers who lied and connived across the front
pages of Watergate was to require all law students to take a course in legal
ethics, the Committee suggested that law schools consider instituting courses
in civility in the law school curriculum. That set me to thinking about what
a syllabus for such a course might look like.

I think it would be appropriate to begin the course with a strong interdisciplinary note, by studying the civility of discourse in other professional call-
ings. Like baseball. Students should be exposed to these examples:

Harry Wendelstedt: "Call me anything... but don't call me Durocher. A
Durocher is the lowest form of living matter."

---

3. CLARENCE DARROW, ATTORNEY FOR THE DAMNED 451 (Arthur Weinburger ed.,
1961). Ananias lied to St. Peter. *See The Acts of the Apostles:* 1–5.

4. GERALD F. UELMEN, SUPREME FOLLY 67 (1990). The lawyer was fined $250 plus $693
in costs for this outburst.

5. The missing letters are on permanent file at the Office of the Dean, Santa Clara University School of Law, Santa Clara, CA., 95053. Please enclose a stamped, self-addressed
envelope.

6. Uelmen, *supra* note 4, at 70. In Schleper v. Ford Motor Co., 585 F.2d 1367 (8th Cir.
1978), the Court held that a response of "**** you" to a written interrogatory could not
be punished by contempt.

7. INTERIM REPORT OF THE COMMITTEE ON CIVILITY OF THE SEVENTH FEDERAL JU-
DICIAL CIRCUIT, INTERIM REPORT, 47 (1991).

"Bugs Bear," describing outfielder Ping Bodie: "His head was full of larceny, but his feet were honest."

Charlie Finley: "I have often called Bowie Kuhn a village idiot. I apologize to all the village idiots of America. He is the nation's idiot."

Umpire Marty Springstead: "The best way to test a Timex would be to strap it to [Earl] Weaver's tongue."[8]

We could also assign the reading of some very articulate law review articles, so students could behold the contribution that legal scholars have made to the preservation of great moments in courtroom history. They could consider an article entitled *Defendant Nomenclature in Criminal Trials,* which collects all the appellations prosecutors have successfully affixed to criminal defendants in closing arguments.[9] My favorite was the Missouri District Attorney who suggested the defendant "ought to be shot through the mouth of a red hot cannon, through a barb wire fence into the jaws of hell," and after that "he ought to be kicked in the seat of the pants by a Missouri mule and thrown into a manure pile to rot."[10]

Most prosecutors seem to favor animal allusions. Cases are collected in which defendants were called dogs, hogs, hyenas, rats, rattlesnakes, skunks, vultures, wolves and worms.[11] It calls to mind the observation Mark Twain offered in the introduction to *Pudd'nhead Wilson. Pudd'nhead,* incidentally, was a lawyer. He said:

> Observe the ass, for instance: his character is about perfect, he is the choicest spirit among all the humbler animals, yet see what ridicule has brought

---

8. King v. Burris, 588 F. Supp. 1152, 1157 n.9 (D. Colo. 1984).

9. Arthur N. Bishop, *Name-Calling: Defendant Nomeclature in Criminal Trials,* 4 Ohio N.U. L. Rev. 38 (1977).

10. *Id.* at 71 (citing State v. Richter, 36 S.W.2d 954, 955–56 (Mo. Ct. App. 1931)).

11. James Gorman suggests that an evolutionary scale can be utilized to assess the level of disgust that animal allusions engender, noting the difference, for example, between calling Ed Meese a "dirty rat," an "insect," and a "slug":

> Part of the answer may lie in evolutionary biology. Evolutionarily, slugs are pretty distant from us, what with all our limbs and our clearly defined ears. And the further things get from us, in evolutionary terms, the creepier they seem. Other mammals may be fearsome, but they're seldom disgusting. Birds are cute. Reptiles at least aren't gooey. Amphibians are pushing it. And once you move outside of the vertebrates, it's yuck city. Insects, spiders, worms, grubs, slugs.

James Gorman, *Does Creepiness Recapitulate Phylogeny?,* Discover, Oct. 1987, at 30–31.

him to. Instead of feeling complimented when we are called an ass, we are left in doubt.[12]

Another contribution to the literature of vilification is entitled *A Study in Epithetical Jurisprudence*.[13] It collects every case in which someone was called a "son of a bitch." A case is reported in which the defendant relied on the defense of truth, and set out to prove that the plaintiff truly was a son of a bitch. As his final witness, he called a tall, lean, sun-tanned gentleman to the stand. In answer to the question, "What is your business or profession?" he testified, "I am an expert judge of sons o' bitches. Out in Texas we got a lot of 'em, and my business is knowing how to spot 'em. I can spot one a mile away on a clear day." He was then asked to carefully observe the plaintiff. He looked, turned to the jury, and said, "Gentlemen, he's a son of a bitch if I ever saw one."[14]

Students who seek to master the art of civil scurrility must also be exposed to the nuances of the law of libel. Use of epithets which are not capable of factual proof or disproof will receive judicial protection. Thus, the coach of the Denver Gold got away with calling a sports agent a "sleazebag who slimed up from the bayou," because it was impossible to prove whether someone is a sleazebag or not.[15] On the other hand, recovery was allowed by a plaintiff who was called a "turkey," because this connotes "ineptitude, dumbness, and ignorance" which can be easily proven or disproven.[16]

A good deal of attention in any effort to raise the level of civility in our profession must be devoted to the simple task of increasing the vocabulary of law students and lawyers. I have a strong suspicion that the perceived decline in civility is simply a decline in the typical lawyer's arsenal of insults. As mo-

---

12. MARK TWAIN, PUDD'NHEAD WILSON 3 (Heritage Press 1974) (1893). *Pudd'nhead Wilson* should also be assigned reading for a course in civility. Mark Twain describes the initial debate among townspeople as to whether the young lawyer was a fool, a damn fool, a lummox, a labrick or a perfect jackass. They finally settled on pudd'nhead, which stuck. While my Funk & Wagnalls describes a lummox as a stupid, clumsy person (*cf. infra*, *schlemiel*, text accompanying note 25), I have been unable to find a definition of labrick anywhere.

Stuart Berg Flexner suggests good reason for Americans to be left in doubt when called an ass:

> Until World War II it was assumed that *ass* for a stupid person referred to jackass, but since 1940 it has increasingly referred to [anus],...(this confusion doesn't exist in England, where *ass* refers to the animal, *arse* to the part of the body).

STUART B. FLEXNER, LISTENING TO AMERICA 321 (1982). Flexner collects and catalogues 87 ways to call someone stupid, an invaluable resource for lawyers and law students.

13. Saul Cohen, *A Study in Epithetical Jurisprudence*, 41 L.A. B. BULL. 374 (1966).

14. *Id.* at 379–80 (footnote omitted).

15. Henderson v. Times Mirror Co., 669 F. Supp. 356, 357 (D. Colo. 1987).

16. Ferguson v. Park Newspapers, 253 S.E.2d 231, 232 (Ga. Ct. App. 1979).

tion picture and television script writers increasingly resort to four letter words for emphasis, the "dumbing down" phenomenon has infected our diatribes as well as our polite discourse. This phenomenon is comparable to that noted by Justice Robert Gardner, in bemoaning the crudeness of the demands currently utilized by American robbers:

> It is a sad commentary on contemporary culture to compare "Don't say a word, don't say a mother-******* word," with "Stand and deliver," the famous salutation of Dick Turpin and other English highwaymen. It is true that both salutations lead to robbery. However, there is a certain rich style to "Stand and deliver." ... The speech of contemporary criminal culture has always been a rich source of color and vitality to any language. Yet, when one compares the "bawds," "strumpets," "trulls," "cut-purses," "knaves" and "rascals" of Fielding and Smollett to the "hookers," "pimps," "Narcs," "junkies" and "snitches" of today's criminal argot, one wonders just which direction we are traveling civilization's ladder.[17]

Justice Gardner's lament is equally applicable to the argot of attorneys. Compare calling the judge a "butt brain" to calling the judge a "mumpsimus" or a "sophronist."[18] Compare calling opposing counsel a "jerk" with calling

---

17. People v. Benton, 142 Cal. Rptr. 545, 546 n.1 (Cal. Ct. App. 1978).

18. A classic source of "words to describe life's indescribable people" is DAVID GRAMBS, DIMBOXES, EPOPTS AND OTHER QUIDAMS (1986). Grambs offers at least ten labels that might be appropriate for judges who occupy the bench at every level:

AGELAST: One who never laughs or smiles; a total deadpan. In Yiddish, a farbissener.

BATTOLOGIST: One who repeats the same thing over and over, like a broken record, *e.g.*, "objection overruled."

CATAGELOPHOBE: One who bristles at the least suggestion of criticism. "May the record reflect that Your Honor is bristling?"

LATITUDINARIAN: One who is broadminded, willing to stretch things a little. Now that "liberal" has become a dirty word, latitudinarian makes a nice substitute. At least it will never be reduced to four letters.

MUMPSIMUS: One who stubbornly persists in error, even after it is rationally and patiently explained. A play on sumpsimus, the stickler for precise correctness. A sumpsimus is a mumpsimus who's right.

MISOLOGIST: Hates rational discussion. You have to reduce your argument to gut level or below.

OPSIMATH: One who learns late in life. It is better that wisdom come late than that it come not at all.

PRETERIST: One who lives totally in the past. Still cites Warren Court precedents.

SOPHRONIST: One who is excessively cautious, wary, and hesitant. "Can you supply points and authorities on that relevancy objection?"

WITWANTON: One who tries to be cleverly amusing, but misses the mark.

opposing counsel a "big-endian," a "cunctator" or a "malapert."[19] Instead of labeling your client a "deadbeat," imagine referring to him as "embusque."[20] Rather than calling a witness a "dirty liar," think how memorable your closing argument would be if you called him a "Vicar of Bray."[21] A "Vicar of Bray" is a col-

---

19. Grambs' collection also includes ten gems that match most lists of the top ten lawyers you love to hate:

ATELOPHOBE: The morbid perfectionist. Ten pages of deposition testimony can be devoted to one typographical error.

BIG-ENDIAN: The anal-retentive with a magnifying glass. The trivial achieves epic proportions. (From *Gulliver's Travels*)

CACOEPIST: Consistently mispronounces words. The CACOGRAPHER consistently misspells them.

CUNCTATOR: The ultimate procrastinator. Never does anything that can be put off.

ERGOTIST: The pedantic reasoner. Every other word is "consequently" or "therefore." Not to be confused with the ERGOPHILE (workaholic) or the ERGOPHOBE (afraid of work).

MALAPERT: Impudent, always sassing back.

PRONEUR: Constant flatterer, a toady who offers nothing but praise. In Yiddish, a *Tochis Lecher.*

QUODLIBETARIAN: The hair-splitter who loves to divide everything into six categories, even the luncheon check.

SNOLLYGOSTER: Totally unprincipled. Keep your hand on your wallet.

ULTRACREPEDARIAN: The overreacher, whose analysis extends far beyond his own comprehension.

20. "Embusque" comes from the French term for draft-dodger. In English, it refers to a shirker who accepts no responsibility whatsoever. I found descriptions in Grambs' catalogue for nine other clients I have represented on occasion:

ATABILARIAN: The gloomy hypochondriac who develops a new symptom every morning and calls to tell you about it.

CASSANDRA: The true prophet of evil, who is never believed.

LAODICEAN: Totally indifferent, nonchalant.

LATITANT: One who's hiding out, lying low. Wants you to take his messages.

MISARCHIST: Dislikes all authority, including that which you occasionally assert.

PANJANDRUM: The pretentious bigwig, very self-important.

PHILOPOLEMIST: Loves being the center of controversy.

PSYCHASTHENIC: Totally indecisive neurotic. "Well what do *you* think I should do?"

SUIST: Not a perennial plaintiff, but one who is simply unfazed by approval or disapproval of others. Simply does his or her "own thing," oblivious of your advice.

21. Nine other ways to call a witness a liar, most drawn from Grambs:

DENTILOQUIST: Speaks through clenched teeth, with real determination.

CHIROSOPHIST: Sleight of hand artist who changes the facts faster than the court reporter can get it down.

GANSER'S SYNDROME: Compulsive inability to give a precise answer. Every answer is preceded by "about" or "approximately."

GREMIAL: The bosom friend through thick or thin. Always good for an alibi.

GRINAGOG: Always smiles even when lying. Opposite of the lachrymist, who cries on cue.

HYDRA: Grows two heads for each one you cut off. When you catch Hydra in a lie, you'll get two more in the explanation.

PHILALETHE: Loves to forget. Favorite answer is "I don't recall."

orful British phrase describing someone whose version of the truth depends completely on who's winning. The Vicar's flexibility, which allowed him to survive King Henry VIII and each of his children, is immortalized in a brief poem:

"And this is the law I will maintain
Until my dying day, Sir,
That whatsoever King shall reign,
I'll still be the Vicar of Bray, Sir."[22]

Just a simple rule that any insult must exceed two syllables would carry us a long way in raising the level of civility in our profession.

We should also devote some time in any respectable civility course to a cross-cultural perspective. I personally think students would gain a great deal by learning the rudiments of Yiddish.[23] A single Yiddish word can capture all the subtle nuances one might need to contemptuously characterize the depths to which an opposing lawyer has sunk. Rather than an indignant objection that "Counsel is deliberately interposing frivolous objections to delay these proceedings," you can simply chortle, "The *nebbish* is *putzing* up this case."

One of the great advantages of Yiddish is that the same word can be used to insult in one context and express admiration in another. *Chachem* can denote a savant of great wisdom, or a foolish jerk, depending on the intonation. Thus, you might greet a judge's overruling of your objection by sighing, "Such a chachem."

Judges have even been known to use Yiddish labels to insult each other, all the while denying that an insult was intended. In one notable California Court of Appeals opinion, a justice responded to a dissent with a footnote in which the first letter of each sentence spelled "SCHMUCK."[24] The German definition of schmuck is a jewel. The Yiddish definition is somewhat less flattering, although equally treasured by some. It refers to the male reproductive organ. The dissenter protested that English dictionaries use the Yiddish definition,

---

PSEUDOLOGIST: The truly systematic liar who constructs an elaborate house of cards.
SYNTONE: Goes with the flow. Will agree with contradictory propositions as long as they're advanced by two different lawyers.

22. WILLARD R. ESPY, O THOU IMPROPER, THOU UNCOMMON NOUN 60 (1978). Espy's etymology of words that once were names includes many expressions that lawyers will find useful. JEDBURGH JUSTICE and LYDFORD LAW are both places that became synonymous with injudicious trials:

"First hang, and then draw.
Then try the case at Lydford law."

Id.

23. *See* Gerald F. Uelmen, *Plain Yiddish for Lawyers*, 71 A.B.A. J. 78 (1985).

24. People v. Arno, 153 Cal. Rptr. 624 (Cal. Ct. App. 1979).

and California law requires that appellate opinions be written in English. The author of the offending footnote, however, included a reference to a German dictionary. Thus, the dexterity of Yiddish insults should be apparent.

Many laws schools have already incorporated some basic Yiddish into their curriculum. Justice William O. Douglas, for example, reported that the most important distinction impressed upon him as a student at Columbia Law School was the difference between a schnook and a schlemiel. He said a schnook is a fellow who gets dressed up in his dinner jacket and goes to a very elegant dinner party and proceeds to spill the soup, and spill the gravy from the entree and then slobbers the chocolate sauce when dessert is served. The schlemiel is the person sitting next to him, upon whom he spills it. Edward Bennett Williams observed that in every case involving multiple defendants represented by separate lawyers, there is always one lawyer who's a schnook, and he makes all the other lawyers look like schlemiels.[25]

Lest we feel too sorry for the schlemiel, however, we should note the difference between a schlemiel, who brings on his own misfortune, and the schlimazel, who is simply plagued by bad luck. When a schlimazel drops a piece of toast, it always lands with the butter side down. When a schlemiel drops a piece of toast, it's only after he has put butter on both sides.[26]

Now that we have a syllabus for our course in civility, the problem is finding a professor to teach it. The traditional Socratic technique, which is undoubtedly the least civil form of dialogue ever devised, will have to be discarded. The teacher will have to serve as a role model of gracious civility. Judging from the civility of their behavior at faculty meetings, most deans will have great difficulty filling this position from their current full-time faculty. They will have to embark on a search to recruit a Professor of Civility.

Finding a role model of civility in today's bench and bar may require an arduous search. Even among the ranks of the justices of the U.S. Supreme Court, I'm informed, oral arguments have become embarrassing displays of sniping and snarling.[27] Ultimately, we may have to employ the services of the Walt Disney Company, to create a professor somewhat like the mechanical Abraham Lincoln at Disneyland. Perhaps we could construct a plastic mechanical replica of John W. Davis to teach the course.

---

25. *The Problems of Long Criminal Trials, A Panel Discussion*, 34 F.R.D. 155, 184 (1963) (statement of Edward Bennett Williams during the Judicial Conference of the Second Circuit of the United States).

26. PAUL HOFFMAN & MATT FREEDMAN, DICTIONARY SCHMICTIONARY 129 (1983).

27. Russell W. Galloway, *Conservative Inquisitors Run the Show*, L.A. DAILY J., June 11, 1991, at 6.

Devising a final examination for this course should be quite simple. The most efficient way to test a student's civility is a multiple choice exam, similar to the format utilized for the Multistate Professional Responsibility Examination. A sample of fifteen questions, utilizing the "quadruple distractor" format highly favored by the National Conference of Bar Examiners, appears as an Appendicitis[28] to this article. Under the "quadruple distractor" format, *no* answer is correct. The student is challenged to select the answer that is least incorrect.

The greatest challenge we will face as legal educators in the decade ahead will be to preserve the great traditions of insult and invective which have always characterized our profession, while still training our students to deliver their insult and invective in a civil way. Law school courses in civility should be designed with this goal in mind.

---

28. An appendicitis is an inflamed appendix.

APPENDICITIS

Multistate Civility Examination
Sample Questions

1. The proper way to address Chief Justice Rehnquist during oral argument is:
   a. Bill
   b. Chief
   c. Your Excellency
   d. Most Honorable and Exalted Lordship, Sir (while drooling)

2. A judge who observes a lawyer picking his nose in the courtroom should:
   a. Publicly rebuke the lawyer
   b. Hold the lawyer in contempt of court and jail him overnight
   c. Call the Bar Association "hot line"
   d. Make a crude joke, like "Hope you pick a winner, Counselor."

3. The proper attire for male attorneys to appear in municipal court is:
   a. Slacks and a sport shirt
   b. An Italian silk suit and alligator shoes
   c. Striped slacks and a swallowtail coat
   d. A Columbo raincoat

4. At a state dinner, U.S. Court of Appeals judges rank:
   a. After U.S. Supreme Court justices and before five-star generals
   b. Between five and four-star generals
   c. Between four and three-star generals
   d. In the kitchen with John Sununu

5. An "aperitif" is:
   a. A vicious breed of dog
   b. The hot towel served on some airlines to wash your hands and face
   c. Two cigars
   d. A partial denture

6. When setting the table for a Bar Association dinner, the napkin should go:
   a. Under the knife, on the left
   b. Under the knife, on the right
   c. Under the spoon
   d. Under the table

7. In addressing a letter to a U.S. Magistrate, the appropriate salutation is:
   a. Dear Magistrate:
   b. Dear U.S.:
   c. Greetings!
   d. To Whom it May Concern:

8. When denouncing a judge's adverse ruling at a press conference, it is appropriate for a lawyer to refer to:
   a. The judge's difficulty in passing the bar exam
   b. The judge's ABA "unqualified" rating
   c. The judge's drunk driving conviction
   d. The judge's Law School Grades.

9. Two days before a long-scheduled deposition of your client, opposing counsel calls to request a continuance, informing you his mother passed away and the funeral is set for the evening of the day of the deposition. The most appropriate response is:
   a. Can you supply a notarized death certificate?
   b. Were you close to her?
   c. Can't you get someone to substitute for you (at the funeral)?
   d. No problem. We'll finish the depo by 5:00 p.m.

10. When opposing counsel is a woman, a male attorney should address her:
    a. Miz (emphasize zzz with slight hiss)
    b. Madam (or Ma'am)
    c. By her first name
    d. Don't address her directly; direct all comments at the wall or the ceiling.

11. Upon receiving contributions from lawyers for his reelection campaign, a judge should:
    a. Not acknowledge receipt
    b. Send a personal note of thanks
    c. Call and pledge undying gratitude
    d. Any or all of the above, depending on the amount

12. The American Inns of Court are:
    a. Slightly sleazy cocktail lounges
    b. A chain of motels
    c. Schools that teach lawyers to speak with a British accent
    d. The fastest growing lawyer's organization since Diner's Club

13. An offer to stipulate to obviously provable facts is:
    a. A sign of weakness
    b. A tactical move best saved for the eve of trial
    c. Revocable at will
    d. Most effective if made in the jury's presence, after opposing counsel has called the witness

14. When a filing clerk refuses to accept a brief because the cover is the wrong color, you should:
    a. Berate the clerk with colorful epithets
    b. File a writ of scire facias
    c. Demand to see the chief judge immediately
    d. Offer the clerk your tickets to the twi-night double-header

15. When you write a nasty letter to opposing counsel, complaining that her secretary disconnected you while you were on "hold," you should:
    a. Send a copy to her client
    b. Send a copy to the judge
    c. Send a copy to the Bar Discipline Committee
    d. Send a copy to the Committee on Civility of the Seventh Federal Judicial Circuit:

    c/o Judge Marvin E. Aspen
    U.S. Courthouse
    219 S. Dearborn Street, Rm. 1946
    Chicago IL 60604

Note: All questions utilize the "quadruple distractor" format highly favored by the National Conference of Bar Examiners. Thus, *no* answer is correct. The challenge is to select the "best" answer, *i.e.*, the one that is least incorrect.

Suing the Devil:
A Guide for Practitioners

*Charles Yablon**

These are precarious times for plaintiffs' lawyers. With most of the asbestos manufacturers safely bankrupt, the tobacco companies looking for a settlement, and even the most gullible investors unable to lose money on Wall Street, there is a serious risk of a defendant shortage. To be sure, people continue to be cheated, harassed, and abused by corporate America in reassuring numbers, but recovering the costs of standard corporate malfeasance is just a job, not an adventure. It provides none of the opportunities for financial windfalls, moral indignation, and national television exposure that come from suing a really despicable defendant. It is somewhat surprising, therefore, that one notorious perpetrator of injury, misery, and wrongful conduct has remained curiously immune from the current onslaught of civil litigation. I am speaking, of course, about the Devil incarnate, Satan, Prince of Darkness.

I know that the concept of a lawsuit, preferably a class action, against the Devil strikes many lawyers as bizarre, perhaps even absurd. I completely understand such concerns. Obviously Satan is a formidable legal opponent. He is well financed, highly intelligent, very aggressive, and completely unscrupulous. I believe he has had formal legal training. Yet the point of this Essay is to show that in a world in which Philip Morris, Microsoft, and Rupert Murdoch are all targets of litigation, the Devil isn't really so tough. Moreover, while Satanic litigation does pose some unique jurisdictional and procedural difficulties, none of them, as I will subsequently demonstrate, poses an insurmountable obstacle to a successful lawsuit.

Indeed, the current climate is just about perfect for the announcement of a Satanic lawsuit to get substantial media attention. While not yet a superstar, the Devil has been getting more public attention in recent years. Luckily, this exposure has done little to increase his popularity. Quite the contrary, it has

* Professor of Law, Benjamin N. Cardozo School of Law. This Essay was previously presented to the Faculty of Law at Birkbeck College, University of London. I want to thank them for their helpful comments and for laughing at the right places.

been more in the nature of a negative media campaign.[1] Elaine Pagels, a noted biblical scholar, published a highly unflattering biography of Satan a few years ago[2] detailing the Devil's long involvement with various right-wing hate groups, like those who organized the Crusades. Dr. Pagels's book is primarily descriptive and historical. Others, however, are trying to increase public awareness of Satan for the same reasons they want more attention paid to global warming, the nuclear capability of Kazakhstan, and sex fiends on the Internet, i.e., because they believe people are not sufficiently scared.

Some scholars, like Professor Andrew Delbanco,[3] have a practical political and social agenda in seeking to increase Satanic visibility. Professor Delbanco evinces a nostalgia for the days when Mephistopheles took a more active role in corrupting humanity. He argues that in Satan's absence we have lost that piquant sense of evil that formerly caused those timorous of fire and brimstone to toe the line and that added a certain danger and zest to sin. Indeed, many feel that, as Satan's public appearances have become less frequent in the twentieth century, evil has tended to become rather banal. Although Satan has become reclusive in recent years, there is little doubt that he continues to play an active and vigorous role in world events and human affairs.[4] He has done absolutely nothing, however, to improve his media image. Except for providing a few quotations of dubious veracity in the kinds of publications generally found in grocery store checkout lines, the Devil has made no public appearances whatsoever. Even Larry King can't get him to appear (and you know Larry wouldn't ask any of the hard questions).

Litigation against the Devil is, in short, an idea whose time has come. Indeed, it is surprising to me that no one has yet instituted such an action. The major difference I can discern between suing the Devil and suing, say, the tobacco industry, is that while there are numerous practical guides for lawyers who wish to sue nicotine merchants for fun and profit, no one has put out a guide to the specific legal problems posed by Satanic litigation. No one, that is, until now.

This Essay is intended to provide such guidance to the harried practitioner looking for new litigation targets. It consists of two Parts. The first takes a good hard look at Satan's prior legal career. It goes beyond the hype that usu-

---

1. For example, Al Pacino's recent portrayal of Satan in The Devil's Advocate (Warner Bros. 1997) was far less sympathetic than his prior depictions of drug dealers, see Scarface (Universal 1983), and mob bosses, see The Godfather (Paramount 1972). Of course, his character in *The Devil's Advocate* was not only the Devil, but a partner at a large law firm.

2. See Elaine Pagels, The Origin of Satan (1995).

3. See Andrew Delbanco, The Death of Satan: How Americans Have Lost the Sense of Evil (1995).

4. Cf. today's news.

ally accompanies celebrity litigators to show that, despite his inflated reputation, the Devil's litigation record is spotty at best. The Devil is no F. Lee Bailey (and vice versa).

The second Part of this Essay analyzes the technical legal problems involved in actually filing and prosecuting a lawsuit against the Devil, an area in which surprisingly little work has been done, given the enormous number of potential plaintiffs. It shows that Satan is clearly amenable to suit in both federal and state courts (particularly in New York, the jurisdiction with which I am most familiar) based on fairly standard jurisprudential principles. Litigation against the Devil is not only possible, but potentially quite lucrative. Aggressive lawyering is very likely to be rewarded with a substantial Mephistophelean settlement offer. As everyone knows, the Devil is always ready to cut a deal, particularly with lawyers.

I. A Legal History of Satan

While I have been unable to ascertain where the Devil received his formal legal education, there seems to be little doubt that he was an excellent law student. This can be seen by the fact that he managed to land, as his first legal job, the highly prestigious position of prosecutor for the Deity. There he was responsible for such high-profile cases as the trial of Job, "a perfect and an upright man."[5] Of course, Satan did lose that case rather badly, which was not really surprising given his inexperience, coupled with the fact that the defendant was completely innocent.[6]

As you know, the Devil subsequently became embroiled in a rather complicated political and legal dispute with his Superior. Although we have an extensive record of the case from Mr. John Milton,[7] as often happens with unofficial reports of early common law actions, the precise nature of the litigation remains unclear. It appears to have been some kind of a hybrid proceeding, an ejectment action that seems to have been resolved by trial by battle. Mr. Milton, unfortunately, is totally unaware of the legal precision necessary in writing on these matters. In any event, the result of the case is clearly reported. The Devil left his prior position with the Deity and set up his own private practice in Hell, a separate jurisdiction (and one with which Heaven apparently has no extradition treaty).

---

5. Job 1:8 (King James).
6. See Job (King James).
7. See John Milton, Paradise Lost (William Zunder ed., 1999) (1667).

After setting down stakes in the Netherworld, Satan embarked on a wide variety of business enterprises. He became quite adept at commercial law, particularly contract negotiation, and most of his litigation from this period involves contractual disputes. The litigation itself was rather routine and will be familiar to anyone who has ever represented a finance company or automobile dealership. The defendant enters into a contract, obtains all the benefits of the Devil's performance under the contract, and then refuses to pay in accordance with the clearly specified terms. Given the straightforward nature of such litigation, it is quite surprising how poorly the Devil has fared in the reported cases.

Satan did manage a decisive victory in his action against Don Juan a/k/a Giovanni,[8] but Mr. Giovanni was not a particularly sympathetic defendant, at least not when the judges were men. More troublesome is the celebrated case of Dr. Faustus. Here Satan also seemed to have a clear-cut winner. There was no question that a contract had been formed and that the material terms were clear. Unfortunately, numerous incomplete and conflicting reports of the case again leave the actual outcome disturbingly unclear.[9] Most commentators agree that the Devil was successful at the trial level, but there are troubling intimations, particularly in Mr. Goethe's reports, that this judgment was reversed on appeal.[10] If true, it would not be surprising if the Devil subsequently began to question his ability to get a fair hearing in a court of law.

An even more egregious miscarriage of justice is reported by Mr. Stephen Benet in Satan's only known appearance in an American court.[11] The defendant, although supposedly only a "poor" New Hampshire farmer, managed to obtain the legal services of Mr. Daniel Webster, the preeminent advocate of his day. Not surprisingly, Mr. Webster, with the home court advantage, made short work of the Devil.

---

8. See Tirso de Molina, The Trickster of Seville and the Stone Guest (Gwynne Edwards trans., 1986) (1630); Wolfgang A. Mozart, Don Giovanni (1787); George Bernard Shaw, Don Juan in Hell (1903) (Act III of "Man and Superman").

9. See Johann Spies, History of the Damnable Life, and Deserved Death of Doctor Johann Faustus (P.F. Gent trans., Da Capo Press 1969) (1587); Christopher Marlowe, The Tragical History of D. Faustus, in 2 The Complete Works of Christopher Marlowe 3 (Roma Gill ed., 1990) (1604) (Text A); Christopher Marlowe, The Tragical History of D. Faustus, in 2 The Complete Works of Christopher Marlowe, supra, at 107 (1616) (Text B); Johann Wolfgang von Goethe, Faust: A Tragedy (Part I) (Stuart Atkins ed. & trans., 1984) (1808).

10. See Johann Wolfgang von Goethe, Faust: A Tragedy (Part II) 121 (Stuart Atkins ed. & trans., 1984) (1832).

11. See Stephen Vincent Benet, The Devil and Daniel Webster (1937).

Since that time, there have been virtually no reported instances of Satanic litigation.[12] This may strike some of you as odd, since the Devil is obviously still heavily involved in commercial activity, and we all know how indispensable the threat of a lawsuit is to maintaining amicable business relations. If he has stopped resorting to the courts, how does Satan keep his business associates in line? After much consideration and research, I believe I have discovered the answer. I can state it in three words: alternative dispute resolution. It appears that the standard-form demonic contract, like the standard securities brokerage contract, now contains an arbitration clause. This explains not only why the Devil no longer resorts to litigation, but also why so many people and institutions these days seem summarily to be going to Hell.

The key point of this history, however, is to show that the Devil's litigation prowess is considerably overrated. Certainly, Satan is no pushover, but how does he really stack up against an aggressive, high-powered lawyer with extensive trial experience? I would be far more frightened of the latter. Indeed, my extensive research into the Devil's prior litigation history has enabled me to pinpoint his three major weaknesses as a trial lawyer.

First is the Devil's curious reluctance to employ outside counsel. Despite the fact that he is the real party in interest in virtually every one of the numerous contract actions he has brought, the Devil invariably seeks to represent himself, often, as we have seen, with unfortunate results. The only exceptions to this practice I have found involve canonization proceedings in ecclesiastical courts. There, the Devil is always represented by his Advocate. Presumably, this is because Satan himself is not admitted to practice in those tribunals.

The Devil's second legal failing is his outdated and overly formalistic approach to contract law. This may not be surprising for someone who went to law school so long ago, but the Devil has clearly not kept up. He seems never to have even read *Corbin* or the *Second Restatement of Contracts,* let alone have any familiarity with doctrines like unconscionability and contracts of adhesion. He does, however, seem to have a good grasp of the basic principles of law and economics.[13]

The Devil's third drawback as an advocate is the fact that he is *responsible*

---

12. There are obscure reports of more recent litigation involving another demonic contract, supposedly resulting in a losing season for the New York Yankees baseball team. I have been unable to find any written records of this case, however, and I suspect that it may involve some understandable confusion between the Devil and George Steinbrenner.

13. Satan appears to share the law and economics view of individuals as primarily a source of appetites and desires. Satan's perspective, however, appears to be a little more empirically grounded.

for all the evil in the world. This tends to put him at a disadvantage, at least in courts of equity.

The Devil, in short, is a deep pocket just waiting to be picked. Although he has recently shown a reluctance to initiate lawsuits, this does not make him any less subject to being sued. In the following Part, we will consider the practical legal questions raised by the prospect of Satanic litigation.

II. Suing the Devil: Procedural Issues

The seminal American case involving suits against the Devil—indeed, the only reported such case—is *United States ex rel. Gerald Mayo v. Satan and His Staff*.[14] Mr. Mayo sought to assert a class action on behalf of himself, and all others similarly situated, against "Satan and his staff" for deprivation of his civil rights under federal law. Mr. Mayo alleged in his complaint that "Satan has on numerous occasions caused plaintiff misery and unwarranted threats, against the will of plaintiff, that Satan has placed deliberate obstacles in his path and has caused plaintiff's downfall."[15] There seems to be little doubt that Mr. Mayo was sincere and that his complaint was well grounded in fact, since at the time of filing he was in prison and seeking to proceed *in forma pauperis*.

In denying Mr. Mayo's motion to proceed *in forma pauperis*, Judge Gerald Weber expressed misgivings about the viability of his claims. Judge Weber stated:

> [T]he Court has serious doubts that the complaint reveals a cause of action upon which relief can be granted by the court. We question whether plaintiff may obtain personal jurisdiction over the defendant in this judicial district. The complaint contains no allegation of residence in this district. While the official reports disclose no case where this defendant has appeared as defendant there is an unofficial account of a trial in New Hampshire where this defendant filed an action of mortgage foreclosure as plaintiff.[16] The defendant in that action was represented by the preeminent advocate of that day, and raised the defense that the plaintiff was a foreign prince with no

---

14. 54 F.R.D. 282 (W.D. Pa. 1971). Judge Thomas Gee of the United States Court of Appeals for the Fifth Circuit has called this one of the "most delightful" case names he has encountered, deserving comparison with United States v. 11¼ Dozen Packages of Article Labeled in Part Mrs. Moffat's Shoo Fly Powders for Drunkenness, 40 F. Supp. 208 (W.D.N.Y. 1941), and the case in which he made the observation, Easter Seal Society for Crippled Children v. Playboy Enterprises, 815 F.2d 323, 325 n.1 (5th Cir. 1987).

15. *Ex rel. Mayo*, 54 F.R.D. at 283.

16. This is obviously a reference to the questionable decision previously reported by Mr. Benet. See supra note 11 and accompanying text.

standing to sue in an American Court. This defense was overcome by over-whelming evidence to the contrary. Whether or not this would raise an estoppel in the present case we are unable to determine at this time.

If such action were to be allowed we would also face the question of whether it may be maintained as a class action. It appears to meet the re-quirements of [Fed. R. Civ. P. 23] that the class is so numerous that joinder of all members is impracticable, there are questions of law and fact common to the class, and the claims of the representative party is [sic] typical of the claims of the class. We cannot now determine if the representative party will fairly protect the interests of the class.

We note that the plaintiff has failed to include with his complaint the re-quired form of instructions for the United States Marshal for directions as to service of process.

For the foregoing reasons we must exercise our discretion to refuse the prayer of plaintiff to proceed in forma pauperis.[17]

The *Ex rel. Mayo* case is obviously not an entirely helpful precedent, but Judge Weber's opinion is not as damning as it may first appear. Judge Weber did not actually dismiss the action, but merely refused to give the plaintiff the fee waivers associated with *in forma pauperis* treatment. Since the actual ground for his ruling was failure to provide instructions for service of process, all the other disparaging remarks about the case may be characterized as mere dicta.[18] Furthermore, it seems from some of Judge Weber's statements that he was not taking this case entirely seriously. Finally, I would note that Mr. Mayo was not represented by counsel when he made his motion, and, thus, the strongest arguments for the viability of his lawsuit were never made. (I reject the claim of a commentator in the *Yale Law Journal* who suggested that Mr. Mayo was unable to find counsel because asking a lawyer to sue the Devil would constitute an "obvious conflict of interest."[19])

Let us put *Ex rel. Mayo* aside, then, and carefully consider the actual legal issues that might be raised in a well-litigated lawsuit against Beelzebub. One naive objection we can easily dispose of is what I call the "ontological defense." Only a very foolish or untrained jurist would suggest that the Devil may not be sued because he does not really exist, that he is merely a fictitious entity wholly created by human imaginations to embody their darkest, most malev-

---

17. *Ex rel. Mayo*, 54 F.R.D. at 283.

18. But for an argument relying on *Ex rel. Mayo* to support the proposition that Gozer the Destructor (from the *Ghostbusters* movie) is not subject to personal jurisdiction, see Christine Alice Corcos, "Who Ya Gonna C(S)ite?" *Ghostbusters* and the Environmental Reg-ulation Debate, 13 J. Land Use & Envtl. L. 231, 262 & n.147 (1997). It's amazing what gets published in law reviews these days.

19. James D. Gordon III, How Not to Succeed in Law School, 100 Yale L.J. 1679, 1687–88 (1991).

olent impulses. The flaw in this argument will be immediately obvious to anyone with a modicum of legal training. Whether or not the Devil "really" exists is, of course, completely irrelevant from a legal point of view. For most
corporate lawyers, myself included, the vast majority of our clients do not "really" exist, but are similarly fictitious entities, many of whom have indeed been
created by humans out of some rather malevolent impulses. None of these
fictitious entities, however, have the slightest trouble suing or being sued in a
court of law. Existence is simply not a predicate for legal action.[20] Courts are
more than happy to consider claims against such nonexistent entities as corporations, nations, deceased persons, and sunken ships, not to mention the
ubiquitous John Doe and Jane Roe.[21]

The critical question for determining amenability to suit is not whether the
defendant "really" exists, but simply whether there are agents acting on the
defendant's behalf in the relevant jurisdiction. Where the defendant is the
Devil, and the relevant jurisdiction is New York, can there be any serious dispute?

The amenability of the Devil to suit in New York, however, does not resolve the question of service of process. As we know, the Devil has been laying low,[22] perhaps seeking to avoid such service, and while Satan has plenty
of agents in New York, it is not at all clear that he has authorized any of them
to accept service of process on his behalf.[23] This is indeed a problem, but I believe it can be solved by invoking the provisions of Section 308(5) of the New
York Civil Practice Law and Rules, which permit a plaintiff to obtain an order

---

20. But see Water Energizers Ltd. v. Water Energizers, Inc., 788 F. Supp. 208, 211
(S.D.N.Y. 1992) ("Existence is surely a necessary requisite for this court's exercise of personal jurisdiction."). Significantly, the only authority cited in support of this dubious
proposition is the erroneously decided *Ex rel. Mayo.* See id.

21. See any casebook on, respectively, Corporations, International Law, Trusts and Estates, and Admiralty.

22. Under the Federal Rules of Civil Procedure, a defendant must be served personally
or by leaving copies of the service with someone at the defendant's "dwelling house or usual
place of abode." Fed. R. Civ. P. 4(e)(2). New York has a similar rule, although it also permits service at the defendant's actual place of business. See N.Y. C.P.L.R. §§ 308(1)–(2)
(McKinney 1990). It is unclear, however, whether Satan maintains a permanent dwelling
place or an actual place of business in New York. Times Square, which many out-of-town-
ers frequently mistook for the outskirts of Hades, has been cleaned up by Mayor Rudolph
Giuliani and the Walt Disney Company. Hell's Kitchen, a neighborhood on the west side
of Manhattan that would have been another obvious place to look for a Satanic residence,
has since been renamed "Clinton," which may explain some recent events in Washington.

23. Service can only be made on "an agent authorized by appointment or by law to receive service of process." Fed. R. Civ. P. 4(e)(2); see N.Y. C.P.L.R. §§ 308(3), 318 (McKinney 1990).

authorizing service by publication when it can be shown that service by other means is not feasible.

I have given the question of the appropriate publication some thought. I am not at all sure whether the Devil is more likely to read the *New York Times* or a tabloid like the *Daily News*. After some reflection, I believe the most appropriate order would be one authorizing service by publication in the *Wall Street Journal* and *People* magazine.

Once service of process is effected, there remains the troublesome issue of sovereign immunity. As the court in *Ex rel. Mayo* suggested, Satan's repeated use of the self-description "Prince of Darkness" does raise this question, although it is unclear whether the term denotes actual status as a sovereign with true political and executive authority or whether it is merely an honorific along the lines of "Aretha Franklin, Queen of Soul," "Tarzan, King of the Jungle," or "Al Gore, Vice-President of the United States." Once again, however, this issue turns out to be irrelevant, because whether the Devil is actually the sovereign of the Underworld, the United States does not appear to have ever formally recognized the Government of Hell nor established diplomatic relations with it (although it must be admitted that some of the records from the Nixon years remain under seal).

We have seen, then, that notwithstanding Judge Weber's skepticism in the *Ex rel. Mayo* case, there are really no serious obstacles to suing the Devil in a New York court. Indeed, it might be just the thing to light a fire under old Lucifer.

And what would be the substance of the claims brought against the Devil in such a lawsuit? I originally thought this would be the easiest part of my research. After all, Satan is responsible for all sorts of human misery. Think of all the fires, famines, wars, pestilence, typhoons, and tornadoes for which the Devil is responsible, not to mention ozone depletion and low sperm counts. My legal research has revealed, however, that not one of these horrendous events constitutes a viable legal claim against the Devil. It turns out that, from a legal point of view, fires, wars, famines, etc. are all classified as "acts of God."[24]

After giving the matter careful consideration, I do *not* recommend a lawsuit against the Deity. This is not because such a lawsuit would lack substan-

---

24. The United States Supreme Court has stated that "[e]xtraordinary floods, storms of unusual violence, sudden tempests, severe frosts, great droughts, lightnings, earthquakes, sudden deaths and illnesses, have been held to be 'acts of God.'" Gleeson v. Virginia Midland R.R., 140 U.S. 435, 439 (1891). A few years later, the Court held that damage to luggage from a leaky porthole did not constitute such an "act of God.'" See The Majestic, 166 U.S. 375, 386–87 (1897). Although this latter decision might provide some basis for a lawsuit, it doesn't really seem sufficient to sue the Devil for water damage.

tial merit. On the contrary, any careful observer of world events will readily agree that God has much to answer for. I have reluctantly concluded, however, that it will simply not be possible to get a fair hearing for such claims given the improper influence exercised by the Deity over the federal and state judiciaries. To cite just the most blatant example, in many New York courtrooms the words "In God We Trust" are prominently displayed on the wall behind the judge. Even in proceedings in the highest court in the land, the Deity is frequently requested to "save" not only the United States, but "this honorable Court." It is hard to imagine a more brazen violation of the principle of judicial neutrality. Given such blatant favoritism, I would stick with suing the Devil you know.

But if we cannot sue the Devil for acts of God, what is the basis of his liability? The problem turned out to be more complicated than I had originally thought. I needed to find some wrongful acts that could be appropriately attributed to the Devil. Since we are seeking to bring a class action, it must be something that has caused serious injury to large numbers of people. I wanted something shocking and disturbing, yet readily classifiable under existing causes of action and legal precedents. With major catastrophes already excluded, I found myself at a loss, until I remembered Satan's fundamental attribute.

The Devil is a trickster, a deceiver, a demon not to be trusted. Obviously, the Devil is liable to an action for fraud.

But what exactly has the Devil lied about? Remember, I needed a widespread and pervasive lie, a monumental lie, a lie that wreaks havoc in its path, and yet a lie that virtually everyone believes. And then, sitting in a real estate broker's office in Manhattan, I had my revelation. The immensity and horror of the Satanic deception became clear to me while contemplating mortgage rates and closing costs. It is the Devil who makes us all believe that we can be happy.

Think about it—the perfect fraudulent scheme—totally untrue, and yet we cannot stop believing it. We rely on the representations, again and again, that the next apartment, or the next job, or the next lover, or the next election will finally bring us the satisfaction and happiness that have thus far eluded us. Such lies are clearly actionable under principles of common law fraud. The belief in human happiness is obviously false and equally obviously made with knowledge of its falsity. Yet we rely on it and continue to strive for happiness based on Satan's ridiculous representations. But are we thereby injured? Injured? The search for happiness leaves us scarred, bruised, beaten, run though the wringer, and left out to dry, or as I might say it in the complaint, "the class of humanity has suffered serious mental and physical injury in an amount to be determined at trial, but believed to exceed," oh, I don't know, how about "all the money in the world."

But even though this claim seems highly promising, it is subject to various defenses. Did the Devil really make us do it or have we brought these injuries on ourselves? The defense will claim that *in pari delicto*, contributory negligence, and assumption of risk all bar our way to recovery. Truth to tell, the evidence on this issue is far from clear. We will obviously need some expert witnesses on the subject of Satanic influence and human downfall. Luckily, such people are readily available. I wonder what Jim and Tammy Faye Bakker are doing these days?

In short, although the case against Satan is not a clear winner, it is certainly worth taking a shot. I am cautiously optimistic, particularly if the action can be brought to a final verdict before a finder of fact. My research indicates that the Devil is not expected to do well on Judgment Day.

Finally, then, we come to the question of recovery. Assuming that our action is successful, will it actually be possible to collect on the judgment? At the present time I am looking into this question to try to determine whether it is possible to garnish the Wages of Sin. Such a remedy would be nice, but I don't think it's essential. If anyone manages to actually get a judgment against the Devil in a court of law, there will undoubtedly be Hell to pay.

IV. Judges

Regina v. Ojibway

Anonymous

(In the Supreme Court)

BLUE, J.   AUGUST, 1965

BLUE, J.:— This is an appeal by the Crown by way of a stated case from a decision of the magistrate acquitting the accused of a charge under the Small Birds Act, R.S.O., 1960, c.724, s.2. The facts are not in dispute. Fred Ojibway, an Indian, was riding his pony through Queen's Park on January 2, 1965. Being impoverished, and having been forced to pledge his saddle, he substituted a downy pillow in lieu of the said saddle. On this particular day the accused's misfortune was further heightened by the circumstance of his pony breaking its right foreleg. In accord with Indian custom, the accused then shot the pony to relieve it of its awkwardness.

The accused was then charged with having breached the Small Birds Act, s.2 of which states:

> 2. Anyone maiming, injuring or killing small birds is guilty of an offence and subject to a fine not in excess of two hundred dollars.

The learned magistrate acquitted the accused holding, in fact, that he had killed his horse and not a small bird. With respect, I cannot agree.

In light of the definition section my course is quite clear. Section 1 defines "bird" as "a two legged animal covered with feathers". There can be no doubt that this case is covered by this section.

Counsel for the accused made several ingenious arguments to which, in fairness, I must address myself. He submitted that the evidence of the expert clearly concluded that the animal in question was a pony and not a bird, but this is not the issue. We are not interested in whether the animal in question is a bird or not in fact, but whether it is one in law. Statutory interpretation has forced many a horse to eat birdseed for the rest of its life.

Counsel also contended that the neighing noise emitted by the animal could not possibly be produced by a bird. With respect, the sounds emitted by an animal are irrelevant to its nature, for a bird is no less a bird because it is silent.

Counsel for the accused also argued that since there was evidence to show accused had ridden the animal, this pointed to the fact that it could not be a bird but was actually a pony. Obviously, this avoids the issue. The issue is not whether the animal was ridden or not, but whether it was shot or not, for to ride a pony or a bird is of no offence at all. I believe counsel now sees his mistake.

Counsel contends that the iron shoes found on the animal decisively disqualify it from being a bird. I must inform counsel, however, that how an animal dresses is of no concern to this court.

Counsel relied on the decision in *Re Chicadee*, where he contends that in similar circumstances the accused was acquitted. However, this is a horse of a different colour. A close reading of that case indicates that the animal in question there was not a small bird, but, in fact, a midget of a much larger species. Therefore, that case is inapplicable to our facts.

Counsel finally submits that the word "small" in the title Small Birds Act refers not to "Birds" but to "Act", making it The Small Act relating to Birds. With respect, counsel did not do his homework very well, for the Large Birds Act, R.S.O. 1960, c. 725, is just as small. If pressed, I need only refer to the Small Loans Act R.S.O. 1960, c. 727 which is twice as large as the Large Birds Act.

It remains then to state my reason for judgment which, simply, is as follows: Different things may take on the same meaning for different purposes. For the purpose of the Small Birds Act, all two legged, feather-covered animals are birds. This, of course, does not imply that only two-legged animals qualify, for the legislative intent is to make two legs merely the minimum requirement. The statute therefore contemplated multi-legged animals with feathers as well. Counsel submits that having regard to the purpose of the statute only small animals "naturally covered" with feathers could have been contemplated. However, had this been the intention of the legislature, I am certain that the phrase "naturally covered" would have been expressly inserted just as 'Long' was inserted in the Longshoreman's Act.

Therefore, a horse with feathers on its back must be deemed for the purposes of this Act to be a bird, and *a fortiori*, a pony with feathers on its back is a small bird.

Counsel posed the following rhetorical question: If the pillow had been removed prior to the shooting, would the animal still be a bird? To this let me answer rhetorically: Is a bird any less of a bird without its feathers?

Appeal allowed.

Reported by: H. Pomerantz
               S. Breslin

The Common Law Origins of the Infield Fly Rule

Aside

The[1] Infield Fly Rule[2] is neither a rule of law nor one of equity; it is a rule of baseball.[3] Since the[4] 1890's it has been a part of the body of the official rules

---

1. 11 OXFORD ENGLISH DICTIONARY 257–60 (1961).

2. OFF. R. BASEBALL 2.00 & 6.05(e). Rule 2.00 is definitional in nature and provides that:

> An INFIELD FLY is a fair fly ball (not including a line drive nor an attempted bunt) which can be caught by an infielder with ordinary effort, when first and second, or first, second and third bases are occupied, before two are out. The pitcher, catcher, and any outfielder who stations himself in the infield on the play shall be considered infielders for the purpose of this rule.
>
> When it seems apparent that a batted ball will be an Infield Fly, the umpire shall immediately declare "Infield Fly" for the benefit of the runners. If the ball is near the baselines, the umpire shall declare "Infield Fly, if Fair."
>
> The ball is alive and runners may advance at the risk of the ball being caught, or retouch and advance after the ball is touched, the same as on any fly ball. If the hit becomes a foul ball, it is treated the same as any foul.
>
> NOTE: If a declared Infield Fly is allowed to fall untouched to the ground, and bounces foul before passing first or third base, it is a foul ball. If a declared Infield Fly falls untouched to the ground outside the baseline, and bounces fair before passing first or third base, it is an Infield Fly.

Rule 6.05(e) gives operational effect to the definition, by providing that the batter is out when an Infield Fly is declared.

Depending upon the circumstances, other rules which may or may not apply to a particular situation include, *inter alia,* FED. R. CIV. P., Rule Against Perpetuities, and Rule of *Matthew* 7:12 & *Luke* 6:31 (Golden).

3. Although referred to as "Rules" both officially and in common parlance, if the analogy between the conduct-governing strictures of baseball and a jurisprudential entity on the order of a nation-state is to be maintained, the "rules" of baseball should be considered to have the force, effect, and legitimacy of the statutes of a nation-state. The analogy would continue to this end by giving the "ground rules" of a particular baseball park the same status as the judge-made rules of procedure of a particular court.

4. Note 1 *supra.*

of baseball.[5] In its inquiry into the common law origins[6] of the rule, this Aside does not seek to find a predecessor to the rule in seventeenth-century England. The purpose of the Aside is rather to examine whether the same types of forces that shaped the development of the common law[7] also generated the Infield Fly Rule.

As a preliminary matter, it is necessary to emphasize that baseball is a game of English origin, rooted in the same soil from which grew Anglo-American law and justice.[8] In this respect it is like American football and unlike basketball, a game that sprang fully developed from the mind of James Naismith.[9] The story of Abner Doubleday, Cooperstown, and 1839, a pleasant tribute to American ingenuity enshrined in baseball's Hall of Fame, is not true.[10] The myth reflects a

---

5. It is only with the greatest hesitation that one hazards a guess as to *the* year of origin of the Infield Fly Rule. Seymour considers it to have been 1893. 1 H. SEYMOUR, BASEBALL 275 (1960). Richter, on the other hand, in an opinion which *The Baseball Encyclopedia* joins, considers the rule to have entered the game in 1895. F. RICHTER, RICHTER'S HISTORY AND RECORDS OF BASEBALL 256 (1914); THE BASEBALL ENCYCLOPEDIA 1526–27 (1974). Finally, Voigt considers 1894 the correct year. 1 D. VOIGT, AMERICAN BASEBALL 288 (1966).

Although independent investigation of primary sources has led to the belief that the rule first developed in 1894 and 1895, notes 25–35 *infra* & accompanying text, a certain sense of justice would be satisfied if the rule developed as a result of play during the 1894 season. For that season was the first of the championship seasons of the Baltimore Orioles, the team that developed what is now known as "inside baseball," including such plays as the Baltimore chop and the hit-and-run. The Orioles not only played smart baseball; they played dirty baseball. "Although they may not have originated dirty baseball they perfected it to a high degree. In a National League filled with dirty players they were undoubtedly the dirtiest of their time and may have been the dirtiest the game has ever known." D. WALLOP, BASEBALL: AN INFORMAL HISTORY 88 (1969); *accord,* L. ALLEN, THE NATIONAL LEAGUE STORY 68 (1961); *see* R. SMITH, BASEBALL 136–46 (1947). Even if the Infield Fly Rule was not developed as a result of the event of the 1894 season, perhaps it should have been.

6. For a discussion of origins, *see generally* Scopes v. State, 154 Tenn. 105, 289 S.W. 363 (1927); *Genesis* 1:1-2:9. *But see even more generally* Epperson v. Arkansas, 393 U.S. 97 (1968); R. ARDREY, AFRICAN GENESIS (1961); C. DARWIN, THE DESCENT OF MAN (1871); C. DARWIN, THE ORIGIN OF SPECIES (1859).

7. For a discussion of common law in a non-baseball context, see W. HOLDSWORTH, A HISTORY OF ENGLISH LAW (1903–1938); O.W. HOLMES, THE COMMON LAW (1881).

8. *Cf.* Palko v. Connecticut, 302 U.S. 319, 325 (1937).

9. R. BRASCH, HOW DID SPORTS BEGIN? 41 (1970).

10. R. HENDERSON, BAT, BALL AND BISHOP 170–94 (1947). The Doubleday theory of origin is outlined in 84 CONG. REC. 1087–89 (1939) (remarks of Congressman Shanley) *(semble)*. Congressional approval of the theory, however, was never forthcoming. H.R.J. Res. 148, 76th Cong., 1st Sess. (1939), seeking to designate June 12, 1939, National Baseball Day, was referred to the Committee on the Judiciary, never again to be heard from. 84 CONG. REC. 1096 (1939). Nor did the Supreme Court formally adopt the Doubleday theory. Flood v. Kuhn, 407 U.S. 258, 260–61 (1972) (opinion of Blackmun, J.) (not explicitly

combination of economic opportunism,[11] old friendship,[12] and not a small element of anti-British feeling.[13] The true birthplace of the game is England; thence it was carried to the western hemisphere, to develop as an American form.[14]

The original attitude toward baseball developed from distinctly English origins as well. The first "organized" games were played in 1845 by the Knickerbocker Base Ball Club of New York City,[15] and the rules which governed their contests clearly indicate that the game was to be played by gentlemen. Winning was not the objective; exercise was.[16] "The New York club players were 'gentlemen in the highest social sense'—that is, they were rich.... The earliest clubs were really trying to transfer to our unwilling soil a few of the seeds of the British cricket spirit."[17] This spirit, which has been variously described as the attitude of the amateur, of the gentleman, and of the sportsman,[18] would have kept the rules simple and allowed moral force to govern the game.[19] Such an attitude, however, was unable to prevail.

As baseball grew, so did the influence of values that saw winning, rather than exercise, as the purpose of the game.[20] Victory was to be pursued by any means possible within the language of the rules, regardless of whether the tactic violated the spirit of the rules.[21] The written rules had to be made more and more specific, in order to preserve the spirit of the game.[22]

---

rejecting the theory either). An interesting, if unlikely, explanation, offerable as an alternative to both the Doubleday and English theories of origin, is found in J. HART, HEY! B.C. 26 from the back (unpaginated, abridged & undated ed.).

11. R. BRASCH, *supra* note 9, at 31–32.

12. R. HENDERSON, *supra* note 10, at 179. The chairman of the commission suggested by A.G. Spalding to investigate the origins of the game was A.G. Mills, who had belonged to the same military post as Abner Doubleday.

13. R. SMITH, *supra* note 5, at 31.

14. *See generally* H. SEYMOUR, *supra* note 5; D. VOIGT, *supra* note 5. The American qualities of the game are also revealed in other than historical or legal contexts. *Cf.* M. GARDNER, THE ANNOTATED CASEY AT THE BAT (1967); B. MALAMUD, THE NATURAL (1952).

15. R. SMITH, *supra* note 5, at 32–35.

16. KNICKERBOCKER BASE BALL CLUB R. 1 (1845), *reprinted in* R. HENDERSON, *supra* note 10, at 163–64, *and in* F. RICHTER, *supra* note 5, at 227.

17. R. SMITH, *supra* note 5, at 37

18. Keating, *Sportsmanship as a Moral Category,* 75 ETHICS 25, 33 (1964).

19. R. SMITH, *supra* note 5, at 68–69.

20. 1 D. VOIGT, *supra* note 5, at xvii; *cf. Hearings on S. 3445, Federal Sports Act of 1972, Before the Senate Committee on Commerce,* 92d Cong., 2d Sess. 94–95 (1973) (statement of H. Cosell). *See generally* Keating, *supra* note 18, at 31–34.

21. Perhaps the most glaring example of this attitude is contained in the career of Mike "King" Kelly. When the rules permitted substitutions on mere notice to the umpire, Kelly inserted himself into the game after the ball was hit in order to catch a ball out of reach of any of his teammates. R. SMITH, *supra* note 5, at 89–90.

22. *Cf. id.* 68–69; 1 D. VOIGT, *supra* note 5, at 204–05.

The Infield Fly Rule is obviously not a core principle of baseball. Unlike the diamond itself or the concepts of "out" and "safe," the Infield Fly Rule is not necessary to the game. Without the Infield Fly Rule, baseball does not degenerate into bladderball[23] the way the collective bargaining process degenerates into economic warfare when good faith is absent.[24] It is a technical rule, a legislative response to actions that were previously permissible, though contrary to the spirit of the sport.

Whether because the men who oversaw the rules of baseball during the 1890's were unwilling to make a more radical change than was necessary to remedy a perceived problem in the game, or because they were unable to perceive the need for a broader change than was actually made, three changes in the substantive rules, stretching over a seven-year period, were required to put the Infield Fly Rule in its present form. In each legislative response to playing field conduct, however, the fundamental motive for action remained the same: "To prevent the defense from making a double play by subterfuge, at a time when the offense is helpless to prevent it, rather than by skill and speed."[25]

The need to enforce this policy with legislation first became apparent in the summer of 1893. In a game between New York and Baltimore, with a fast runner on first, a batter with the "speed of an ice wagon"[26] hit a pop fly. The runner stayed on first, expecting the ball to be caught. The fielder, however, let the ball drop to the ground, and made the force out at second.[27] The particular occurrence did not result in a double play, but that possibility was apparent; it would require only that the ball not be hit as high. Although even the Baltimore Sun credited the New York Giant with "excellent judgment,"[28] the incident suggested that something should be done, because by the play the defense obtained an advantage that it did not deserve and that the offense could not have prevented. Umpires could handle the situation by calling the batter out,[29] but this was not a satisfactory solution; it could

---

23. *See* Yale Daily News, Oct. 29, 1966, at 1, col. 1.

24. NLRB v. Insurance Agents Int'l Union, 361 U.S. 477, 488–90 (1960).

25. 1 H. SEYMOUR, *supra* note 5, at 276.

26. Baltimore Sun, May 24, 1893, at 6, col. 2. Raised by this statement is the issue of the speed of an ice wagon in both relative and absolute terms. Such inquiry is beyond the scope of this Aside.

27. *Id.* The fielder who made the play was Giant shortstop and captain John Montgomery Ward, who became a successful attorney after his playing days ended. 1 D. VOIGT, *supra* note 5, at 285.

28. Baltimore Sun, May 24, 1893, at 6, col. 2.

29. *E.g.*, the Chicago-Baltimore game of June 8, 1893. "In the second inning...Kelley hit a pop fly to short-stop. Dahlen caught the ball, then dropped it and threw to second

create as many problems as it solved.[30] The 1894 winter meeting responded with adoption of the "trap ball" rule, putting the batter out if he hit a ball that could be handled by an infielder while first base was occupied with one out.[31]

The trap ball rule of 1894, however, did not solve all problems. First, although the rule declared the batter out, there was no way to know that the rule was in effect for a particular play. The umpire was not required to make his decision until after the play, and, consequently, unnecessary disputes ensued.[32] Second, it became apparent that the feared unjust double play was not one involving the batter and one runner, but one that, when two men were on base, would see two baserunners declared out.[33] The 1895 league meeting ironed out these difficulties through changes in the rules.[34] The third problem with the trap ball rule of 1894, one not perceived until later, was that it applied only when one man was out. The danger of an unfair double play, however, also exists when there are no men out. This situation was corrected in 1901, and the rule has remained relatively unchanged since that time.[35]

The Infield Fly Rule, then, emerged from the interplay of four factors, each of which closely resembles a major force in the development of the common law. First is the sporting approach to baseball. A gentleman, when playing a game, does not act in a manner so unexpected as to constitute trickery;[36] in

---

base, a runner being on first. The muff was so plain that Umpire McLaughlin refused to allow the play and simply called the batsman out." Baltimore Sun, June 9, 1893, at 6, col. 2.

30. Text accompanying notes 45–46 *infra*.

31. Baltimore Sun, Feb. 27, 1894, at 6, col. 3. The rule stated that "the batsman is out if he hits a fly ball that can be handled by an infielder while first base is occupied and with only one out." *Id.* Apr. 26, 1894, at 6, col. 2.

32. Baltimore Sun, Apr. 26, 1894, at 6, col. 2.

33. 1 H. Seymour, *supra* note 5, at 275–76. Seymour developed yet another reason for the change in the rule: that "teams got around it by having outfielders come in fast and handle the pop fly." *Id.* 276. This does not appear to be a valid thesis because, from the beginning, the rule referred not to whether an infielder, as opposed to an outfielder, *did* handle the chance, but to whether an infielder *could* handle it. Note 31 *supra*.

34. Baltimore Sun, Feb. 18, 1895, at 6, col. 4. *Id.* Feb. 28, 1895, at 6, col. 5.

35. The Baseball Encyclopedia 1527 (1974). The current rule is set forth in note 2 *supra*.

36. *See, e.g.,* Pluck (the wonder chicken).

particular he does not attempt to profit by his own unethical conduct.[37] The gentleman's code provides the moral basis for the rule; it is the focal point of the rule, just as the more general precept of fair play provides a unifying force to the conduct of the game. The principle of Anglo-American law analogous to this gentleman's concept of fair play is the equally amorphous concept of due process, or justice[38] itself.

Baseball's society, like general human society, includes more than gentlemen, and the forces of competitiveness and professionalism required that the moral principle of fair play be codified so that those who did not subscribe to the principle would nonetheless be required to abide by it.[39] Thus the second factor in the development of the Infield Fly Rule—a formal and legalistic code of rules ensuring proper conduct—was created.[40] In the common law, this development manifested itself in the formalism of the writ system.[41] Conduct was governed by general principles; but to enforce a rule of conduct, it was necessary to find a remedy in a specific writ.[42] The common law plain-

---

37. In the law, this belief is reflected in the clean hands doctrine, which "is rooted in the historical concept of [the] court of equity as a vehicle for affirmatively enforcing the requirements of conscience and good faith." Precision Instrument Mfg. Co. v. Automotive Maintenance Mach. Co., 324 U.S. 806, 814 (1945). For a statutory codification of the clean hands rule, see CAL. HEALTH & SAFETY CODE § 28548, ¶ 2 (West 1967) (requiring food service employees to "clean hands" before leaving restroom). See generally Z. CHAFEE, SOME PROBLEMS OF EQUITY, chs. 1–3 (1950).

To be contrasted with the doctrine of "clean hands" is the "sticky fingers" doctrine. The latter embodies the reaction of the baseball world to the excitement caused by the emergence of the home run as a major aspect of the game. Applying to the ball a foreign substance, such as saliva, made the big hit a difficult feat to achieve. As a result, in 1920, the spitball was outlawed. L. ALLEN, supra note 5, at 167. The banning of the spitball was not, however, absolute. Seventeen pitchers were given lifetime waivers of the ban, id., possibly because the spitball had become an essential element of their stock-in-trade, and depriving them of the pitch would in effect deny them the right to earn a living. See Adams v. Tanner, 244 U.S. 590 (1917); McDermott v. City of Seattle, 4 F. Supp. 855, 857 (W.D. Wash. 1933); Winther v. Village of Weippe, 91 Idaho 798, 803–04, 430 P.2d 689, 694–95 (1967); cf. RESTATEMENT (SECOND) OF CONTRACTS § 90 (Tent. Drafts Nos. 1–7, 1973). But see Ferguson v. Skrupa, 372 U.S. 726, 730–31 (1963).

38. See generally, e.g., U.S. CONST. amends. V & XIV and cases citing thereto; Poe v. Ullman, 367 U.S. 497, 539–55 (1961) (Harlan, J., dissenting); J. RAWLS, A THEORY OF JUSTICE (1971); Bentley, John Rawls: A Theory of Justice, 121 U. PA. L. REV. 1070 (1973); Michelman, In Pursuit of Constitutional Welfare Rights: One View of Rawls' Theory of Justice, 121 U. PA. L. REV. 962 (1973); Scanlon, Rawls' Theory of Justice, 121 U. PA. L. REV. 1020 (1973); cf., e.g., Byron R. "Whizzer" White (1962–), Hugo L. Black (1937–71), & Horace Gray (1881–1902) (Justices). But cf., e.g., Roger B. Taney (1836–64) (Chief Justice).

39. Keating, supra note 18, at 30. See also R. SMITH, supra note 5, at 68–69.

40. Text accompanying notes 25–35 supra.

41. 2 F. MAITLAND, COLLECTED PAPERS 477–83 (1911).

42. F. POLLOCK, THE GENIUS OF THE COMMON LAW 13 (1912); 2 F. POLLOCK & F. MAITLAND, HISTORY OF ENGLISH LAW 558–65 (2d ed. 1952).

tiff had no remedy if the existing writs did not encompass the wrong complained of; and the baseball player who had been the victim of a "cute" play could not prevail until the umpire could be shown a rule of baseball squarely on point.

To the generalization set forth in the preceding sentence there is an exception, both at common law and at baseball. At common law, the exception was equity, which was able to aid the plaintiff who could not find a form of action at law.[43] At baseball, the exception was the power of the umpire to make a call that did not fit within a particular rule.[44] The powers of equity and of the umpire, however, were not unlimited. The law courts circumscribed the power of the chancellor to the greatest extent possible, and this process of limitation has been defended.[45] Likewise, the discretionary power of the umpire has been limited: Additions to the written rules have reduced the area within which the umpire has discretion to act. Strong policy reasons favor this limitation upon the umpire's discretionary power. Because finality of decision is as important as correctness of decision, an action that invites appeal, as broad discretion in the umpire does, is not valued. The umpire must have the status of an unchallengeable finder of fact.[46] Allowing challenges to his authority on matters of rules admits the possibility that he may be wrong, and encourages a new generation of challenges to findings of fact.

The fourth element in the development of the Infield Fly Rule is demonstrated by the piecemeal approach that rules committees took to the problem. They responded to problems as they arose; the process of creating the Infield Fly Rule was incremental, with each step in the development of the rule merely a refinement of the previous step. Formalism was altered to the extent necessary to achieve justice in the particular case; it was not abandoned and replaced with a new formalism. Anglo-American law has two analogies to this process. The first is the way in which common law precedents are employed to mold existing remedies to new situations. Although the rigid structure of the common law was slow to change, it did change. The substantive change took place not only as a result of judicial decision; it was also caused by legislation, which is the second analogy. The legislation, however, was to a great extent directed at specific defects perceived to exist in the system.[47] Adjustment of the law, not its reform, was the goal of the legislative process. The

---

43. F. Maitland, Equity 4–5 (1909).
44. Note 29 *supra.*
45. 2 F. Maitland, *supra* note 41, at 491–94.
46. Off. R. Baseball 4.19.
47. F. Pollock, *supra* note 42, at 72.

rules of baseball and of Anglo-American jurisprudence are thus to be contrasted with the continental system of complete codes designed to remedy society's ills with a single stroke of the legislative brush.[48]

The dynamics of the common law and the development of one of the most important technical rules of baseball, although on the surface completely different in outlook and philosophy, share significant elements. Both have been essentially conservative, changing only as often as a need for change is perceived, and then only to the extent necessary to remove the need for further change. Although problems are solved very slowly when this attitude prevails, the solutions that are adopted do not create many new difficulties. If the process reaps few rewards, it also runs few risks.

---

48. *Cf.* H. GUTTERIDGE, COMPARATIVE LAW 77–78 (2d ed. 1949).

Don't* Cry** over Filled Milk: The Neglected Footnote Three to *Carolene Products****

Aside

> *Membership on the* Law Review *is an invaluable learning experience both in substantive law and in the skills of research, analysis and expression. Recognition of the value of this experience by the legal profession generally makes membership on the* Law Review *a goal for most students.*[1]

The famous footnote four to *United States v. Carolene Products Co.*[2] has

---

* *But cf.* Posner, *Goodbye to the Bluebook,* 53 U. CHI. L. REV. 1343, 1350 (1986) (citing refusal to use contractions as an example of "anti-lessons" that law reviews drum into the heads of law students).

** *See* Ely, *The Wages of Crying Wolf: A Comment on* Roe v. Wade, 82 YALE L.J. 920 (1973).

*** United States v. Carolene Prods. Co., 304 U.S. 144 (1938). This Aside commemorates the fiftieth anniversary of *Carolene Products,* April 25, 1988.

1. THE LAW SCHOOL, UNIVERSITY OF PENNSYLVANIA, PENN: BULLETIN OF THE LAW SCHOOL, UNIVERSITY OF PENNSYLVANIA 1987–1989, at 43 (Sept. 1986). *But see* FCC v. Pacifica Found., 438 U.S. 726, 753 (1978) (Appendix to Opinion of the Court) ("I've had that shit up to here.").

2. 304 U.S. 144, 154 n.4 (1938).

generated significant and plentiful scholarly discussion.[3] The equally impor-

---

3. *See, e.g.*, J. Ely, Democracy and Distrust 75–77, 148–53, 221 n.4, 243–44 n.17, 248–49 n.52, 255 n.84 (1980) (footnote four is important); W. Lockhart, Y. Kamisar & J. Choper, Constitutional Law: Cases-Comments-Questions 1252 (5th ed. 1980) (same); 2 R. Rotunda, J. Nowak & J. Young, Treatise on Constitutional Law: Substance and Procedure § 15.4 (1986) (same); L. Tribe, American Constitutional Law 567, 573 n.7, 613 n.30, 1001, 1077 n.1 (1978) (same); Ackerman, *Beyond* Carolene Products, 98 Harv. L. Rev. 713, 713 (1985) [hereinafter Ackerman, *Beyond* Carolene Products] (same); Aleinikoff, *Constitutional Law in the Age of Balancing*, 96 Yale L.J. 943, 962–63 n.116 (1987) (same); Attanasio, *The Constitutionality of Regulating Human Genetic Engineering: Where Procreative Liberty and Equal Opportunity Collide*, 53 U. Chi. L. Rev. 1274, 1312–17 (1986) (same); Baker, *Outcome Equality or Equality of Respect: The Substantive Content of Equal Protection*, 131 U. Pa. L. Rev. 933, 945 n.40 (1983) (same); Ball, *Judicial Protection of Powerless Minorities*, 59 Iowa L. Rev. 1059, 1060–64 (1974) (same); Brilmayer, *Carolene, Conflicts, and the Fate of the "Inside-Outsider"*, 134 U. Pa. L. Rev. 1291, 1291 (1986) (same); Caplan, *The History and Meaning of the Ninth Amendment*, 69 Va. L. Rev. 223, 261–62 n.161 (1983) (same); Cover, *The Origins of Judicial Activism in the Protection of Minorities*, 91 Yale L.J. 1287, 1287–1307 (1982) (same); Ely, *supra* note **, at 933–35 (same); Estreicher, *Platonic Guardians of Democracy: John Hart Ely's Role For the Supreme Court in the Constitution's Open Texture*, 56 N.Y.U. L. Rev. 547, 552–57 (1981) (same); Fiss, *The Supreme Court, 1978 Term—Foreword: The Forms of Justice*, 93 Harv. L. Rev. 1, 6–7, 16 (1979) (same); Gerety, *Children in the Labyrinth: The Complexities of* Plyler v. Doe, 44 U. Pitt. L. Rev. 379, 393 (1983) (same); Hazard, *Rising Above Principle*, 135 U. Pa. L. Rev. 153, 176 (1986) (same); Hovenkamp, *The Economics of Legal History*, 67 Minn. L. Rev. 645, 696 (1983) (same); Karst, *Woman's Constitution*, 1984 Duke L.J. 447, 498 & n.202 (1984) (same); Lawrence, *The Id, the Ego, and Equal Protection: Reckoning with Unconscious Racism*, 39 Stan. L. Rev. 317, 345–46 (1987) (same); Lee, *Gerrymandering and the Brooding Omnipresence of Proportional Representation: Won't It Go Away?*, 33 UCLA L. Rev. 257, 268–70 (1985) (same); Lowe, *Public Safety Legislation and the Referendum Power: A Reexamination*, 37 Hastings L.J. 591, 630 (1986) (same); Lusky, *Footnote Redux: A* Carolene Products *Reminiscence*, 82 Colum. L. Rev. 1093, 1093 (1982) (same); McKay, *The Preference for Freedom*, 34 N.Y.U. L. Rev. 1182, 1184, 1191–93 (1959) (same); Osakwe, *Equal Protection of Law in Soviet Constitutional Law and Theory—A Comparative Analysis*, 59 Tul. L. Rev. 974, 1009 n.70 (1985) (same); Pollak, *Racial Discrimination and Judicial Integrity: A Reply to Professor Wechsler*, 108 U. Pa. L. Rev. 1, 27–28 (1959) (same); Powell, Carolene Products *Revisited*, 82 Colum. L. Rev. 1087, 1087 (1982) (same); Schoenbrod, *The Delegation Doctrine: Could the Court Give It Substance?*, 83 Mich. L. Rev. 1223, 1287–89 (1985) (same); Schuck, *The Transformation of Immigration Law*, 84 Colum. L. Rev. 1, 65 n.364 (1984) (same); Seidman, *Public Principle and Private Choice: The Uneasy Case for a Boundary Maintenance Theory of Constitutional Law*, 96 Yale L.J. 1006, 1033–38 (1987) (same); Shane, *School Desegregation Remedies and the Fair Governance of Schools*, 132 U. Pa. L. Rev. 1041, 1080 n.128 (1984) (same); Taylor, Brown, *Equal Protection, and the Isolation of the Poor*, 95 Yale L.J. 1700, 1731–32 (1986) (same); Williams, *The Constitutional Vulnerability of American Local Government: The Politics of City Status in American Law*, 1986 Wis. L. Rev. 83, 137 n.283 (1986) (same); *The Supreme Court, 1971 Term: Constitutional Law*, 86 Harv. L. Rev. 1, 82 (1972) (same); Note, *The Constitutionality of Excluding Desegregation from the Legal Services Program*, 84 Colum. L. Rev. 1630, 1647 n.122 (1984) (same); Note, *Beyond* Youngsberg: *Protecting the Fundamental Rights of the Mentally Retarded*, 51 Fordham L. Rev. 1064, 1070–71 (1983) (same); Note, *Public Use, Private Use, and Judicial*

tant footnote three in Justice Stone's opinion,[4] however, has not attracted as much attention from the academic community.[5] This is an unfortunate oversight. Footnote three illustrates in microcosm many of the issues on the forefront of modern legal debate.[6] It provides a starting point for an examination of the importance of footnotes in general to the world in which we live; for a study of the vital importance of dairy jurisprudence to the general field of bovine law, and by extension to American law; and for speculation that cozy assumptions as to the legal system's human origins may be sadly mistaken.

Part I of this Aside describes footnote three's contribution to the development of citation overkill in American law and the impending triumph of form over vulgar functionalism. Part II does not exist. Part III discusses footnote three's influence on legal interpretation as exemplified in the law of dairy products, and of barnyard animals in general. Part IV examines footnote three's origins and concludes that it was drafted by authorities hitherto ignored by "respectable" legal scholars.

I. Toward a Theory of Deontological Citational Dialecticism: Footnote Three and Deconstructive Footnote Teleology

A. *Citation: The Sincerest Form of Flattery*

Footnote three is divided into two parts.[7] The first paragraph contains a discrete and independent branch of the footnote's constitutional theory. It reads:

> There is now an extensive literature indicating wide recognition by scientists and dietitians of the great importance to the public health of butter

---

Review in Eminent Domain, 58 N.Y.U. L. Rev. 409, 428–29 (1983) (same); Note, *Political Protest and the Illinois Defense of Necessity*, 54 U. Chi. L. Rev. 1070, 1085 (1987) (same); Comment, *Still Newer Equal Protection: Impermissible Purpose Review in the 1984 Term*, 53 U. Chi. L. Rev. 1454, 1455–56 n.4 (1986) (same); Comment, *The Tenth Amendment After Garcia: Process-Based Procedural Protections*, 135 U. Pa. L. Rev. 1657, 1671–72 (1987) [hereinafter *Tenth Amendment After* Garcia] (same); Note, *Voter Registration: A Restriction on the Fundamental Right to Vote*, 96 Yale L.J. 1615, 1620 (1987) (same); Note, *Choosing Representatives By Lottery Voting*, 93 Yale L.J. 1283, 1284–85 (1984) (same); Note, *On Reading and Using the Tenth Amendment*, 93 Yale L.J. 723, 740 n.87 (1984) (same).

4. *Carolene Prods.*, 304 U.S. at 150 n.3.

5. *See, e.g.,* .

6. *See infra* note 64.

7. *Cf.* 7 I. Caesaris, Bello Gallico 1 (1972) ("Gallia est omnis divisa in partis tris").

fat and whole milk as the prime source of vitamins, which are essential
growth producing and disease preventing elements in the diet. See Dr. Henry
C. Sherman, The Meaning of Vitamin A, in Science, Dec. 21, 1928, p. 619;
Dr. E.V. McCollum et al., The Newer Knowledge of Nutrition (1929 ed.), pp.
134, 170, 176, 177; Dr. A.S. Root, Food Vitamins (N. Car. State Board of
Health, May 1931), p. 2; Dr. Henry C. Sherman, Chemistry of Food and Nutrition (1932) p. 367; Dr. Mary S. Rose, The Foundations of Nutrition (1933),
p. 237.[8]

Thus, paragraph one is the source of the doctrine that scientists and dieticians
recognize the importance of butter fat and whole milk to the public health.
It is significant for its modest ratio of four lines of text to six lines of citations.
Paragraph two, on the other hand, is the Court's pinnacle of citation overkill:

> When the Filled Milk Act was passed, eleven states had rigidly controlled
> the exploitation of filled milk, or forbidden it altogether. H.R. 365, 67th
> Cong., 1st Sess. Some thirty-five states have now adopted laws which in
> terms, or by their operation, prohibit the sale of filled milk. Ala. Agri. Code,
> 1927, § 51, Art. 8; Ariz. Rev. Code, 1936 Supp., § 943y; Pope's Ark. Dig. 1937,
> § 3103; Deering's Cal. Code, 1933 Supp., Tit. 149, Act 1943, p. 1302; Conn.
> Gen. Stat., 1930, § 2487, c. 135; Del. Rev. Code, 1935, § 649; Fla. Comp. Gen.
> Laws, 1927, §§ 3216, 7676; Ga. Code, 1933, § 42-511; Idaho Code, 1932, Tit.
> 36, §§ 502–504; Jones Ill. Stat. Ann., 1937 Supp., § 53.020 (1), (2), (3); Burns
> Ind. Stat., 1933, § 35-1203; Iowa Code, 1935, § 3062; Kan. Gen. Stat., 1935,
> c. 65, § 707; Md. Ann. Code, Art. 27, § 281; Mass. Ann. Laws, 1933, § 17-A, c.
> 94; Mich. Comp. Laws, 1929, § 5358; Mason's Minn. Stat., 1927, § 3926; Mo.
> Rev. Stat., 1929, §§ 12408–12413; Mont. Rev. Code, Anderson and McFar-
> land, 1935, c. 240, § 2620.39; Neb. Comp. Stat., 1929, § 81-1022; N. H. Pub.
> L. 1926, v. 1, c. 163, § 37, p. 619; N.J. Comp. Stat., 1911–1924, § 81-8j, p. 1400;
> Cahill's N.Y. Cons. Laws, 1930, § 60, c. 1; N. D. Comp. Laws, 1913–1925, Pol.
> Code, c. 38, § 2855 (a) 1; Page's Ohio Gen. Code, § 12725; Purdon's Penna.
> Stat., 1936, Tit. 31, §§ 553, 582; S. D. Comp. Laws, 1929, c. 192, § 7926-0, p.
> 2493; Williams Tenn. Code, 1934, c. 15, §§ 6549, 6551; Vernon's Tex. Pen.
> Code, Tit. 12, c. 2, Art. 713a; Utah Rev. Stat., 1933, §§ 3-10-59, 3-10-60; Vt.
> Pub. L., 1933, Tit. 34, c. 303, § 7724, p. 1288; Va. 1936 Code, § 1197c; W. Va.
> 1932 Code, § 2036; Wis. Stat., 11th ed. 1931, c. 98, § 98.07, p. 1156; cf. N.
> Mex. Ann. Stat., 1929, §§ 25-104, 25-108. Three others have subjected its sale
> to rigid regulations. Colo. L. 1921, c. 30, § 1007, p. 440; Ore. 1930 Code, v.2,
> c. XII, §§ 41-1208 to 41-1210; Remington's Wash. Rev. Stat., v. 7, Tit. 40, c.
> 13, §§ 6206, 6207, 6713, 6714, p. 360, *et seq.*[9]

Footnote three is an extraordinary display of raw citation power.[10] Although

---

8. *Carolene Prods.*, 304 U.S. at 150 n.3.

9. *Id.*

10. One observer of the federal judiciary notes that the average number of citations in
a Supreme Court opinion only reached 61.9 in 1983, from an average *in 1960* of 39.3. *See*

the statutory citations in paragraph two serve some function by telling the reader which states have controlled the sale of filled milk, the sheer volume of citations, unnecessary to support or clarify any argument in the opinion's text, represents a breathtaking dominance of form over function.

Analysis of footnote three demonstrates why it, or any footnote, matters. Legal citations, especially in the form of footnotes, deserve scholarly attention for several reasons. But in order to engage in such study, one must distinguish between academic and judicial footnotes.

In legal periodicals, footnotes differentiate one piece of work from the mass of other available literature: "Footnoting has evolved from primitive origins and use as a 'pure' reference into an artistic and abstruse discipline that functions as a subtle, but critical, influence in the determination of promotion, tenure, and professional status."[11] A footnote can also contain information useful in understanding the body of the work.[12] Or it can suggest the absence of useful information in the text.[13]

In a judicial opinion, a footnote can provide doctrinal guidance for future courts,[14] or, like *Carolene Products'* famous footnote four,[15] it can cause con-

---

R. Posner, The Federal Courts: Crisis and Reform 112 (1985). Although it could be argued that footnote three counts as one "citation," its 44 individual citations make it a footnote clearly ahead of its time.

11. Austin, *Footnotes as Product Differentiation*, 40 Vand. L. Rev. 1131, 1135 (1987) (footnotes omitted).

12. *See, e.g.,* Martineau, *Considering New Issues on Appeal: The General Rule and the Gorilla Rule*, 40 Vand. L. Rev. 1023, 1057 n.137 (1987) (graphically illustrating exception to rule that eight-hundred-pound gorilla sleeps wherever it wants to).

13. *See, e.g.,* Chused, *Married Women's Property Law*, 71 Geo. L.J. 1359, 1365 n.19 (1983) ("The men's wills were sampled by turning the microfilm crank 10 times and reading the first male will to appear thereafter.").

14. *See, e.g.,* United States v. Socony-Vacuum Oil Co., 310 U.S. 150, 224 n.59 (1940), *cited in, e.g.,* Arizona v. Maricopa County Medical Soc'y, 457 U.S. 332, 351 (1982); McLain v. Real Estate Bd., 444 U.S. 232, 243 (1980); United States v. Citizens and S. Nat'l Bank, 422 U.S. 86, 113 (1975); United States v. Container Corp. of America, 393 U.S. 333, 337 (1969); Hanover Shoe, Inc. v. United Shoe Mach. Corp., 392 U.S. 481, 499 (1968); United States v. Columbia Steel Co., 334 U.S. 495, 537 (1948); Gershman v. Universal Resources Holding Inc., 824 F.2d 223, 229 (3d Cir. 1987); Stone v. William Beaumont Hosp., 782 F.2d 609, 618 (6th Cir. 1986); United States v. Miller, 771 F.2d 1219, 1226 (9th Cir. 1985), *rev'd* Marrese v. American Academy of Orthopedic Surgeons, 471 U.S. 1062 (1985); Marrese v. American Academy of Orthopedic Surgeons, 726 F.2d 1150, 1155 (7th Cir. 1984); St. Bernard Hosp. v. Hospital Serv. Ass'n, 713 F.2d 978, 986 (5th Cir. 1983); Olsen v. Progressive Music Supply, Inc., 703 F.2d 432, 441 (10th Cir.), *cert. denied*, 464 U.S. 866 (1983).

15. *See Carolene Prods.*, 304 U.S. at 154 n.4.

fusion in the lower courts and spawn a new jurisprudence.[16] Or it can simply cause parties a lot of trouble.[17]

One court opined that a judicial footnote "is as important a part of an opinion as a matter contained in the body of the opinion and has like binding force and effect."[18] Courts have been less respectful of academic footnotes. Witness the First Circuit's audacious suggestion that Professor Laurence Tribe's billing of $5,500 for twenty hours' work preparing an eighteen-line footnote for a brief was excessive.[19]

B. *How Life Imitates the Bluebook*[20]

In the final analysis, footnotes are important mainly when they guide the reader to authority for a stated proposition. Citation is the highest form of legal discourse. It has a history as long and rich as that of the law itself.[21] The first codification of rules for legal citation occurred as early as the late fifteenth century.[22] It is no coincidence that Europe's Renaissance was contemporaneous with the rise of legal citation manuals.

The civilizing influence of citation systems reached its highest point with

---

16. *See, e.g.*, Sedima S.P.R.L. Inc. v. Imrex Co., 473 U.S. 479, 496 n.14 (1985) (discussing elements of "pattern of racketeering activity" for purposes of Racketeer Influenced and Corrupt Organizations Act, 18 U.S.C. §§ 1961–1968 (1982 & Supp. IV 1987)), *cited in, e.g.*, Marshall-Silver Const. Co. v. Mendel, 835 F.2d 63, 65 (3d Cir. 1987); Sun Sav. & Loan Ass'n v. Dierdorff, 825 F.2d 187, 191 (9th Cir. 1987); Montesano v. Seafirst Commercial Corp., 818 F.2d 423, 424 (5th Cir. 1987); Madden v. Gluck, 815 F.2d 1163, 1164 n.1 (8th Cir. 1987); International Data Bank, Ltd. v. Zepkin, 812 F.2d 149, 154–55 (4th Cir. 1987); Marks v. Pannell Kerr Forster, 811 F.2d 1108, 1110 n.1 (7th Cir. 1987); *id.* at 1112 (Cudahy, J., concurring); Torwest DBC, Inc. v. Dick, 810 F.2d 925, 928 (10th Cir. 1987); United States v. Ianniello, 808 F.2d 184, 190 (2d Cir. 1986), *cert. denied*, 107 S. Ct. 3230 (1987).

17. *See* United States v. Ofshe, 817 F.2d 1508, 1516 n.6 (11th Cir.) (suggesting prosecuting attorney be disciplined), *cert. denied*, 108 S. Ct. 451 (1987); *see also* Uviller, Presumed Guilty: The Court of Appeals Versus Scott Turow (forthcoming in 136 U. PA. L. REV. (1988)) (criticizing *Ofshe's* criticism of the prosecuting attorney's prosecution).

18. Melancon v. Walt Disney Prods., 127 Cal. App. 2d 213, 214 n.1, 273 P.2d 560, 562 n.1 (1954).

19. *See* Grendel's Den, Inc. v. Larkin, 749 F.2d 945, 954–55 (1st Cir. 1984).

20. *Cf.* T. BOSWELL, HOW LIFE IMITATES THE WORLD SERIES: AN INQUIRY INTO THE GAME (1983) (the only link between this Aside and *The Common Law Origins of the Infield Fly Rule*, 123 U. PA. L. REV. 1474 (1975)).

21. *See generally* Cooper, *Anglo-American Legal Citation: Historical Development and Library Implications*, 75 LAW LIBR. J. 1, 33 (1982) (given the long history of Anglo-American citations, "we are on the threshold of exciting opportunities for improved bibliographic control.").

22. *See id.* at 20–21.

the development of *A Uniform System of Citation* ("the Bluebook").[23] The Bluebook was first published in 1926,[24] during a period of unprecedented national prosperity. Again, it cannot be mere coincidence that the ultimate citation manual originated at such a salubrious moment in history.

The Bluebook did not gain widespread acceptance immediately, of course. It "was not widely adopted [by academic journals] until the 1930s,"[25] and it did not provide citation forms for statutes until the twelfth edition in 1976.[26] Therefore, the Court did not write *Carolene Products*, including footnote three, under the Bluebook's auspices. This is a pity, because footnote three, unnecessarily long as it is, could have been even longer had the Court used modern bluebooking techniques. Stronger formalistic scrutiny would have allowed the footnote to obscure further the residual functionalism of the second paragraph.

For, while misguided commentators may scoff,[27] one must cite each unofficial state statutory compilation with the prescribed abbreviation and give the name of its publisher in parentheses.[28] Adherence to this rule would have enhanced the length and massiveness of footnote three.[29] Similarly, inclusion of the date of each statutory compilation and relevant supplement would have lengthened the footnote without adulterating it with particularly useful information. For example, if modern bluebooking techniques were used, the statement "Md. Ann. Code, Art. 27, § 281" would read "MD. ANN. CODE art. 27, § 281 (1924)."[30] And if footnote three were written today, the same statute would be cited "MD. HEALTH-GEN. CODE ANN. § 21-1210 (1987)."[31]

The addition of different typefaces within the same citation lends an element of welcome unreadability to modern footnotes. Although some argue that LARGE AND SMALL CAPITALS are unnecessary when citing statutes or books

---

23. COLUMBIA LAW REVIEW, HARVARD LAW REVIEW ASS'N, UNIVERSITY OF PENNSYLVANIA LAW REVIEW, YALE LAW JOURNAL, A UNIFORM SYSTEM OF CITATION (14th ed. 1986) [hereinafter BLUEBOOK].

24. *See* Cooper, *supra* note 21, at 21.

25. *Id.*

26. *See id.* at 21 n.143.

27. *See* Axel-Lute, *Legal Citation Form: Theory and Practice*, 75 L. LIBR. J. 148, 152 (1982) ("[I]t may make sense to specify West or Deering in California and McKinney or Consol. in New York, but no one in New Jersey should bother to add West to an N.J.S.A. citation — nor should they, or do they, bother to write it as N.J. Stat. Ann. And there is not much point anywhere in the United States in adding West to a U.S.C.A. citation or Law. Co-op. to U.S.C.S.").

28. *See* BLUEBOOK, *supra* note 23, Rule 12.3(d) at 59.

29. *See infra* note 66.

30. *See* BLUEBOOK, *supra* note 23, at 191.

31. *See id.* at 191–92. Moreover, "Burns Ind. Stat., 1933, § 35-1203" would now be IND. CODE ANN. § 16-6-6-2 (Burns 1984). *See id.* at 187.

in law review footnotes,[32] such arguments reflect the type of permissiveness that leads us down the road to barbarism.[33] Ever since Gutenberg printed the Bible, hard-to-produce typefaces have represented advances in Western civilization.[34]

C. If We Will Not Cite Ourselves, Who Will Cite Us?[35]

As demonstrated, footnote three is a fine model for studying the triumph of form over mere function in footnotes. But it is also a good example of how to pad the amount of support for an assertion. Footnote three contains voluminous citations in support of two factual statements.[36] This highlights the critical importance of providing support for as many assertions as possible, no matter how self-evident many of them may seem. Respected federal judges have scoffed at the modern habit of documenting the most innocuous assertions.[37] But they fail to recognize that the more propositions that need documentation, the more sources that can be cited. Decreasing the number of footnotes would rob many legal publications of their *raisons d'etre*—being cited.[38]

---

32. *See, e.g.,* BIEBER'S CURRENT AMERICAN LEGAL CITATIONS 22 (M. Prince 2d ed. 1986) (Maryland statute should be cited "Md. Health-Gen. Code § 21-1210 (1987)"); Posner, *supra* note 1, at 134 (criticizing practice of using separate typefaces).

33. [FIND SUPPORT]

34. *Id.*

35. *See* 4 THE BABYLONIAN TALMUD (SEDER NEZIKHIN), *Aboth*, ch. I, 14 (I. Epstein ed. 1961) ("If I am not for myself, who is for me, but if I am for my own self [only], what am I, and if not now, when?" (footnotes omitted)).

36. *See infra* note 39.

37. *See* Mikva, *Goodbye to Footnotes,* 56 U. COLO. L. REV. 647, 653 (1985); Posner, *supra* note *, at 1350.

38. One measure of the success of a law review is the frequency with which it is cited in Supreme Court opinions. *See generally* Sirico & Margulies, *The Citing of Law Reviews by the Supreme Court: An Empirical Study,* 34 UCLA L. REV. 131 (1986). There is some gratification, however, in seeing one's work used to support arguments in the opinions of lower courts, or, for that matter, in other law journals. For examples of pieces that use support, see Altman, *The Reconciliation of Retirement Security and Tax Policies: A Response to Professor Graetz,* 136 U. PA. L. REV. 1419 (1988); Cornell, *Institutionalization of Meaning, Recollective Imagination and the Potential for Transformative Legal Interpretation,* 136 U. PA. L. REV. 1135 (1988); Donohue, *Further Thoughts on Employment Discrimination Legislation: A Reply to Judge Posner,* 136 U. PA. L. REV. 523 (1987); Fitts, The Vices of Virtue (forthcoming in 136 U. PA. L. REV. (1988)); Francione, *Experimentation and the Marketplace Theory of the First Amendment,* 136 U. PA. L. REV. 417 (1988); Freedman, Client Confidences and Client Perjury (forthcoming in 136 U. PA. L. REV. (1988)); Johnson & Siegel, *Corporate Mergers: Redefining the Role of Target Directors,* 136 U. PA. L. REV. 315 (1987); Kreimer, *Releases, Redress, and Police Misconduct: Reflections on Agreements to Waive Civil Rights Actions in Exchange for Dismissal of Criminal Charges,* 136 U. PA. L. REV. 851 (1988); Lev-

III. Dairy Products and Distrust: Footnote Three and Meaning

The statutes cited in footnote three all deal in some way with the question "What is filled milk," and by extension, "What is milk." Footnote three symbolizes the key to understanding "law": interpreting terms. Unless there is

___

more, *Recharacterizations and the Nature of Theory in Corporate Tax Law*, 136 U. PA. L. REV. 1019 (1988); Lipton, *Corporate Governance in the Age of Finance Corporatism*, 136 U. PA. L. REV. 1 (1987); Pine, *Speculation and Reality: The Role of Facts in Judicial Protection of Fundamental Rights*, 136 U. PA. L. REV. 655 (1988); Posner, *The Efficiency and the Efficacy of Title VII*, 136 U. PA. L. REV. 513 (1987); Revesz & Karlan, *Nonmajority Rules and the Supreme Court*, 136 U. PA. L. REV. 1067 (1988); Schwartz, *Justice, Expediency, and Beauty*, 136 U. PA. L. REV. 141 (1987); Stern, *Revealing Misconduct By Public Officials Through Grand Jury Reports*, 136 U. PA. L. REV. 73 (1987); Uviller, *supra* note 17; Wachter & Cohen, *The Law and Economics of Collective Bargaining: An Introduction and Application to the Problems of Subcontracting, Partial Closure, and Relocation*, 136 U. PA. L. REV. 1349 (1988); Aside, *Don't Cry over Filled Milk: The Neglected Footnote Three to* Carolene Products, 136 U. PA. L. REV. 1553 (1987); Comment, *Revolutionaries Beware: The Decline of the Political Offense Exception Under the 1986 United States-United Kingdom Supplementary Extradition Treaty*, 136 U. PA. L. REV. 1515 (1988); Comment, *The Influence of the Islamic Law of Waqf on the Development of the Trust in England: The Case of Merton College*, 136 U. PA. L. REV. 1231 (1988); Comment, *What Films We May Watch: Videotape Distribution and the First Amendment*, 136 U. PA. L. REV. 1263 (1988); Comment, *Preemption and Punitive Damages: The Conflict Continues Under FIFRA*, 136 U. PA. L. REV. 1301 (1988); Comment, *Contractual Shifting of Defense Costs in Private Offering Securities Litigation*, 136 U. PA. L. REV. 971 (1988); Comment, *Help Wanted: An Expansive Definition of Constructive Discharge Under Title VII*, 136 U. PA. L. REV. 941 (1988); Comment, *Affirmative Action and the Remedial Scope of Title VII: Procedural Answers to Substantive Questions*, 136 U. PA. L. REV. 625 (1987); Comment, *Federal Common Law Power to Remand a Properly Removed Case*, 136 U. PA. L. REV. 583 (1987); Comment, *Giving Substance to the Bad Faith Exception of* Evans v. Jeff D.: *A Reconciliation of* Evans *with the Civil Rights Attorney's Fees Awards Act of 1976*, 136 U. PA. L. REV. 553 (1987); Comment, *When Bright Lines Break Down: Limiting* New York v. Belton, 136 U. PA. L. REV. 281 (1987); Comment, *Limiting Corporate Directors' Liability: Delaware's Section 102(b)(7) and the Erosion of the Directors' Duty of Care*, 136 U. PA. L. REV. 239 (1987); Comment, *Politics and Purpose: Hide and Seek in the Gerrymandering Thicket After* Davis v. Bandemer, 136 U. PA. L. REV. 183 (1987); Comment, *The Tenth Amendment After* Garcia, *supra* note 3; Comment, *Yellow Rows of Test Tubes: Due Process Constraints on Discharges of Public Employees Based on Drug Urinalysis Testing*, 135 U. PA. L. REV. 1623 (1987); Comment, *Child Care Land Use Ordinances — Providing Working Parents with Needed Day Care Facilities*, 135 U. PA. L. REV. 1591 (1987); Comment, *A New Category of Free Exercise Claims: Protection for Individuals Objecting to Governmental Actions that Impede Their Religions*, 135 U. PA. L. REV. 1557 (1987); Comment, *Insights into Lender Liability: An Argument for Treating Controlling Creditors as Controlling Shareholders*, 135 U. PA. L. REV. 1321 (1987); Comment, *Commissioned Works as Works Made for Hire Under the 1976 Copyright Act: Misinterpretation and Injustice*, 135 U. PA. L. REV. 1281 (1987); Comment, *Reason and the Rules: Personal Knowledge and Coconspirator Hearsay*, 135 U. PA. L. REV. 1265 (1987).

common understanding, there can be no communication.[39] And without communication, there can be no informed debate or adversarial process. Defining the operative words is crucial to legal analysis. As one legal scholar put it, "[a]ll words are different. That's why we have different words."[40]

Footnote three is a fitting starting point for a study of legal interpretation, because *United States v. Carolene Products*[41] was part of a most esteemed body of law: dairy jurisprudence, or those judicial decisions dealing with milk and its byproducts.[42] Before *Carolene Products*,[43] the most intriguing American dairy case was the 1912 decision, *United States v. 11,150 Pounds of Butter*.[44] There, the Eighth Circuit held that the presence of an abnormal amount of moisture in butter did not make it "adulterated butter" according to a Minnesota health statute.[45] Since then, dairy cases have contributed to the development of constitutional law,[46] commercial law,[47] "slip-and-fall" torts,[48] securities regulation,[49] and family law.[50]

Although dairy jurisprudence is vitally significant in its own right, one

---

39. *See supra* note 6.

40. Statement of Professor Gary Francione to first year Torts class, University of Pennsylvania Law School (September 1985).

41. 304 U.S. 144 (1938).

42. *Cf.* G. CHAPMAN, J. CLEESE, T. GILLIAM, E. IDLE, T. JONES & M. PALIN, MONTY PYTHON'S THE LIFE OF BRIAN 9 (Methuen ed. 1979) (arguing that Christ's remark in the Sermon on the Mount, "Blessed are the cheesemakers," was not meant literally, but rather "refers to any manufacturers of dairy products.").

43. *Cf.* Ackerman, *Beyond* Carolene Products, *supra* note 3.

44. 195 F. 657 (8th Cir. 1912).

45. *See id.* at 659.

46. *See, e.g., Carolene Prods.*, 304 U.S. at 154 n.4; Setzer v. Mayo, 150 Fla. 734, 740, 9 So. 2d 280, 282–83 (Fla. 1942) (upholding constitutionality of Florida filled milk statute on grounds similar to those used in *Carolene Products); see also* Great Atl. & Pac. Tea Co. v. Cottrell, 424 U.S. 366, 372 (1976) (per curiam) (noting that "[a]djudication of Commerce Clause challenges to the validity of local milk regulations burdening interstate milk is not a novel experience for this Court," and citing five leading cases without which American federalism might have been udderly different).

47. *See, e.g.*, Neu Cheese Co. v. FDIC, 825 F.2d 1270, 1272 (8th Cir. 1987) (dealing with waiver of security interest in milk and its proceeds under U.C.C. § 9-306(2) (1977)).

48. *See, e.g.*, Cook v. Great Atl. & Pac. Tea Co., 244 A.D.2d 63, 64, 278 N.Y.S. 777, 778 (1935) (plaintiff slipped on cottage cheese); Burke v. Wegman's Food Markets, 1 Misc. 2d 130, 146 N.Y.S.2d 556 (N.Y. Sup. Ct. 1955) (plaintiff slipped on cheese).

49. *See, e.g.*, Activator Supply Co. v. Wurth, 239 Kan. 610, 620, 722 P.2d 1081, 1089 (1986) (promise of "from Milk to Profit with Lactic Cultures" gave rise to expectation of profit for purpose of applicability of state securities laws); *Review of Supreme Court's Term*, 56 U.S.L.W. 3119, 3121 (1987) ("While it may be appropriate for dairy farmers to boast that they make butter the old fashioned way — 'we churn it' — such claims should be avoided by stockbrokers in the handling of customer accounts.").

50. *See, e.g.*, Butters v. Butters, 353 Mass. 751, 230 N.E.2d 913 (1967).

should treat it as a distinct subset of the wider field of cow law.[51] Cattle have affected our legal tradition through a broader range of cases than those decided under dairy jurisprudence.[52] Cow law has been on the cutting edge of legal development since *Sherwood v. Walker*.[53] It has entered into judicial analysis of such doctrines as the insanity defense[54] and cautionary jury instructions.[55]

Having placed dairy jurisprudence in its proper context under the rubric of bovine jurisprudence,[56] this Aside can now proceed with its inquiry into

---

51. *Cf.* 2 The Babylonian Talmud (Seder Khodashim), *Chullin*, ch. VII, at 576–647 (I. Epstein ed. 1961) (discussing separation of milk and meat on grounds that consuming them together would be unholy because they are distinct proceeds of the same animal). There is some confusion in the Bankruptcy Courts as to the relationship between milk and cows. *Compare In re* Jackels, 55 Bankr. 67, 69 (Bankr. D. Minn. 1985) ("While there can be no doubt that in agricultural parlance milk is a product of a cow, that is not the meaning of the word product in the context of security interests"); Pigeon v. Production Credit Ass'n of Minot (*In re* Pigeon), 49 Bankr. 657, 660 (Bankr. D.N.D. 1985) (holding that milk is not a "product" of a cow within the meaning of 11 U.S.C. § 552(b) (1982)); *In re* Serbus, 48 Bankr. 5, 8 (Bankr. D. Minn. 1984) (same) *with* Smith v. Dairymen, Inc., 790 F.2d 1107, 1112 (4th Cir. 1986) (holding that milk is, in fact, the product of a cow); *In re* Delbridge, 61 Bankr. 484, 488–90 (Bankr. E.D. Mo. 1985) (same); *In re* Rankin, 49 Bankr. 565, 567 (Bankr. W.D. Mo. 1985) (same); *In re* Johnson, 47 Bankr. 204, 207 (Bankr. W.D. Wis. 1985) (same).

52. Compare the traditional filled milk scenario as illustrated in *Carolene Products* (in which a dairy *product* is held out for sale when a part of it does not exist as claimed) with the facts of Wheeler v. Commissioner, T.C. Memo 1983–385, 46 T.C.M. (CCH) 642 (1983), in which dairy *cattle* were claimed as a tax loss when they "were nothing more than a 'rent-a-herd' staged to lead [IRS inspectors] into believing they were owned by respondents."

53. 66 Mich. 568, 33 N.W. 919 (1887); *see also* A. Herbert, Uncommon Law 201, 205–06 (new ed. 1969) (discussing an English common law case holding that a cow could be a negotiable instrument).

54. *See* United States v. Chapman, 5 M.J. 901, 903 (A.C.M.R. 1977) (Mitchell, J., concurring in part and dissenting in part) (for determining defendant's "substantial capacity" to appreciate criminality of his act, "substantial means something more than slight or not just a little. But how much more? The age old puzzler: 'When does a calf become a cow'?").

55. *See* United States v. Schatz, 40 C.M.R. 934, 936 (N.B.R. 1969) (instructing factfinder to ignore certain evidence "is like telling a person to stare into the corner for three minutes without at anytime [sic] thinking of a purple cow. It simply cannot be done!").

56. Some of the principles herein discussed may be found in the law of other barnyard animals. See *infra* notes 58–59 and accompanying text. This should not be surprising; after all, cows are not the only animals on a farm. *See In re* Maike, 77 Bankr. 832, 839 (Bankr. D. Kan. 1987) (holding that the "laundry list" of animals in the song "Old McDonald's Farm" is not all-inclusive); Lecture of Margaret Baldwin to Three-Year-Old Class, First Congregational Church Nursery School, Eugene, Oregon (1966) ("Old McDonald had a farm....And on that farm he had some cows....And on that farm he had some ducks.... And on that farm he had some pigs...."); *cf. In re* Delbridge, 61 Bankr. 484, 488 n.7 (Bankr. E.D. Mich. 1986) (citing the judge's kindergarten teacher on the point that "a cow's offspring, i.e., a baby cow, is called a calf—not milk").

legal interpretation. The difficulty in determining what falls under filled milk statutes[57] reflects the main problem in any attempt to define legal concepts: all interpretation is subjective. How can one say objectively what is or is not milk when such an intellect as Judge Friendly had such trouble determining "what is chicken?"[58] Determining the plain meanings of words has always been difficult.[59] In the end, legislatures' attempts, as illustrated in footnote three, to pin down a definition of milk leaves a mystery that presently limited modes of legal thought cannot solve.

IV. Citation Manual of the Gods?

The reason we are unable to unlock the mysteries of footnote three is that we are bound by received wisdom as to its origins. This is true partly because the origin of footnote four is so well documented. Justice Stone's biographer, Alpheus Thomas Mason, revealed that Louis Lusky, Justice Stone's clerk at the time and later a Columbia Law School professor, wrote, in the first draft of *United States v. Carolene Products*,[60] what became the second and third paragraphs of footnote four.[61] Lusky admitted to Mason that he wrote the first draft of footnote four, exclusive of the first paragraph, and that Justice Stone adopted it "almost as drafted."[62] In a published article, Lusky did not state outright who wrote the last two paragraphs of footnote four, but explained how

---

57. *See, e.g.,* Department of Agric. v. Country Lad Foods, Inc., 224 Ga. 683, 683, 164 S.E.2d 110, 111 (1968) (affirming injunction prohibiting department from preventing filled milk producer from putting product on market); Odle v. Imperial Ice Cream Co., 11 Ariz. App. 203, 205, 463 P.2d 98, 100 (1970) (discussing applicability of statute entitled "Prohibition of sale of filled milk labeled imitation dairy products").

58. Frigaliment Importing Co. v. B.N.S. Int'l Sales Corp., 190 F. Supp. 116, 117 (S.D.N.Y. 1960); *see* C. Reitz, Contracts as Basic Commercial Law 7 (1975) ("What does Judge Friendly mean when he says that 'the word "chicken" standing alone is ambiguous'? Doesn't everyone know what a 'chicken' is?"). *But see* R. Dworkin, Taking Reitz Seriously (1977).

The link between *Frigaliment* and cow law is evident in the First Circuit's opinion in A.J. Cunningham Packing Corp. v. Florence Beef Co., 785 F.2d 348, 348 (1st Cir. 1986) ("A quarter century ago Judge Friendly confronted the question of 'what is a chicken.' [sic] Today we are asked to review a case in which the jury had to confront the meatier issue of 'what's the beef.'" [sic] (citation omitted)).

For a description of another chicken case with far-reaching consequences for American jurisprudence, see B. Flanagan, Last of the Moe Haircuts 74–75 (1986).

59. *See* Regina v. Ojibway, 8 Crim L.Q. 137 (1965) (holding that a horse is a "small bird"); *In re* Johnson, 14 Bankr. 14 (Bankr. W.D. Ky. 1981) (holding that a "bus" is a "car").

60. 304 U.S. 144 (1938).

61. *See* A. Mason, Harlan Fiske Stone: Pillar of the Law 513 (1956).

62. *See id.* at 513 & n.9.

the first paragraph was added to the footnote after a suggestion from Chief Justice Hughes.[63]

So we know that footnote four was a team effort among Chief Justice Hughes (or his clerk), Lusky, and Justice Stone. The sources that discuss the origins of footnote four, however, are suspiciously silent about the genesis of footnote three. What accounts for this conspiracy of silence? Who wrote footnote three? Was it Justice Stone? Chief Justice Hughes? Louis Lusky? A combination of the three? Or superintelligent astronauts from another world?

Footnote three is an orgy of legal citation. Accordingly, for evidence about its origins we should look at the original authors of the Bluebook.[64] Only one so impressed with citation and ponderous documentation could have produced such a footnote. Legal literature is fortunately rife with clues as to the Bluebook's true origin.

Judge Richard Posner has written that "[t]he pyramids in Egypt are the hypertrophy of burial. The hypertrophy of law is [the Bluebook]."[65] Judge Posner may, for once, be on to something.[66] The same entities responsible for the pyramids are probably responsible for the advent of the Bluebook. The Egyptian pyramids were, according to strong evidence, actually built by extraterrestrials as navigational aids.[67] Experts in the subject agree that many phenomena, mysterious to the ancients, were caused by the arrival on Earth of an advanced race with technology beyond human understanding.[68]

The Bluebook almost certainly came from such a source. Like the technology of the ancient astronauts, the Bluebook is puzzling to all but an anointed few[69]—who are probably not entirely human—to whom its mysteries are revealed. Who but a truly advanced race would have taken for granted that the title of the Journal of College and University Law would be

---

63. *See* Lusky, *supra* note 3, at 1097–98 (describing Hughes' reaction to the first draft of the opinion); *id.* at 1106 (reproducing Hughes' memorandum to Stone suggesting an addition to what became footnote four).

64. *See supra* note 29.

65. Posner, *supra* note *, at 1343.

66. *See supra* note 36.

67. *See* E. Von Däniken, Chariots of the Gods? 74–79 (Bantam ed. 1974) (explaining that pyramids could not have been built by humans and are perfectly placed as guides to aerial navigation); A. Landsburg & S. Landsburg, In Search of Ancient Mysteries 118–19 (1974) (in examining Egyptian, as well as Mayan, Aztec and Toltec pyramids, authors found "nothing that could demolish any of the various speculations about helpful beings from another planet.").

68. *See* E. Von Däniken, *supra* note 67, at 7–12.

69. In ancient Greece, these beings were known as "demigods" and "oracles." Anthropologists categorize them as "shamans" or "medicine men." Nowadays, they are often referred to as "Production Editors."

abbreviated "J.C. & U.L.?"[70] Only a population with an intelligence far greater than our own would have produced a citation manual that requires its own instructional guide.[71]

Evidence of the extraterrestrials' presence permeates the annals of legal history. For example, what was Justice Holmes' "brooding omnipresence in the sky"?[72] Could it have been the Bluebook authors, watching over us? And what was Justice Stewart talking about when he mentioned the "orbit of the common law?"[73] Although some Justices might try to cover up their knowledge of the cosmos by pretending, for example, that the "substance of the Milky Way" is "unknown,"[74] the truth is visible to those who have the courage to look for it.

The fact that the Bluebook is "the *universally* accepted standard for citations"[75] reveals its extraterrestrial origin. The Bluebook has yet to conquer the entire world of law,[76] and its rules still leave uncertain the citation of particular sources.[77] Only recognition of the special origins of the Bluebook and of

---

70. *See* BLUEBOOK, *supra* note 23, Rule 16.2 at 94 ("If the periodical you wish to cite is not given in full on this list, you may determine the proper abbreviation by looking up each word in the periodical's title on this list and on the list of geographical abbreviations found on the inside back cover. Put together the abbreviations for each word to form the full abbreviated title."); *id.* at 99 (abbreviation for "Journal" is J.); *id.* at 96 (abbreviation for "College" is C.); *id.* at 104 (abbreviation for "University" is U.); *id.* at 100 (abbreviation for "Law" is L.). Following the Bluebook's abbreviation rules, the name of the University of Southern North Dakota at Hoople Quarterly Forum of Eastern Law, if it existed, would be abbreviated "U.S.N.D. (HOOP.) Q.F.E.L."

71. *See generally* E. MAIER, HOW TO PREPARE A LEGAL CITATION (1986) (cover blurb: "Your complete guide to... Using *A Uniform System of Citation* (Bluebook)").

72. Southern Pac. Co. v. Jensen, 244 U.S. 205, 222 (1917) (Holmes, J., dissenting).

73. Rosenblatt v. Baer, 383 U.S. 75, 93 n.4 (1966) (Stewart, J., concurring) (quoting I. BRANT, THE BILL OF RIGHTS: ITS ORIGIN AND MEANING 502–03 (1965); *see also* Vlandis v. Kline, 412 U.S. 441, 460 (1973) (Burger, C.J., dissenting) (noting that an equal protection doctrine had fallen into "the orbit of the Due Process Clause").

74. Ginzburg v. United States, 383 U.S. 463, 480 (1966) (Black, J., dissenting).

75. M. RAY & J. RUMSFELD, LEGAL WRITING: GETTING IT RIGHT AND GETTING IT WRITTEN 35 (1987) (emphasis added).

76. *Compare* BLUEBOOK, *supra* note 23, Rule 2.2 at 8 (definition of *see* as signal in footnotes) *with* 26 U.S.C. § 7806(a) (1982) (definition of "see" as having no legal effect in Internal Revenue Code).

77. *Compare* Singer, *The Player and the Cards: Nihilism and Legal Theory*, 94 YALE L.J. 1, 237 (citing "Sting, *De Do Do Do, De Da Da Da*, recorded on THE POLICE, ZENYATTA MANDATTA. Courtesy and copyright. [sic] 1980 Virgin Music (Publishers) Ltd. Published in the U.S.A. and Canada by Virgin Music Inc. All Rights Reserved.") *with* Van Alstyne, *Cracks in "The New Property": Adjudicative Due Process in the Administrative State*, 62 CORNELL L. REV. 445, 470 (1977) (citing "M. Jagger & K. Richard, *You Can't Always Get What You Want* ((c) 1969, Abkco. Music, Inc.)"). The mere failure to account for every possibility does not make the Bluebook suspect. "Every document except perhaps the Ten Commandments has

footnote three will cause such a conquest and remedy such ambiguities. Only then can we live up to the imprecation of the ancient philosophers: *Verba tene, res sequetur.*[78]

its flaws, and maybe if you worked at it you could find flaws in that too." *Burger on Constitution: 'It Isn't Perfect',* U.S.A. Today, May 14, 1987, at 1A, col. 2.

78. Loosely translated, "Form over substance." *But see* CAIUS JULIUS VICTOR, ARS RHETORICA, I (4th century A.D.) (quoting Marcus Porcius Cato (Cato the Elder)), *quoted in* J. BARTLETT, FAMILIAR QUOTATIONS 95 (15th ed. 1980) ("Rem tene, verba sequentur," or, "Grasp the subject, the words will follow.").

Great Cases in Utopian Law

*David Eccles Hardy**

Rumplestilskin v. Beautiful Princess,
Utopian Higher Court, 1691

GRIMM, J. The facts of this case may be stated briefly. Once upon a time, a dwarf of questionable character, Rumplestilskin by name (appellant herein), entered into a contract with a Beautiful Princess (respondent herein). No written contract was ever drawn up by the parties. However an oral agreement was reached under the terms of which Rumplestilskin agreed to instruct the Beautiful Princess in the lost art of spinning gold from straw, in return for which the Beautiful Princess promised to deliver to Rumplestilskin, upon demand, her first-born child, as yet naught but a twinkle in respondent's eye. At this particular time, respondent was in what might be considered a rather tight spot, having entered into a particularly demanding contract under the terms of which she was to furnish spun gold from rather low-grade straw. If respondent was successful in producing the gold, she was to be granted yet a little more time upon this fair land of ours. If her efforts proved unsuccessful…well, suffice it to say the executioner's axe would make the breach permanent.

Appellant duly instructed respondent, thus preventing the feared breach (above all between respondent's head and shoulders), and causing, as a consequence, the Beautiful Princess' rather rapid rise to fame and fortune.

Several years then passed during which the Beautiful Princess married a handsome prince, conceived, and completely forgot about her promise to the dwarf. Upon the birth of respondent's child, appellant appeared and demanded the same claiming legal right thereto, to which respondent vehemently objected. Rumplestilskin, somewhat softened by respondent's obvious affection for the child, reached an accord with the Beautiful Princess to the effect that if she were able to ascertain his name within three attempts she would be permitted to keep the infant. Upon the third attempt respondent was successful, but foul play was proven and thus the accord was breached.

---

* J.D. Candidate, 1980, University of Utah.

Appellant thereafter brought suit seeking specific performance under the original agreement. The lower court, however, held for respondent, finding the oral agreement to be unenforceable under the Statute of Frogs. Appellant now brings this appeal.

The question presented to the court is this: Can appellant be permitted to take possession under the terms of the oral agreement, or is the contract unenforceable under the Statute of Frogs?

Section 639.1, *Utopian Civil Code* (1603) states:

> No action shall be brought to charge any Beautiful Princess upon any agreement entered into with a dwarf which is not to be performed within one year from the making thereof unless the parties shall witness such agreement by stepping upon a frog until the same shall expire.

This important statute dates back to the early years of Utopia when, it is recorded, a prominent Beautiful Princess, about to enter into a questionable contract with an ambitious young dwarf and concerned lest her handsome prince discover and thwart her plans, ordered the dwarf to exterminate a particularly aristocratic-looking frog (perhaps it was the monocle?) intently observing the tete á tete, exclaiming, "stomp on it—quickly! You never can tell—he's pulled that one before." Thus the Statute of Frogs has ever governed the contractual relations between Beautiful Princesses and dwarfs.

Counsel for the Beautiful Princess argues correctly that because the agreement in question was not to be performed within one year, its enforceability required that a frog be stepped upon "until the same shall expire." Section 639.1, *Utopian Civil Code* (1603).

M. Goose on Shady Deals, § 210(a) at 67 [2nd rev. ed. (1688)] deals precisely with this problem:

> Our courts as of late have been virtually jammed with a multitude of cases dealing almost exclusively with breached contracts between beautiful princesses and dwarfs, calling for the payment of some seemingly unimportant item, such as a first-born child, in return for instruction in some art, long forgotten except among those sundry dwarfs who eagerly seek out such offers. Having witnessed time and again beautiful princesses' late surfacing instinct to keep their first-born children, it has become quite clear that any dwarf worth his beard will demand that all agreements entered into be witnessed by a stomped frog, or suffer the consequences of an unenforceable contract under the Statute of Frogs.

Thus we must agree with the lower court and find the oral agreement between the parties to be wholly unenforceable under the Statute of Frogs.

However appellant contends, and with this contention we must agree, that to deny him recovery under these facts would result in respondent's unjust enrichment at appellant's expense. This claim was set forth in the alternative in Count II of appellant's complaint. The trial court appears to have been somewhat confused as to the exact nature of appellant's second cause of action, referring to it by several different names: unjust enrichment, restitution, disgorgement and queasy-contract, to name but a few. This court desires to follow the example set by our sister court in the recent case of *Three Bears v. Goldilocks,* 43 U.L.2d 377 (2d Realm 1689), to refer to such a claim as one in queasy-contract. It will be remembered that in that case the court had a difficult time properly defining the Bears' claim that Goldilocks had been unjustly enriched by the vast quantities of their porridge that she had eaten. The court struck upon the term "disgorgement," but feeling a little nauseous at the thought of what this remedy might entail, elected to term the action as one in queasy-contract.

The respondent contends that she received no material benefit from appellant, and that any fame and fortune that may have resulted from her, shall we say, special abilities on the spinning wheel was unasked for and, indeed, has made her life miserable. She thus claims that she has not been unjustly enriched and likens her situation to that of the defendants in the landmark case *B. B. Wolf Wrecking Co. v. Three Little Pigs,* 98 U.L. 6 (1st Realm 1667) in which this court upheld the trial court's ruling that Mr. Wolf's efforts in "huffing and puffing and blowing down" two of defendant pigs' houses had not resulted in the pigs' unjust enrichment.

We think that *Pigs* is clearly distinguishable from the situation now before us. In the former, the defendants were pigs; in the present, a beautiful princess. In addition to this, the benefits visited upon respondent as a result of appellant's diligent instruction can hardly be compared to having one's house mistakenly razed due to the fact that a wrecking company "got the addresses a little mixed up."

Having determined that to leave the parties where they presently are would result in respondent's unjust enrichment at appellant's expense, the only question remaining to be resolved is the amount by which respondent has been unjustly enriched.

Appellant contends that he should be able to recover the value of all the spun gold that respondent has been able to produce and submits the gold valuation analysis set forth in the recent case of *Commissioner v. King Midas,* 455 U.T.C. 396 (Utopian Tax Court 1690). We think this is an improper measure of respondent's unjust enrichment. Furthermore, it is clear that the gold valuation analysis employed by the Tax Court in *Midas* is wholly inapplicable, as the question before the Tax Court was the valuation of "reorganized" gold in terms of the King's earnings and profits for the fiscal year 1689. This bears little relation to the value of spun gold on the open market.

A second theory advanced by the appellant is that he should recover the actual value of his instructions in the art of spinning gold from straw. Due to the fact, though, that there is no "market" for instruction in this lost art, and there are extremely few individuals (person or otherwise) competent to testify as to the value of such instruction, the court may have a very complicated question to deal with. In such case, the third theory advanced—that appellant's instruction was worth the value of respondent's very life—may be a surer guide to follow, for it has been often stated with authority in this court that "in these times, beautiful princesses in Utopia are a dime a dozen,"[1] thereby clearly allowing appellant to recover .083¢ plus interest.

Reversed and remanded to the lower court for determination of the issue of the reasonable value of respondent's unjust enrichment. We further instruct the lower court to diligently seek that solution which will allow the parties to live happily ever after.

With this opinion Brothers, J., and Talu, C.J., concur.

---

1. *Cinderella v. Handsome Prince*, 40 U.L.2d 606 (2d Realm 1688) and cases therein cited.

Legislative and Judicial Dynamism in Arkansas: *Poisson v. d'Avril*

Jasper Bogus McClodd* and Pepe Le Peu**

Few cases have ever rocketed forth from appellate courts to literally stun the English-speaking world, and few have possessed such sweeping significance for the law of a single jurisdiction as has the recent Arkansas decision of *Poisson v. d'Avril*.[1] Overnight, in a manner which might well be successfully emulated in other jurisdictions, this decision of the Arkansas Supreme Court to apply the clearly expressed intent of the state legislature swept away decades of statutory effluvia, restored much of the beauty of the common law in its pristine glory, and eradicated legislative acts which would literally tear at the vitals of a less gutsy jurisdiction. Legal scholars now gaze in awe at the magnificent destruction wrought by the Arkansas legislature and bravely carried out by the state supreme court. Seldom if ever has such an amazing display of cerebral prowess and un-inhibited vision emanated from any legislative body at any time or in any place.

I. The Case

Consider, if you will once again, the now hallowed and familiar situation which confronted the Arkansas court in this landmark case which, due to its everlasting prominence in the galaxy of select opinions which law students will

* B.A., Chill Wills Modern School of Dance, Hollywood, California; J.D., Kumquat Correspondence University, Sodbuster, Idaho; Partner in the firm of Hopp, Skipp, McClodd & McThudd, Greasy Corner, Arkansas.

** Charles DeGaulle Professor of Napoleonic Juridical Thought, L'Ecole de Droit Parisien, Paris, France; Visiting Lecturer in Girls' Physical Education and Hygiene, Needmore Senior High School, Needmore, Arkansas.

1. 244 Ark. 478A (1968). *See* note 2, *infra*.

hereafter know by rote, is printed in full in an appendix to this article.[2] The case appeared to be "routine," as the court pointed out, in that Poisson had attempted to enforce an oral land sales agreement against d'Avril and the latter had pleaded the statute of frauds. At this point, Poisson let him have it with a veritable "bombshell," as the court notes.[3] He asserted the now famed "Omnibus Repealer," an Arkansas innovation which surely will take its place in the forefront of such other established legislative devices as writing special acts so that they look like general acts and attaching fake emergency clauses. Sneaky though it may have been, the "Omnibus Repealer" was virgin pure in its clarity and intent. It said simply: "All laws and parts of laws, and particularly Act 311 of the Acts of 1941, are hereby repealed."[4] There you have it. Act 311 of 1941,[5] which was apparently especially obnoxious and was thereby singled out, was shot down in flames. Along with it, however, (and this was the beauty of it) went "[a]ll laws and parts of laws."[6] It is enough to warm the heart of every collegiate anarchist and nouveau nihilist from Berkeley to Boston.

The court found the language of the legislature to be expressed "plainly, clearly, unmistakably, decisively," and to "hardly [call] for judicial interpretation."[7] Being a court, however, it successfully overcame its expressed reluctance, recognizing no doubt that the case was a "biggie" that deserved an opinion which would rise to the occasion. (After all, what if John Marshall had been asleep at the switch when *Marbury v. Madison*[8] rolled around the bend?) Marching swiftly toward greatness, the Arkansas court seemingly recognized that its moment had come.

The court, in a masterful opinion by Justice George Rose Smith, found no doubt in its review of previous Arkansas precedents that it would have to follow the statute literally and without regard to consequences, even if such consequences might be harsh or absurd. Steadied by the prophets from its own past, the court found its duty clear: "'We shall not,' in Churchill's words (nor in anyone else's), 'flag or fail.'"[9]

---

2. This case appeared in the Arkansas advance sheets for decisions handed down by the Arkansas Supreme Court on April 1, 1968. For reasons which have never been adequately explained, the opinion has apparently been omitted from the official reporter and the regional reporter.

3. 244 Ark. at 478A.

4. No. 17, [1945] Ark. Acts 34.

5. This act dealt with the vacation of alleys in cities of the first and second class. It conflicted with Act 17, *supra* note 4, which the legislature was in the process of adopting.

6. *Supra* note 4.

7. 244 Ark. at 478B.

8. 5 U.S. (1 Cranch) 137 (1803).

9. 244 Ark. at 478C.

Nonetheless, the court was confronted with at least one genuine interpretive issue which necessitated some first-rate agonizing: Did "laws" mean only statutes, thus "leaving all judge-made law unmonkeyed with,"[10] or did the word also encompass the common law? Had the legislature only gutted its predecessors or had it also laid siege to the venerable Coke?[11] The latter thought was more than any Anglo-American court could bear and is hardly one which is inclined to cast a favorable light on legislatures. Jurisprudes around the world no doubt thrilled as the Arkansas court rose, Wellington-like, to the challenge. It uttered these immortal phrases:

> After much anxious study we have concluded that the legisature intended for the Omnibus Repealer to apply only to statutes, not to the common law. We are simply unable to believe that the General Assembly would do away with judge-made law. That law is obviously too wonderful to be lightly tampered with. In the immortal words of Lord Coke (himself, as it happens, a judge): "Reason is the life of the law; nay, the common law itself is nothing else but reason...."[12]

Reason aside, the court found a sound basis for holding that the common law remained intact in the fact that the statute used the word "laws" rather than the singular, "law." This mark of particular care on the part of the legislature would seem clearly to refer to statutes when considered by any reasonable man (and one might assume that judges, being eminently reasonable men, would know what a reasonable man would think, or if they were unreasonable or out of sorts on that day, they might bring in a reasonable man off the street — possibly an Alabama taxi driver if one were available — to deliberate with them and demonstrate the mental workings of a reasonable man). In any event, "laws" was interpreted to mean statutes, as it most certainly must, since lawyers and other reasonable men are inclined to view cases as expressing "law," but not "laws," whereas we speak of "the laws of Texas" which clearly means the statutes. Of course, it may be pointed out that we also speak of "statutory law" so that the word in the singular *may* refer to statutes, but we use the word, "laws," *only* to refer to statutes and never to cases. Considering all of this, the court found the letter "s" in laws to be possibly "the most significant 's' in legal literature," pointing out that "[a]t least,

---

10. *Id.*

11. Sir Edward Coke's Institutes and his Commentary on Littleton are an authoritative expression of the common law as it existed in England around the time of the first settlements in the New World. The writings of Coke had great impact upon the development of law in the United States. *See* 3 Pound, Jurisprudence 428 (1959).

12. 244 Ark. at 478C.

counsel have not cited a more significant 's,' nor has our own research disclosed one."[13]

One last consideration seems to have entered into the holding. If anarchy were to be avoided, the common law must be preserved. Statutory law, the court found, was "not equally essential...because the common law, always fluid in nature, will at once seep into the temporary vacancy left by the evaporation of the statutes and keep the ship of state safely on the right track."[14] As for "last-ditch arguments" and "imaginary perils"[15] expressed by counsel for the appellee, these would not be permitted to deter the Court from its duty:

> It is said, for instance, that to give full effect to the Omnibus Repealer (hereinafter called the Omnibus Repealer) will nullify such pillars of government as the sales tax law and the income tax law, both of which antedated 1945. We daresay, however, that the general public can and will face that catastrophe with that serene equanimity born of courage. Again, it is argued, with a veiled threat, that wholesome recreational activities such as horse racing will be abolished by the Repealer. Not so! In its wisdom the common law permits such contests, prohibiting only the secondary practice of betting on the outcome of the races. We need not extend this opinion by discussing one by one the various bugbears envisaged by counsel's vivid imagination. The truth is that in nearly every instance the purposes served by the Omnibus Repealer are praiseworthy and beneficent. We are calling the act to the attention of the Commissioners on Uniform Laws, who may well be inclined to make similar model legislation available to all the states.[16]

Although the opinion ends on that progressive note, it is unfortunate that only Justice Smith, who wrote the opinion, joined in the majority. Justice Fogleman dissented on the basis that he disagreed, and this dissent was concurred in by Justices Ward, Brown and Jones. Chief Justice Harris would have affirmed, and Justice Conley Byrd was disqualified for reasons which do not appear. Thus, the result was a 1–5 decision in which Justice Smith constituted a majority of one. It can only be concluded that his position prevailed due to the unassailable reasoning, impeccable analysis, and admirable courage which he employed. Confronted with such stuff as this, the other members of the court had no choice except to devalue their own opinions to the point that Justice Smith's one vote counted more than the other five.[17]

---

13. *Id.* at 478D.

14. *Id.*

15. *Id.*

16. *Id.* at 478D-E.

17. This is possibly the first instance in which the maxim de minimis non curat lex has been applied by judges to their own opinions. At least, diligent research has failed to dis-

II. The Effects of the Case

Despite the words of the majority opinion that "statutes which were on the books when the Omnibus Repealer was adopted in 1945 can, for the most part, be spared,"[18] the fact is that the impact of the case upon the Arkansas law was quite substantial. All statutes enacted prior to the effective date of the Act[19] were rendered no longer in force. We will not quibble here with the fact that the Arkansas tax structure was emasculated, for as the court observes, the public in general will not mind. There never was enough revenue to do much with anyway. The effect upon the executive branch, moreover, should be salutary, since no one can ever again be accused of seeking the governor's office for ulterior reasons or of profiting at the state's expense. Only persons with the purest of altruistic motives and with ample wealth to accomplish whatever their program may be will seek public office. The federal government, moreover, is certain to step in and fill the financial gap on programs which it deems essential, such as highways. The supreme court can continue its work with retired lawyers and with attorneys donating part of their time to deciding appellate cases as a means of public service. Some of the posh Little Rock law firms, in fact, could take turns subsidizing or providing legal talent for the court, with qualified associates just out of law school serving an apprenticeship period by staffing the court as justices. Similar efforts could be made on the trial court level. Some research assistance might be provided by the University of Arkansas Law School, which would now be subsidized by the Ford Foundation, resulting *eo instante* in a trebling of its budget. The lack of tax monies would have absolutely no effect upon service in the legislature, of course, since legislative salaries in Arkansas have always been somewhat below the poverty level.[20] Legislators have historically served for the kicks they get out of introducing bills such as that giving Miller County, Arkansas, to the

---

close any other instances. It would, however, be presumptuous of us to assume that humility may not on occasion affect judges in the same manner as lesser mortals.

18. 244 Ark. at 478D.

19. The Act was approved on February 6, 1945, and contained an emergency clause.

20. Under Article 5, Section 16, (as amended by Amendment 5) to the Arkansas Constitution of 1874, legislators received six dollars per day during the first sixty days of the regular session and nothing for any extension thereof. They received ten cents per mile travel allowance, and received three dollars per day during the first fifteen days of extraordinary sessions and the same mileage allowance. This was superseded by paragraph three of Amendment 15, which fixed a regular salary of $1,000 per year for members, $1,100 for the Speaker, a travel allowance of five cents per mile, and six dollars per day for special sessions. Amendment 37 upped the salaries to $1,200 per year for members and $1,350 per year for the Speaker, leaving the mileage and special session per diem intact.

state of Texas,[21] or converting colleges into paper "universities,"[22] or making speeches against demon rum.[23] Since relieving them of their salaries does not eliminate the motivating factor for legislative service, Arkansas should have just as much fun out of the legislature as in the good old days, and legislators should be even freer than in the past to select subjects for legislation which appeal to their seemingly insatiable senses of humor. Having only recently spawned an outstanding young novelist with a wry sense of humor in Charles Portis,[24] and a modern folk singer in Glen Campbell,[25] Arkansas should contribute even more to the entertainment field with the legislature serving as a veritable vaudeville and with performers ascending to its hallowed halls from every portion of the state. Perhaps, ever after, the capitol will take its place beside "Argenta," "Dogtown," and other Little Rock colloquialisms to be known as "the Follywood Palace."

A. Some Ill Effects

As beneficial as these results may be, some effects of the case are less salutary. The Arkansas statutes, down through the years, have acquired some laws which have stood as pillars of modern jurisprudence for an enlightened people. These have gone down the drain as a result of *Poisson,* and in some in-

---

21. This was not seriously urged, of course, but was just a typical legislative thigh-slapper.

22. ARK. STAT. ANN. § 80-3105.2 (Supp. 1967). *See also* Arkansas Gazette, Jan. 18, 1967, at 1A, cols. 5–8; *and* Arkansas Gazette, Jan. 19, 1967, at 6A, col. 1 (editorial entitled, *A New 'University'—In Name Only*).

23. *See* Arkansas Gazette, Feb. 10, 1967, at 1A, cols. 3–4; at 2A cols. 1–4, in which is described the defeat of proposed bills to permit local option elections at Little Rock and Hot Springs on the sale of mixed drinks. One representative is purported to have pointed out that he "had seen home after home destroyed by drink" and that the times were "similar to the days just before the fall of Rome." *Id.* at 2A, cols. 2–3. Another viewed it as a question of "right or wrong" and a "moral issue," pointing out that personally he was one who "drinks a little wet and votes a little dry." *Id.* at 2A, col. 3. A representative of the Christian Civic Foundation, apparently worried that the forces of darkness would flock in immediately, feared that the bill would "make our state a gathering place for out of state drunks." *Id.* at 2A, col. 4.

See also Arkansas Gazette, Mar. 2, 1967, at 1A, cols. 4–6, in which the fear was expressed that No. 120, [1967] Ark. Acts 326 making it a felony for anyone to give liquor to a minor, might cause Episcopal and Roman Catholic clergymen to become felons if they used wine in Holy Communion.

24. Portis, formerly of Hamburg, Arkansas, and now living in Little Rock, wrote the novel, TRUE GRIT, a best-seller now being made into a John Wayne movie, and an earlier novel, NORWOOD, which is also slated for motion picture production.

25. Campbell, formerly of Delight, Arkansas, recently hosted the Summer Brothers Smothers Show on CBS-TV. He will appear in the movie version of TRUE GRIT.

stances the impact almost shocks the conscience. A few of these landmarks of Arkansas statutory law, to which reference is made, are these:

1. Sunday horseracing. This statute,[26] which time has hallowed, provides in part that "[e]very person who shall, on...Sunday, be engaged in...the running of any single horse, for any bet...or for pastime, or for amusement without any bet or wager...shall be adjudged guilty of a misdemeanor...." Previously, as the statute clearly says, the police were able to enforce the public policy and deter a hardened criminal or juvenile delinquent from running his horse. Now it seems apparent that anyone can run a horse on Sunday with impunity while law enforcement officers must stand idly by, with their hands tied, and law-abiding citizens must suffer the awful sound of hoofbeats breaking the quiet and tranquility of an afternoon of televised pro football. Surely this will contribute further to the breakdown of law and order in America.

2. The driving of blindfolded cattle. Act 381 of 1911 provided that "[t]he driving of a cow or any kind of cattle or stock upon any of the public highways in this state, with a board or any other contrivance placed in front to prevent said cow, cattle or stock from seeing their way shall be a misdemeanor."[27] Needless to say, the absence of this provision will provide considerable hazard for motorists on Arkansas highways as the outlawed, but apparently quite popular, practice of blindfolding cattle and turning them out on the highways and byways is resumed. Since it has always been traditional in Arkansas not to enforce the stock laws, perhaps on the grounds that cattle which could see where they were going would have enough sense to get out of the way (a rule known as the "reasonable cow" doctrine), this venerated canon provided the only barrier against unwise use of the highways by our four-footed friends. Thus, if it might be argued that Arkansas' respect for rights of cows almost approached that of the Hindus, it could be answered with equal and persuasive force that the "reasonable cow" dogma was evidence that this would not be carried beyond the bounds of good sense. The fall of the "reasonable cow" rule will be oft-lamented by future sages as they weave their Sting Rays, Cougars, Mustangs and Roadrunners among the hordes of blindfolded cattle released on the public highways by various and sundry wags (such as Arkansas legislators having their fun between sessions).

3. Cockfighting and playing cards on Sunday. The fall of these statutes must certainly be viewed with alarm by all those who believe that ours should be a moral society and who reverence the sanctity of motherhood, the home and

---

26. ARK. STAT. ANN. § 41-3807 (Repl. 1964).
27. ARK. STAT. ANN. § 41-3302 (Repl. 1964).

the flag. A landmark of Arkansas law[28] which was adopted in 1853, a much more enlightened age than our own, provided that every person who on the Sabbath engaged in any game of cards[29] "known by any name now known to the laws, or with any other new name, for any bet or wager on such games, or for amusement, without any bet or wager" would be fined. Arkansas will lament the good old days when the police would crack down with raids on neighborhood bridge games on Sunday evenings and haul all and sundry who were participating off to the pokey. Those days are now past and vice may well run rampant as the spread of Sunday bridge and gin rummy clutches at the very soul of a basically puritanical citizenry.[30] Similarly, the statute forbidding Sunday horseracing[31] also banned cockfighting on Sunday, whether for wager or not. It will not be a happy day for the old red rooster, as Arkansans by the thousands shatter the Sabbath with the clash of fighting cocks. (We've got trouble, my friends, right here in River City.)

4. *Altering the teeth of livestock.* One of the great abuses in Arkansas, among canny vendors of livestock, was to have the teeth of mules, horses and live-stock altered in order to deceive the purchaser. This practice was banned in 1937,[32] and as a result, this foul deceit could no longer be perpetrated. (It is an unfortunate footnote to legal history in the state to observe that the pressure for this vital statute may have come from society bluenoses who were tired of waiting in the dentist's office while a mule was occupying the chair.) Now, of course, widespread abuses may result, although it is possible that the basic rules of equity and the common law with respect to fraud will provide some relief.

5. *Stallions, jacks and seed horses.* Probably some of the most important pieces of legislation in the state of Arkansas and possibly in the English-speak-

---

28. Ark. Stat. Ann. § 41-3809 (Repl. 1964).

29. Specifically designated were such games as "brag, bluff, poker, seven-up, three-up, twenty-one, vingtun, thirteen cards, the odd trick, forty-five, whist...." Whist is the game on which bridge is based, and this fact, plus the catch-all words of the statute, leave no doubt that bridge is forbidden. It is the understanding of the authors that people outside the state are less familiar with such popular games as brag, bluff, and vingtun, which are of course quite popular locally. The authors wish to state publicly, however, that they deny any knowledge of the game known as "the odd trick."

30. Fortunately, the 1965 General Assembly, in its wisdom, passed a law banning the sale on Sunday of a number of specified items. Ark. Stat. Ann. §§ 41-3812–3823 (Supp. 1967). Roadside markets selling souvenirs, novelties and handicraft items were exempted, possibly due to the demonstrated superior morality of selling souvenirs as compared to clothing (which was banned). Ark. Stat. Ann. § 41-3817 (Supp. 1967).

31. Ark. Stat. Ann. § 41-3807 (Repl. 1964).

32. Ark. Stat. Ann. § 41-1922 (Repl. 1964).

ing world were the Arkansas stallion, jack and seed horse statutes.[33] Under these provisions, if any seed horse or unaltered mule or jack of more than two years of age were found running at large, any citizen could take him into custody and, if the animal were not claimed within two days, castrate him. For the services rendered in the castration, the public-spirited citizen performing it was entitled to collect the sum of three dollars from the owner. As a safeguard, it was provided that such "be done in the usual manner, so that the life of the animal shall be endangered as little as possible."[34] The statute did not define "the usual manner," but since no appellate cases ever interpreted this widespread practice, it may be assumed that "the usual manner" was well-known to bounty-hunting castrators. Whether this entailed the use of anesthesia or whether a rope and a Barlow knife were sufficient to do the trick, we will not speculate here. Suffice it to say that the need to alleviate the situation resulting from the demise of this statute, essential as it is to the public welfare, might provide a productive and forward-looking platform for one of the candidates in the next gubernatorial campaign. An issue may well be drawn between the pro-castration and anti-castration forces, if any be so foolish as to adopt the latter position.

6. *Sinful activities around churches and schools.* Being a society fully dedicated to the virtues of bedrock Calvinism, Arkansans moved many years ago to deal with the temptation offered to the young, innocent and wayward due to horseracing near to churches and schools. An Act of November 5, 1875, made it illegal to run a horserace, whether for wager or for sport, within one-quarter mile of any church or schoolhouse, or any public road or highway.[35] Similarly, Act 72 of 1913 prohibited the operation of soft drink stands near religious gatherings where such activities were so close as to disturb the meeting.[36] This sound legislation has an obvious moral purpose which requires no elaboration. If a person is consorting with the Devil by watching a horse race when he should be in church or school, or is guzzling a big orange drink when he should be listening to the perorations of one of his brethren, then society is not doing its part by letting him stray. Moreover, how can any soul enjoy the majestic strains of *In the Sweet By and By,* as warbled by some goodly matron of his community, when a band of clods is busily cheering at a nearby horserace or gulping down cola and uncola by the case at a close-by dispensary? The soundness of such statutes is unassailable.

---

33. ARK. STAT. ANN. §§ 78-1136–1139 (Repl. 1957).
34. ARK. STAT. ANN. § 78-1138 (Repl. 1957).
35. ARK. STAT. ANN. § 41-1417 (Repl. 1964).
36. ARK. STAT. ANN. § 41-1418 (Repl. 1964).

7. The teaching of evolution. Arkansas is in for it now. Since 1928, it had as-
siduously protected the youth of the state against the teaching or instruction
in any state-supported college or public school of "the theory or doctrine that
mankind ascended or descended from a lower order of animals" and had prohibited the use of textbooks expressing the same fallacious and sin-filled
view.[37] This latter provision, of course, eliminated most of the science books
written in this century and thereby assured that sound learning would flourish. Thus did Arkansas deal with the shocking theory of the discredited biol-
ogist, Charles Darwin,[38] and assure that its youth would not be exposed to
such calumnies. Approved by the same supreme court which gave us the *Poisson* case in another landmark opinion,[39] the Arkansas evolution statute stood
as a monument to the triumph of virtue in all its nobility and to the fundamental soundness of the official, unexpurgated William Jennings Bryan interpretation of Holy Writ. It may be a valid criticism of the court that in its
rush to approve the clear, concise legislative verbiage in the Omnibus Repealer
and to sweep away the many barnacles on the statutory ship of state, the court
failed to notice that it was omitting the evolution statute from Arkansas jurisprudence. Surely had it recognized this fact, the significance of its act would
have come home to the court in a striking manner, and some attempt would
have been made to preserve this essential and undeniably virtuous statute.
The court in all its collective wisdom might then have made an *exception* to
the application of the Omnibus Repealer to the evolution statute on the same
reasoning which it applied to the common law: The evolution statute is simply a thing too wonderful to be tampered with. Under this line of reasoning,
the legislature, although it did not say so, must surely have not intended to
invade and desecrate this temple. Had the court reached this conclusion, it
would not be necessary for the legislature to re-enact the evolution statute as
Act 1 of the next session, as it most assuredly will.[40]

---

37. ARK. STAT. ANN. § 80-1627 (Repl. 1960).
38. *See* 7 ENCYCLOPEDIA BRITTANICA 83, 85 (1967). Charles Robert Darwin
(1809–1882), the English naturalist, in his work, THE ORIGIN OF SPECIES, developed the
theory of natural selection and the concept that living things evolved over millions of years.
This is obviously fallacious since everyone knows that the Good Book says that the world
is only about 6,000 years old.
39. State v. Epperson, 242 Ark. 922, 416 S.W.2d 322 (1967).
40. Editor's Note: After this article was accepted for publication and was prepared for
printing, the Supreme Court of the United States handed down its decision in Epperson
v. Arkansas, — U.S. —, 89 S. Ct. 266 (1968), reversing the ruling of the Arkansas court and
declaring the Arkansas evolution statute to be a violation of the First Amendment to the
United States Constitution. When the authors of this article were contacted about this decision, they responded: "The Federal opinion is simply another illustration of what this

8. *Operating lunch counters, shooting galleries and doll racks on Memorial Day.* Of only slightly less importance than the foregoing was the statute providing that no one could erect any lunch counter, shooting gallery, doll rack, swing or other device for profit within a half mile of any national or Confederate cemetery on May 30 or 31 or on any other national or Confederate decoration day.[41] This had been a particularly serious problem in the state due to the tendency of fun-lovers to engage in these festivities around cemeteries on Memorial Day. Although the General Assembly saw no harm in their fun-packed graveyard antics on other occasions, such as Halloween and Guy Fawkes day,[42] enough was enough. This statute will doubtlessly also be re-enacted at an early date.

9. *Dancing and walking marathons.* Originally enacted in 1935 to prevent the deleterious effects of "walking, rocking, running, dancing, and other forms of contests [which were] injurious to the health of the participants and detrimental to the morals and welfare of the public,"[43] this statute made such endurance contests unlawful if they lasted for more than twelve hours.[44] Admittedly, there has not been much of this since the days of Kay Kyser, the Big Apple and the Cliquot Club Eskimos. Observe, however, the value of the statute in dealing with modern civil rights marches! Both the court and the legislature are in serious political trouble when the loss of this valuable tool becomes known to people generally and to the White Citizens Councils in particular.

10. *The blind tiger law.* In its eternal omniscience, the General Assembly of 1883 adopted a provision making it illegal for anyone owning or using a house or tenement to sell or give away "any alcohol, ardent or vinous or malt liquors, or any compound or tincture, commony [sic] called bitters or tonics, whether the same be sold or given away openly or secretly by such device as is known as the 'Blind Tiger.'"[45] This is not to be confused, of course, with the "Flying Tigers" of World War II fame, although it seems probable that those who made

country is coming to. The Supreme Court demonstrated first of all, its ignorance in not realizing that *Poisson* had already done away with the evolution statute, but that wasn't enough for them. They had to go on and get in their licks at good, sound, basic, bedrock spiritual thought." (The balance of the authors' comments were deleted in the interest of good taste.)

41. Ark. Stat. Ann. §41-3710 (Repl. 1964).

42. Guy Fawkes (1570–1606) was an Englishman who conspired to blow up Parliament in 1605. The day (November 5) is celebrated in England with fireworks. 9 Encyclopedia Brittanica 124 (1967).

43. No. 64, [1935] Ark. Acts 143.

44. Ark. Stat. Ann. §41-3306 (Repl. 1964).

45. Ark. Stat. Ann. §48-1001 (Repl. 1964).

use of the "Blind Tiger" device to purchase such spirits were soon in the same category. At any rate, this is clearly a statute which should be once again adopted by the legislature due to the widespread knowledge of the "Blind Tiger" device among Arkansans and the tendency of many scurrilous individuals to make use of it.[46] Some towns have adopted ordinances directed against it,[47] and certainly the legislature should also do its bit. Similarly, other important liquor laws which have been repealed under the *Poisson* decision should be re-enacted at an early date in order that the morals of our people will not begin to deteriorate. To paraphrase the immortal Carrie Nation, there can be no compromise with the devilment wrought by the consumption of hard beverages.

11. The reception statute. To devotees of the law of real property, perhaps the most serious consequence of *Poisson* would seem to be the repeal of the reception statute,[48] through which our law received the common law of England and all statutes of the British Parliament "made prior to the fourth year of James the first...of a general nature" and not inconsistent with our laws. It would appear at first blush that a great many hoary goodies have passed into antiquity as a result of the loss of this statute. The venerable and hallowed Rule in Shelley's Case came in as the result of this statute,[49] for example, and the statute of charitable uses of 1601 was inherited in this same manner. It is likely, however, that the court, when and if confronted with this problem, will hold that most of this English common law has already passed into our own common law as the result of well over a century of decisions. As the court in *Poisson* indicated, the common law is much too wonderful to be dealt with cavalierly. This English common law has *already become Arkansas common law* and, as such, whether inherited or not, it continues in full blossom. But the English statutes, which came to us through the Arkansas reception statute, must surely fall.[50] The result, moreover, is to reverse such Arkansas cases as *Furth v. Furth,*[51] which invalidated common-law marriages under an Arkansas

---

46. *See* Kinnane v. State, 106 Ark. 337, 153 S.W. 264 (1913), in which sales on a boat in the middle of a river were held violative of the statute.

47. *See* Champion v. State, 110 Ark. 44, 160 S.W. 878 (1913), involving an ordinance against the "blind tiger" device adopted by the City of Hartford, Arkansas.

48. Ark. Stat. Ann. § 1-101 (Repl. 1956).

49. *See* Horsley v. Hilburn, 44 Ark. 458 (1884), *and* Hardage v. Stroope, 58 Ark. 303, 24 S.W. 490 (1893).

50. *See* Poisson v. d'Avril, 244 Ark. 478A (1968). Thus, *e.g.,* Biscoe v. Thweatt, 74 Ark. 545, 86 S.W. 432 (1905), recognizing the English statute of charitable uses, is no longer valid.

51. 97 Ark. 272, 133 S.W. 1037 (1911).

enactment, since the clear indication of the Arkansas court was that this *was* a part of our law *except for* that (now repealed) statute.

Other statutes in the property area must also fall, but the result, as in the *Furth* case, is to permit the common law to bubble forth in all its unspoiled elegance. The Arkansas fee tail statute,[52] having now vanished, permits the return of the fee tail, affected to some degree, of course, by the Rule in Shelley's Case.[53] Unfortunately, the Arkansas Constitution of 1874, a document too modern to suit the wishes or needs of most of us, states that all lands are allodial and that feudal tenures are prohibited.[54] *Poisson* having not affected this provision, a constitutional amendment eliminating it may be needed to achieve the true symmetry of the feudal system.

In any event, it may be concluded that while the repeal of the reception statute might appear on the surface to be disastrous, the previous incorporation and conversion of the English common law into the Arkansas common law protects against such an unfortunate eventuality.

B. Other Beneficial Effects of Poisson

The one-man majority opinion of the Arkansas Court pointed out some of the favorable results of the *Poisson* decision, and those will not be reiterated here. Some consideration might be given, however, to some other beneficial aspects of the situation. For one thing, it is still illegal to export Rana Catesleiana (bullfrogs) out of the state of Arkansas under Act 23 of 1945,[55] a major piece of remedial legislation passed by the same General Assembly which came up with the Omnibus Repealer. In addition, the Arkansas statute providing that anyone who curses or swears profanely shall forfeit one dollar[56] has been repealed. This is well and good, since the General Assembly may now re-enact this hallowed rule and up the penalty to twenty-five dollars per violation in keeping with the inflationary spiral. This same statute provided that if such offense were committed in the presence and hearing of any jus-

---

52. ARK. STAT. ANN. § 50-405 (1947). But ARK. STAT. ANN. §§ 50-405.1–.3 (Supp. 1967), having been adopted in 1957, remain in full force and effect.

53. The Rule in Shelley's Case applies where land is conveyed to an individual for life with a remainder to that person's heirs or the heirs of his body. *See* BURBY REAL PROPERTY 338 (3d ed. 1965). ARK. STAT. ANN. § 50-405 (1947), had eliminated the application of the rule in the fee tail situation. *See* Hardage v. Stroope, 58 Ark. 303, 24 S.W. 490 (1893).

54. ARK. CONST. art. 2, § 28.

55. ARK. STAT. ANN. § 47-508 (Repl. 1964).

56. ARK. STAT. ANN. § 41-1409 (Repl. 1964). *See* Bodenhamer v. State, 60 Ark. 10, 28 S.W. 507 (1894), holding that an indictment which did not set out the exact words but charged that the accused "did profanely swear and curse" was sufficient.

tice of the peace, mayor or judge, while holding a court, the offender could
forthwith be fined without any additional proof of guilt. This happy proviso
should be retained in the new law. Only a relatively short time ago, Justice of
the Peace Farkleberry Hicks set up court in the student lounge of the University law school and collected $347 in thirty-one minutes, including $17
from one faculty member. If the fine were increased, more of this admirable
work might be carried on.

Poisson had an important effect also upon the civil procedure of the state,
and for the benefit of those judges and lawyers who have chosen to follow the
rules of procedure, some mention might be beneficial here. The others, who
rely on sniffing the air or on whether their bunions ache or on ouija boards,
need not be concerned.

One part of the Civil Code[57] provided that no act could amend or repeal
any part of the Code unless the intent to do so was expressly stated, with the
portion to be repealed or changed specifically set forth. Apparently, then, the
Omnibus Repealer would not affect the original or amended provisions of the
Civil Code of 1868. Thus, the common law forms of action would remain
abolished and the provisions relative to pleadings would still be intact.[58] Other
laws relating to civil procedure, passed prior to the effective date of the Omnibus Repealer, would be affected, however. The statute providing that
Arkansas courts "shall take judicial knowledge of the laws of other States"[59]
goes down the drain, much to the pleasure of those of us who recognize the
innate superiority of Arkansas law. The statute allowing a change of venue on
the basis that a fair and impartial trial cannot be obtained[60] vanishes from the
books. This is no loss since every lawyer is aware that only some of his trials
are fair anyway (these being the ones which he wins). The statute permitting
joinder of persons as plaintiffs or defendants where it is asserted that they are
jointly or severally liable or liable for or entitled to the same relief[61] also goes
out the window. This statute will hardly be lamented since it permits plaintiffs' lawyers a second or third bite at the apple and allows defense attorneys
an additional fee. The joinder rule had the taint of collectivism about it and
was clearly socialistic anyway. Similarly, the interpleader device[62] is now no
longer available, so that where there are two or more adverse claimants to

57. ARK. STAT. ANN. § 27-134 (Repl. 1962).
58. *E.g.*, ARK. STAT. ANN. §§ 27-1113, 27-1115, 27-1117, 27-1121, 27-1123, 27-1125, 27-
1131, 27-1134 (Repl. 1962).
59. ARK. STAT. ANN. § 28-109 (Repl. 1962).
60. ARK. STAT. ANN. § 27-701 (Repl. 1962).
61. ARK. STAT. ANN. § 27-806 (Repl. 1962).
62. ARK. STAT. ANN. § 27-816 (Repl. 1962).

money or property, the remedy now is to pay one or the other or just thumb the nose at both of them. Litigation will be on the rise, and a new and happy day will dawn for the legal profession.

One beneficial effect on the Omnibus Repealer mentioned in the *Poisson* opinion is the repeal of many of the tax laws of the state. Among those left intact are the severance tax,[63] the horse racing tax,[64] the greyhound racing tax,[65] and the use tax.[66] Certainly, these taxes should provide more than ample revenue for a growing, dynamic society such as Arkansas'.

If the forces of Good in the state, whose devil-in-the-bottle philosophy has served us so well down through the years in the passage and handling of our liquor laws, should prevail in the abolition of horse and dog racing, the state can always retrench by simply lopping off those lazy louts who presently clog the welfare rolls. There is nothing wrong with the Arkansas tax structure that a little economy in government would not correct.

Also fortunate is the fact that one of the most favored foundations of the Arkansas legal system, the fair trade liquor law,[67] was enacted after the effective date of the Omnibus Repealer and thereby continues in full force and effect. Some of the expressions contained in this statute are enough to make strong men weep for joy at the vision which motivated its enactment. The statute flat-footedly states with foursquare fervor:

> It is hereby declared to be the policy of the State to stabilize liquor prices for the purpose of stabilizing public revenues and of avoiding price wars which would materially affect the revenues of the State, attempts at monopolies, and the demoralization of the legally controlled sale of liquors in this State which grows out of unfair price manipulation.[68]

It might have been better if the drafters had said that it is "hereby declared to *ever* be the policy," but we should not quibble over minor details. Certainly, the genius of the legislature is demonstrated in its desire, in situations involving liquor, to avoid the harmful competition which sometimes results in connection with sales of gasoline. This abuse clearly works the "demoralization" mentioned in the statute, as Arkansans from all walks of life and of all conditions, colors and creeds are forced to pay smaller prices for gasoline than they otherwise would in a healthy, non-competitive economy. With this fair

63. ARK. STAT. ANN. §§ 84-2101–2112 (Repl. 1960).
64. ARK. STAT. ANN. §§ 84-2727–2756 (Repl. 1960).
65. ARK. STAT. ANN. §§ 84-2816–2842 (Repl. 1960).
66. ARK. STAT. ANN. §§ 84-3101–3128 (Repl. 1960).
67. ARK. STAT. ANN. §§ 48-1201–1215 (Repl. 1964).
68. ARK. STAT. ANN. § 48-1201 (Repl. 1964).

trade statute remaining in effect, Arkansas' proud people can still point with ever-increasing pleasure to the fact that our liquor prices are second to none. Moreover, fundamentalist sects of all persuasions can draw vast comfort from the fact that if Arkansawyers want to consort with the devil, they will find it indeed costly to do so. Seldom, if ever, has a more popular law, designed only to benefit the public welfare, graced our statute books.

III. Conclusion

It has been said that the drafters of the American Constitution "writ more than they knew."[69] One could hardly make that assertion about the Arkansas legislature. In its wisdom, it gave us the Omnibus Repealer; and the Arkansas Supreme Court courageously backed it up in *Poisson v. d'Avril*. The resulting problems which have been delineated in this article are not so serious as to offset the advantages. Moreover, these problems can easily be corrected. In the meantime, the common law flows on like an historic stream, and we are blessed with the distillation of truth. There can be little doubt that Utopia is just around the corner.

---

69. The authors cannot remember who said this, but they are sure that somebody did. The possibilities include Al Capp, Stokely Carmichael, Bishop Pike, and Lester Maddox.

APPENDIX

J. R. POISSON v. Etienne d'AVRIL
Opinion delivered April 1, 1968

Appeal from Hot Springs Chancery Court, *Burl R. Hutch*, Chancellor; reversed.

J. R. Poisson, pro se.
Etienne d'Avril, pro se.

George Rose Smith, Justice. This case—on the surface a routine suit for specific performance of an oral contract for the sale of land—presents, when probed in depth (as we have probed it), the most far-reaching question ever submitted to this court, perhaps to any court in the English-speaking world. The awesome issue confronting us is that of determining to what extent, if any, the common law and the statute law of this State were set aside and annulled by what we will call the Omnibus Repealer, adopted by the legislature in 1945.

The facts are wholly insignificant. Poisson brought this suit against d'Avril to enforce an oral agreement by which d'Avril sold Poisson forty acres of bottom land in the Hot Springs Mountains. D'Avril, as might be expected, pleaded the Statute of Frauds, insisting that under that statute an oral contract for the sale of land cannot be enforced. But Poisson countered by dropping a judicial bombshell. He alleged that the venerable Statute of Frauds, which was adopted in 1838—soon after Arkansas became a State—had been nullified (along with the rest of our laws) by the Omnibus Repealer of 1945. The learned chancellor, appalled by the enormity of the question presented to him, took the case under advisement and finally delivered an opinion rejecting Poisson's sweeping contention, thereby preserving the status quo pending this appeal. The case has now been submitted to us for final decision.

The Omnibus Repealer was appended to Act 17 of 1945—an otherwise innocuous bit of legislation—and reads as follows: "All laws and parts of laws, and particularly Act 311 of the Acts of 1941, are hereby repealed." Period.

Fundamentally, the Repealer hardly calls for judicial interpretation. The legislature has spoken: Plainly, clearly, unmistakably, decisively. "All laws and parts of laws…are hereby repealed." Under many prior decisions of this court it is unquestionably our solemn duty to give effect to the General Assembly's magnificently comprehensive command. It will suffice to quote two of our earlier pronouncements of the subject.

"It is a well-settled rule of law that, where the will of the Legislature is clearly expressed, the court should adhere to the literal expression of the enactment *without regard to consequences*, and every construction derived from a consideration of its reason and spirit should be *discarded*, for it is *dangerous* to interpret a statute contrary to its express words, where it is not obvious that the makers meant something different from what they have said." (Italics supplied.)" *Walker v. Allred*, 179 Ark. 1104, 20 S.W.2d 116 (1929).

"There are certain elemental rules of construction to be observed in the interpretation of statutes from which we will *not* depart. One is that, where a law is plain and unambiguous, there is no room left for construction, and neither the exigencies of the case nor a resort to extrinsic facts will be permitted to alter the meaning of the language used in the statute. *Even where a literal interpretation of the language used will lead to harsh or absurd consequences,* that meaning can not be departed from unless the whole of the statute furnishes some other guide." (Italics supplied.) *Cunningham v. Keeshan*, 110 Ark. 99, 161 S.W. 170 (1913).

Our duty is clear. "We shall not," in Churchill's words (nor in anyone else's), "flag or fail." Nonetheless, it does occur to us that the pivotal word "laws" in the Omnibus Repealer is open to two interpretations. On the one hand, giving "laws" a strict construction, it may be said to mean statutes only, leaving all judge-made law unmonkeyed with. On the other hand, the word "laws," if given a broad and liberal connotation, may well encompass the common law as well as the digest of statutes, annotated.

In the study of this question we have devotedly worked our law clerks to the bone and, indeed, have lost some sleep ourselves. As far as our research discloses, no other legislative body has ever taken the bold course of repealing all laws — and parts of laws. The nearest parallel we have been able to find, which is persuasive but not binding, is an observation by the great French[1] essayist Montaigne in Chapter 13 of his essay, Of Experience: "I am further of opinion that it would be better for us to have no laws at all than to have them in so prodigious numbers as we have."

After much anxious study we have concluded that the legislature intended for the Omnibus Repealer to apply only to statutes, not to the common law. We are simply unable to believe that the General Assembly would do away with judge-made law. That law is obviously too wonderful to be lightly tampered with. In the immortal words of Lord Coke (himself, as it happens, a judge): "Reason is the life of the law; nay, the common law itself is nothing else but reason...The law, which is perfection of reason." See Bartlett's Familiar Quotations, p. 110 (13th ed. 1955).

---

1. As it happens, the parties to this suit are, significantly, French.

In reaching our conclusion we attach much weight to the legislature's use of the plural "laws" rather than the singular "law." Had the act undertaken to repeal "all law," it might well be argued that the intent was to abrogate the common law as well as the statutes. Put in the Omnibus Repealer, which gives every indication of careful draftsmanship, the lawmakers were careful to refer to "laws" rather than to "law." Thus it may well be true that the letter "s" in "laws" is the most significant "s" in legal literature. At least, counsel have not cited a more significant "s," nor has our own research disclosed one.

Both reason and authority support our interpretation of the Repealer. It is essential that the common law be preserved if we are to avoid anarchy — that state of society where there is no law. The statutory law is not equally essential. Indeed, it will be found that the statutes which were on the books when the Omnibus Repealer was adopted in 1945 can, for the most part, be spared. This is true simply because the common law, always fluid in nature, will at once seep into the temporary vacancy left by the evaporation of the statutes and keep the ship of state safely on the right track.

Counsel for the appellee make the usual last-ditch arguments that are so frequently heard when a court is called upon to perform its stern duty, despite the demands of expediency and wishy-washiness. All sorts of imaginary perils are conjured up. It is said, for instance, that to give full effect to the Omnibus Repealer (hereinafter called the Omnibus Repealer) will nullify such pillars of government as the sales tax law and the income tax law, both of which antedated 1945. We daresay, however, that the general public can and will face that catastrophe with that serene equanimity born of courage. Again, it is argued, with a veiled threat, that wholesome recreational activities such as horse racing will be abolished by the Repealer. Not so! In its wisdom the common law permits such contests, prohibiting only the secondary practice of betting on the outcome of the races. We need not extend this opinion by discussing one by one the various bugbears envisaged by counsel's vivid imagination. The truth is that in nearly every instance the purposes served by the Omnibus Repealer are praiseworthy and beneficent. We are calling the act to the attention of the Commissioners on Uniform Laws, who may well be inclined to make similar model legislation available to all the states.

The decree must be reversed.

HARRIS, C. J., would affirm the decree.

JOHN A. FOGLEMAN, Justice, dissenting. I dissent because I disagree.

WARD, BROWN, and JONES, JJ., concur in the dissent.

BYRD, J., disqualified.

V. Legal Scholarship

Rave Reviews:
The Top Ten Law Journals
of the 1990s

*Ronald L. Brown**

Tonight, I am fortunate to address a group of people who has shown foresight; the foresight to become law review editors.

The ever increasing number of legal journals in recent years certainly indicates that you are on the ground floor of one of the true growth areas of the law for the 1990s. Therefore, I would like to praise you, with the words of no less an historical figure than the immortal knight guarding the holy grail in *Indiana Jones and the Last Crusade,* when he said, "You have chosen, wisely."

At one time, being a law review editor was a stepping stone to the most lucrative law firms, the most prestigious clerkships. But that was all in the past. Although a law review editorship will remain as prized a position as always, in the law school of the 1990s it will be a stepping stone to, yes, permanent jobs as law review editors.

To prepare you for your future, this brave new world of law reviews, I will share with you tonight my predictions for the top ten law journals of the 1990s.

The Journal of Legal Acronyms

Lawyers and those who write about law can be verbose. Sensitive to criticism that they use all too many words, and that some of these words simply use too many letters, the legal profession has developed an elaborate system

* Ronald L. Brown is Research and Reference Librarian, New York University School of Law. He received his JD 1972, Harvard; MLS 1978, Rutgers; BA 1966, Rochester; R&R 1967, Europe.

Most of this article was delivered at *The 1991 Conference of Law Reviews*, Detroit, April 4, 1991. Legal Reference Services Quarterly, Vol. 12(1) 1992 © by The Haworth Press, Inc. All rights reserved.

of shorthand codes. As the ultimate source of abbreviated legal speech, in the 1990s I predict we will see the *Journal of Legal Acronyms*; or, as it will be commonly known, *J. Leg. Acron.*

Both law schools and commercial publishers are vying for the rights to this *J.* The schools include *BU, BYU, LSU* and *NYU* (which is exploring a joint venture with the *ACLU*). The commercial houses include *CCH, CIS* and, surprisingly, the *GPO* (publisher of the *USC* and *CFR),* which boasts it will put the *J.* on a *CD.* Neither the publishers of *ALR, CJS,* nor *ILP,* seem interested.

Articles involving federal regulatory agencies will fit this *J* to a *T.* The editors have already received material on the *S&L* crisis; on the *IRS,* focusing on Subchapter *J* and *S* corporations; and on the *PR* problems of the *INS.* Expected are pieces on the *FTC, FCC, FPC, FDA, FBI, AM, FM,* and the *A&P.* Regulations *Q, U, M, E, L, G, J, R* and *V* are also sure to be covered.

Other areas of interest include commercial law, focusing on *IOUs* under the *UCC;* family law, on *X*-spouses; evidence, on *I*-witness; and medical malpractice, focusing on *OBGYNs* from *HMOs* who fail to establish an *IV* during a *C* section, resulting in *DAMAGES.*

Although editors of the *J. Leg. Acron.* will have to mind their *Ps* and *Qs,* the articles promise to be so short, that they will be expected to do their work *PDQ*; but be permitted to write while watching *TV* in their *BVDs* (or *BRAs),* eating *M&Ms.*

The Journal of the Jurisprudence of Fruit

I also predict that in the 1990s law review connoisseurs will be able to taste from *The Journal of the Jurisprudence of Fruit.* I expect it to be published at the Citrus Belt Law School in Orange County California. I believe it will be their first entry into the field.

Among the subjects covered will of course be "tainted fruit" and "the fruit of the poisonous tree doctrine."

But, for its premier issue, *The Journal of the Jurisprudence of Fruit* will publish a symposium on lemon laws; harvesting a sampling from the prolific law review literature already in existence on this succulent subject. The editors have picked three categories from the available crop of articles, the three categories closely paralleling the very processes of nature.

First, will be articles on the *ripeness* issue, a concept which lies at the core of the jurisprudence of fruit. The editors thank, for example, *Rutgers Law Jour-*

nal, for its 1987 article, "New Jersey's Lemon Law, a Statute Ripe for Revision."[1]

Second, the symposium will turn to extracting juice from the lemon. Although featured will be an article entitled "Putting the Squeeze on Lemons;"[2] because of cross-pollination, the journal will also reprint the following two law review pieces: "Squeezing Consumers: Lemon Law, Consumer Warranties and a Proposal for Reform;"[3] and, as one might expect, an article entitled, "Lawyer Squeezes Fees from Lemon Law Suits."[4]

Third, the symposium will focus on the end product, lemon consumption. The editors have pruned out one of the many articles on lemon-aid, in this case, "Unconscionability as Lemon-Aid," published by *Pace Law Review.*[5]

To deal with the problem alluded to in an article entitled, "State Lemon Law Sours...,"[6] the symposium will offer the solution proposed by *The University of Toledo Law Review* in its article, "Sweetening the Fate of the Lemon Owner."[7]

And, for the conundrum posed by the *University of Richmond Law Review,* which asked what was the best treatment for "Car Owner's Canker?",[8] the editors offer the answer given in the 1990 volume of the *Journal of Dispute Resolution,* "Consumers[,] Swallow Another Lemon..."[9]

To round out this initial issue of the *Journal of the Jurisprudence of Fruit* its editors will also reprint a bunch of articles on sunshine laws. There are different forecasts among the states. For example, although the title of a 1985 article in the *University of Kansas Law Review* indicated that they were "letting the sunshine in..."[10] in that state; and the title to an *Oklahoma Law Review*

---

1. *New Jersey's Lemon Law, a Statute Ripe for Revision: Recent Developments and a Proposal for Reform,* 19 RUTGERS L.J. 97 (1987).

2. Allen, *Putting the Squeeze on Lemons,* 6 CAL. LAW. 15 (Dec. 1986).

3. Vogel, *Squeezing Consumers: Lemon Laws, Consumer Warranties, and a Proposal for Reform,* 1985 ARIZ. ST. L.J. 589 (1985).

4. Maher, *Lawyer Squeezes Fees From Lemon Law Suits,* 11 PA. L.J. REP., p.1, col.2, March 28, 1988.

5. *Unconscionability As Lemon-Aid,* 6 PACE L. REV. 195 (1986).

6. Pauker, *State Lemon Law Sours With Legal Problems,* 12 PA. L.J. REP., p.3, col. l, June 5, 1989.

7. *Sweetening the Fate of the Lemon Owner: California and Connecticut Pass Legislation Dealing With Defective New Cars,* 14 U. TOL. L. REV. 341 (1983).

8. Nance, *Virginia's Lemon Law: The Best Treatment for Car Owner's Canker,* 19 U. RICH. L. REV. 405 (1985).

9. *Consumers Swallow Another Lemon: Agency Consent Order Preemption of State Law Standards for Informal Dispute Resolution,* 1990 J. DIS. RES. 163 (1990).

10. Frederickson, *Letting the Sunshine In: An Analysis of the 1984 Kansas Open Records Act,* 33 U. KAN. L. REV. 205 (1985).

piece suggested that there might be "sunshine in the sunbelt;"[11] the editors of the *Missouri Law Review* have questioned whether there is "sunshine or shade"[12] in Missouri; and the editors of the *Mississippi College of Law Review* have pondered whether there is "a cloud over the[ir] sunshine."[13]

Nevertheless, the sun would seem to shine the brightest, in the law review literature, in the state of Florida. A *Nova Law Journal* article, for example, talks about "a right to sunlight in [that] sunshine state."[14] But, perhaps most revealing, *The Florida Bar Journal*, has seen fit to advise its legal community that the state of Florida has, indeed, developed, as the title to one article reads, a "sunshine state of mind."[15]

Citrus Belt Law School move over.

The Lyrical Law Review

Phrases like "Role Over Beethoven" or "What's Love Got To Do With It?" would generally conjure up images of rock and roll singers, like Chuck Berry or Tina Turner. Law review editors, however, are more apt to associate these riffs with critical legal studies or feminist jurisprudence. Would articles bearing titles such as "Role Over Beethoven"[16] or "What's Love Got To Do With It?"[17] be as likely to appear in the 1990s in journals bearing names such as "Stanford" or "Harvard," as they did in the 1980s? I think not. Instead, they would find true harmony in *The Lyrical Law Revue*.

What type of lyrics will be sung most frequently in the lilting pages of this rave revue?

Capital University Law Review offers some feedback. In 1987, its editors played a classic, and sang a sad song, entitled, "Singing the Blues" bemoaning "The Confused Legal Status of Blue Cross/Blue Shield Companies in Ohio."[18]

---

11. *Legislation: Sunshine in the Sunbelt: Oklahoma's New Open Meeting Act*, 34 OKLA. L. REV. 362 (1981).

12. *Sunshine or Shade? — The University and the Open Meetings Act...*, 49 MO. L REV. 867 (1984).

13. *The Personal Matters Exception to the Mississippi Open Meetings Act — A Cloud Over the Sunshine...*, 7 MISS. C.L. REV. 181 (1987).

14. *Solar Access Rights in Florida: Is There a Right to Sunlight in the Sunshine State?*, 10 NOVA L.J. 125 (1985).

15. *Access in Florida: The Sunshine State of Mind*, 56 FLA. B.J. 233 (Mar. 1982).

16. Gabel and Kennedy, *Roll Over Beethoven*, 36 STAN. L. REV. 1 (1984).

17. Fraser, *What's Love Got to Do With It? Critical Legal Studies, Feminist Discourse, and the Ethic of Solidarity*, 11 HARV. WOMEN'S L.J. 53 (1988).

18. *Singing the Blues: The Confused Legal Status of Blue Cross/Blue Shield Companies in Ohio*, 16 CAP. U. L. REV. 701 (1987).

Other journals have also intoned this original American music format. *Notre Dame Law Review,* for example, recently lamented the passing of a legal concept which had been on the top 10 charts for decades, by reviving another blues oldie. As the 1980s witnessed the rejection of collective bargaining agreements by bankruptcy courts, a 1988 article wailed, "Labor Discovers It Ain't Necessarily So."[19]

But, let's return to rock and roll, which, of course, is synonymous with Elvis. And no one knows better than law review editors that "Elvis" is a word with special legal meaning, as indicated by the often-heard phrase "Elvis citings." One Elvis citing was recently noted by the *Loyola Entertainment Law Journal,* in a 1987 article on criminal copyright infringement. It was entitled, "...Music Pirates Don't Sing the Jailhouse Rock When They Steal From the King."[20]

Securities law was really hip in the 1980s. However, by 1987, it was time to face the music, according to one article. It was entitled, "Heard It Through The Grapevine...,"[21] focusing on insider trading. All the unsuspecting former law review editors could be heard saying was, "ain't that a pip."

So, if you ever find yourself humming along and tapping your feet as you compose footnote number 9, number 9,[22] don't turn a Def Leppard's Ear; instead, slip out the back Jack, join the chorus Dolores,[23] and follow the beat to Beale Street, and the home of the pulsating pages of *The Lyrical Law Review.*

The Joys of Jewish Cooking
and the Law Journal

One of the most popular, and perhaps the most delicious, law journals of the 1990s will be *The Joys of Jewish Cooking and the Law Journal.* There has been some fuss in deciding exactly which street corner would be the best take-out location for this journal. Although few would quibble with New York City as the most mouth-watering selection, it is hard to deny the linguistic claim

---

19. *Bankruptcy Law—The Standard for Rejecting Collective Bargaining Agreements in Bankruptcy: Labor Discovers It Ain't Necessarily So,* 63 NOTRE DAME L. REV. 79 (1988).

20. *Criminal Copyright Infringement: Music Pirates Don't Sing the Jailhouse Rock When They Steal From the King,* 7 LOY. ENT. L.J. 417 (1987).

21. Murdock, *Heard It Through the Grapevine: The Future of Insider-Trading Laws,* 73 A.B.A. J. 100 (Oct. 1987).

22. Hear, "Revolution Number 9," in The Beatles' *The White Album.*

23. Hear also, Simon, "Slip-Slidin Away."

that *The Joys of Jewish Cooking and the Law Journal* be situated at *Nova* University Law School, in Fort Lauderdale, Florida.

What legal subjects will be on the menu? The whole schmear, from soup (chicken soup of course) to nuts; including an article from the *Boston University Journal of Tax Law*, subtitled, "Soup to Nuts," dealing with cafeteria plans (a Kosher cafeteria no doubt).[24]

One article which seems to have been carefully prepared for this journal was displayed in the 1985 edition of *Ocean Development and International Law*. It was entitled "Lox et Lex,"[25] the law of lox, focusing on the raw ingredient itself, protecting Atlantic Salmon stocks.

Naturally, the "Pickle Amendment" will be included, as well articles on herring. However, since the editors were unable to find any existing law review article on "pickled herring," they have agreed to accept for reprint an article from the *Journal of Energy Law and Policy* on a "red herring;"[26] even though, as a side dish, it also discussed the use by western energy developers of a new water rights doctrine developed by environmentalists.

Some authors have indicated the great lengths to which they are willing to go to be seated in the *Joys of Jewish Cooking and Law Journal*. Take, for example, a 1986 article in the *European Intellectual Property Review* on interim relief under the competition rules of the Rome treaty. It is entitled, "Cameras, Chemicals, Cars and [added with a hyphen] - Salami."[27]

Finally, by focusing on the culinary aspects of law, this journal will serve up solutions to some of society's most intractable problems. Let's examine, for example, the meaning of the title of a 1986 article involving constitutional limits on the regulation of religious employers. The title poses the following question: "Serving God or Caesar?"[28] Perhaps in the world of constitutional law the choice may be difficult; but if you think in terms of appetizer, the problem melts away. You can serve God and serve Caesar.

By the way, the editors have informed me that you don't have to be Jewish to subscribe.

---

24. Demos, *Section 125: Cafeteria Plans—Soup to Nuts,* 3 B. U. J. TAX L. 43 (1985).

25. Lyman, *Lox et Lex,* 15 OCEAN DEV. INT'L L. 1 (1985).

26. Tarlock and Fairfax, *Federal Proprietary Rights for Western Energy Development: An Analysis of a Red Herring,* 3 J. ENERGY L. & POL. 1 (1982).

27. *Ferry, Of Cameras, Chemicals, Cars—and Salami: A Fresh Look at Interim Relief Under the Rome Treaty,* 8 EUR. INTELL. PROP. REV. 337 (Nov. 1986).

28. *Serving God or Caesar: Constitutional Limits on the Regulation of Religious Employers…,* 51 MO. L. REV. 779 (1986).

The Journal of Legal Lingerie

In an attempt to borrow from the prestigious trapping of university law reviews, attorneys have always wanted their own journals.

To dress up the appearance that the practice of law has become a business, clothing it instead in more fashionable garb, legal practitioners in the 1990s will design, manufacture and retail *The Journal of Legal Lingerie*.

From a stylistic viewpoint, to handle this most sensitive (if not ticklish) area of the law, the *Journal of Legal Lingerie* will show a back-to-basics, no-frills look, publishing some of the bare documents which undergird the practice of law. Although the word "lingerie" is customarily associated with women's attire, the *Journal of Legal Lingerie* will be tailored to the dress needs of both sexes: offering briefs for the men and slip opinions for the women.

However, so as not to be hemmed in, and not to skirt its more analytical functions, this journal will also be shaped to include a department spotting issues which surface in various types of suits, ranging from labor law's doubled-breasted suits, discussed for example in a *University of Dayton Law Review* article,[29] to one of the vested mainstays of the attorney's wardrobe, "The Prosecutors Blue Suit."[30]

This article, published in 1983, is a legislative history of the trend-setting federal "Blue Suit Act," which, I have been told, is frequently cited by attorneys from "white shoe" firms representing clients with "deep pockets."

I predict that the Blue Suit Act will not be a mere passing fad, but will become a model statute, displaying the dress code of the 1990s for attorneys nationwide, and in Paris.

Journal of Star-Paging

Law review editors are all too familiar with star-paging, for its use in finding jump-cites. But, in the 1990s, this innovative concept in legal research will live up to its true, and literal, meaning, in the *Journal of Star-Paging*. Its editors will page the movie stars and admit all who respond within its glittering covers.

The curtain rises on the *Journal of Star-Paging* with an article from *Columbia Law Review*, published in 1990, purportedly on nonconsensual removal

---

29. *Double-Breasted Operations in the Construction Industry: A Search for Concrete Guidelines*, 6 U. DAYTON L. REV. 45 (1981).

30. Zimmerman, *The Prosecutor's Blue Suit*, CASE & COM. 40 (July–Aug. 1983).

of cadaver organs, but which is in fact entitled, "She's Got Bette Davis['s] Eyes."[31]

Another star in the wonderful show of law reviews is James Bond. Indeed, James Bond has had frequent roles on the law review stage. Although the titles are disguised to hide his real identity, the trained eye will quickly spot the physical prowess of agent 007 in *Yale Law Journal's* 1987 article on "Bond Workouts";[32] in the frequent articles on performance bonds;[33] and in a note published in *Western New England Law Review,* seemingly on the rights of putative fathers, but with a title that is a dead give-away that the protagonist is none other than Ian Fleming's superspy, in its reference to "Mankind's Strongest Bond."[34]

I don't have to tell this audience about the horrors of law review editing. This theme will also be featured in the *Journal of Star-Paging.* For example, several articles, masquerading as expositions on the right of publicity, show their true color, and bite, in their title. Consider the article: "Dracula: Still Undead. Unresolved Right-of-Publicity Questions…Haunt the Courts."[35] It discusses a 1985 California statute nullifying the "Bela Lugosi decision" and allowing, in the words of the author, "deceased personalities…[to] reach out from the grave to demand compensation…."[36]

Another monster from the silver screen who has made several appearances on the law review stage is Frankenstein; his debut introduced by a 1979 article, published by the *Harvard Law Review,* "Frankenstein Monsters and Shining Knights: Myth, Reality, and the Class Action Problem."[37] Frankenstein's law review career has spanned into the 1980s as well, thanks to an article in *Kansas Law Review,* seemingly on multi-state class actions, but in fact entitled, "The Supreme Court Meets the Bride of Frankenstein."[38]

---

31. *She's Got Bette Davis['s] Eyes: Assessing the Nonconsensual Removal of Cadaver Organs Under the Takings and Due Process Clauses,* 90 COLUM. L. REV. 528 (1990).

32. Roe, *The Voting Prohibition in Bond Workouts,* 97 YALE L.J. 232 (1987).

33. One episode is, Hinchey, *Payment and Performance Bond Coverages and Claims,* 41 ARB. J. 25 (June 1986).

34. *Constitutional Law—The Law's Strongest Presumption Collides With Mankind's Strongest Bond: A Putative Father's Right to Establish His Relationship to His Child,* 8 W. NEW ENG. L. REV. 229 (1986).

35. Rohde, *Dracula: Still Undead. Unresolved Right-of-Publicity Questions Are Sure to Haunt the Courts,* 5 CAL. LAW. 51 (April 1985).

36. *Id.* at p. 51.

37. Miller, *Frankenstein Monsters and Shining Knights: Myth, Reality, and the Class Action Problem,* 92 HARV. L. REV. 664 (1979).

38. Kennedy, *The Supreme Court Meets the Bride of Frankenstein: Phillips Petroleum Co. v. Shutts and the State Multistate Class Action Problem,* 34 U. KAN. L. REV. 255 (1985).

Finally, the *Journal of Star-Paging* will be home to heroic battles among the superheroes of the law reviews. I refer to articles such as one appearing in the 1989 release of the *University of Miami Institute on Estate Planning*. It was entitled, "Godzilla Meets Rodan: Generation Skipping Transfer Marital Deduction Planning"[39]—sounds like a messy scene to me. And I also refer to, "Bambi Meets Godzilla," appearing in the 1989 version of *Houston Law Review*.[40] Here, Godzilla portrays capitalist contract doctrine, the monster, who overwhelms the Bambi of consumer protection statutes.

By the way, according to the cue card, the *Journal of Star-Paging* will be produced and directed by the L.A. law firm of McKenzie, Brackman.

The Journal of Original Manuscripts

We have in American Law schools that peculiar institution, in which second and third year students decide, through the process of editing, exactly how a law professor's article shall read. Does the edited version resemble what was originally written? Is it necessarily better?

To render these questions irrelevant, I predict that in the 1990s we will see the quintessential faculty-edited law review, the *Journal of Original Manuscripts*. This journal will publish law review articles, as submitted.

Articles appearing in the *Journal of Original Manuscripts* will, in most instances, be published in another law review as well, although as an edited text. However, since it is so unlikely that the two versions will bear any similarity to each other whatsoever, questions regarding preemption and copyright have been summarily dismissed.

What will be the net effect of the *Journal of Original Manuscripts*? The bottom line is that the effect will not be "net," but "gross." Law review production will double, further contributing to the perception, and the reality, that law reviews are a growth industry; and contributing to your future job prospects as permanent law review editors.

Each month the *Journal of Original Manuscripts* will issue multiple volumes. However, each volume will contain a large disclaimer regarding the accuracy of footnotes, under the rubric, "CAVEAT READOR."

---

39. Gutierrez, *Godzilla Meets Rodan: Generation-Skipping Transfer Marital Deduction Planning*, 23 INST. ON EST. PLAN. 255 (1985).

40. Macauley, *Bambi Meets Godzilla: Reflections on Contracts Scholarship and Teaching vs. State Unfair and Deceptive Trade Practices and Consumer Protection Statutes*, 26 HOUS. L. REV. 575 (1989).

Journal of Law Au Naturel

Few in this audience would not agree that law libraries are inhabited by some of the more unusual specimens on the planet. I refer not to the humans, nor to the increasing number of droids which nest in these oases of learning; but to the rare texts on which we spend so much of your tuition dollars. Why do we do it?

I submit that we do it because it is the *natural* thing to do. The literature of the law, breeding like rabbits, embodies the imagery of nature: both fauna, as in *horn*books; and flora, as in loose-*leafs*. The pastoral and zoological overtones of law books have an irresistible lure.

As a guide to the exotic safaris of legal publishers in the 1990s there will be a need for *The Journal of Law Au Naturel*.

One specie of law books which may be undergoing a metamorphosis is *nut*shells. There is already a budding indication that this popular type of legal nourishment is mutating. In 1986, the journal, *Environmental Law*, published an article entitled, "Chicken Law in an Eggshell."[41] It discusses, among other things, the embryonic stages of this funky body of jurisproduce, dating back to the "sick chicken cases" of the 1930s.

Although the law review literature has covered (and uncovered) many shell games over the years,[42] the hatching of an eggshell series will allow for several new hybrids. One is indicated by a 1987 article in the *West Virginia Law Review*, on the subject of "constitutional kindness;" it envisions a "soft law" in a "hard shell."[43]

The *Journal of Law Au Naturel* will not only bear witness to the spawning of new breeds of legal literature, but will also track those threatened with extinction. For example, *Law Library Journal* has recently looked over the horizon in an article published in 1988, entitled, "Has Shepard's Citations Lost Its Flock...."[44] This article offers a new, substantive, approach for teaching law students how to graze in Shepard's.

---

41. Huffman, *Chicken Law in an Eggshell: Pt. 3 — A Dissenting Note*, 16 ENVTL. L. 761 (1986).

42. See, e.g., *Jurisdiction to Expropriate and the Shell Game of Intangible Assets*, 16 CAL. W.L. REV. 373 (1986); and *A Peek Under the Shell: Investment Bank's Equity Position in the Tender Offeror Should Trigger Disclosure Requirements of the Williams Act*, 46 WASH. & LEE L. REV. 689 (1989).

43. McLaughlin, *In Celebration of Constitutional Kindness: Soft Symbolism in a Hard Shell*, 90 W. VA. L. REV. 67 (1987). Will the "poultry" literature on this subject also give birth to a "hard law" in a "soft shell?"

44. Patten, *Has Shepard's Citations Lost Its Flock: Or, Can the Police Smell Probable Cause? A Substantive Lesson Plan*, 80 L. LIBR. J. 131 (1988).

To make a long story short, *The Journal of Law Au Naturel* will aid those charged with stocking the shelves of law libraries to see the forest through the trees, assuming any survive.

Journal of Legal Repetition

Next is a journal which can be described in one brief sentence. To give "full and complete," "clear and unambiguous," "advice and counsel," "regarding or concerning," "each and every," "word, grouping of words, phrases or expressions," "of or connoting," "legal significance or meaning," *The Journal of Legal Repetition,* I repeat, *The Journal of Legal Repetition,* "will or shall," "appear or surface," "for better or for worse" "to have and to hold" "in or during," "the 1990s or thereabouts."

The Journal of Twilight Zoning

There are many dimensions to the law. However, extensive exploration in the wide world of legal periodical literature has failed to unearth a single article explicitly laying claim to the *Fifth* dimension of the law. The Fifth dimension of the law is a dimension as vast as space, as timeless as infinity. It is the middle ground between light and shadow, between science and superstition. It lies between the pit of one's fears and the summit of one's knowledge.[45]

I predict that in the 1990s, to regulate those who boldly trek where no lawyer has gone before, we will experience the *Journal of Twilight Zoning.*

The coverage of this journal will be spacious, because a review of titles in law journals over the past ten years signals that there is virtually no sector in the legal universe that does not have its twilight zone.

Many law review commentators, for example, have peered into the nebulous contours of undeclared war and called it a twilight zone, as did the author of a 1987 *Kentucky Law Journal* piece.[46]

Labor law, to be sure, has its twilight zone. Indeed, according to a 1987 article, in *Detroit College of Law Review,* the very future of labor unions exists in a twilight zone.[47]

Who would deny the need for special protective shelter in space? This need

---

45. Zicree, *Twilight Zone Companion* (1973), "The First Season," p. 31.
46. Mikva, *The Political Question Revisited: War Powers and the Zone of Twilight,* 76 KY. L.J. 329 (1987/88).
47. Raskin, *Twilight Zone for Unions?,* 1987 DET. C.L. REV. 637 (1987).

extends to a form of shelter one would most certainly expect to find in the twilight zone, the tax shelter. This phenomenon was observed in a 1984 article in the journal *TAXES* entitled "Reaching for the Outer Limits in Tax Shelters: The Right Stuff or the Twilight Zone."[48]

Tax law has also been seen orbiting in other areas of space. Indeed, the Internal Revenue Service has been waging an intergalactic battle to enhance its authority to impose tax penalties, according to a 1990 article entitled, "The Empire Strikes Back."[49]

Finally, it would seem apparent that an article which appeared in *The Harvard Law Review* in 1989 on " ... The Curvature of Constitutional Space"[50] has its trajectory set for the twilight zone; its penumbra no doubt.

Conclusion

Those of you who have been counting know that that was number 10; and that's all the predictions I'll inflict upon you tonight.

You've probably been wondering whether there is a serious message to what I have said. If there is, it is this.

During the past half hour you have shown the traits upon which you will need to rely in the future as permanent law review editors. You have listened to a lot of nonsense, claptrap, gibberish and mishogos. You have shown fortitude and perseverance beyond reasonable doubt; courtesy and patience beyond reasonable expectations; and perhaps even a sense of humor.

In short, you deserve to be on law review.

---

48. Kanter, *Reaching for the Outer Limits in Tax Shelters: The Right Stuff of the Twilight Zone?*, 62 TAXES 879 (1984).

49. Banoff, *Determining and Weighing Valid Legal Authority to Avoid Penalties: In IRS Notice 90–20, The Empire Strikes Back,* 68 TAXES 304 (1990).

50. Tribe, *The Curvature of Constitutional Space: What Lawyers Can Learn From Modern Physics,* 103 HARV. L. REV. 1 (1989).

Chicken Law in an Eggshell: Part III[1] — A Dissenting Note

James L. Huffman[2]

I suppose an occasional article on the legal problems encountered by anadromous fish is acceptable.[3] They are good to eat, and it is fun watching them swim by the windows provided for public viewing at the Bonneville Dam.[4] Perhaps it is even acceptable to publish an aperiodic newsletter on the subject of anadromous fish law.[5] But a symposium on the subject? I must dissent. Sure, it is important to make it clear that the concern is for anadromous, not androgynous, fish. Although the way fish do it, they might just as well be androgynous. But let's face it — you see one salmon, you've seen them all.[6] They just swim to the ocean, dodge a few fishing boats, and swim back up-

---

1. Like other tales of adventure and daring-do, we pick this story up midway. Only time and editorial willingness will determine whether the story is ever begun or finished.

2. Professor of Law and Director of the yet-to-be-established Chicken Law Institute, Northwestern School of Law of Lewis and Clark College. J.D., 1972, University of Chicago Law School; M.A., 1969, Fletcher School of Law and Diplomacy, Tufts University; B.S., 1967, Montana State University. The author is indebted to Ms. Karin DeDona who provided research assistance. Of course, she is in no way responsible for anything I have written, although she did evidence some enthusiasm for the topic and thus encouraged me in what a close friend of Ms. DeDona has described as "this fowl project." I am also, as always, indebted to Ms. Lenair Mulford for translating my handwriting to a typed manuscript; notwithstanding that while typing it, she was overheard to quote from Plautus's *Pseudolus:* "By Hercules, do hens also have hands? For a chicken wrote this." I am in no way indebted to my colleague Michael C. Blumm who refused to read or comment on an earlier draft of this Article.

3. *See, e.g.*, Blumm, *Hydropower vs. Salmon: The Struggle of the Pacific Northwest's Anadromous Fish Resources for a Peaceful Co-Existence with the Federal Columbia River Power System,* 11 ENVTL. L. 211 (1981), and Comment, *Odd Man Out: Idaho's Bid for a Fair Share of Columbia River Upriver Anadromous Fish Stocks,* 10 ENVTL. L. 389 (1980).

4. The latter benefit could no doubt be better and more reliably achieved by use of computer simulation or other modern technology. What is wrong with plastic fish?

5. *See* Blumm (ed.) [1979-Present Transfer Binder] ANADROMOUS FISH L. MEMO. (NAT. RESOURCES L. INST.), Northwestern School of Law of Lewis and Clark College, now in its 36th aperiodic appearance.

6. In 36 issues, the *Anadromous Fish Law Memo* has yet to print a centerfold, no doubt an effort to avoid revealing this truth.

stream four or five years later. What takes them so long? Surely we can focus our attention on the legal problems of some critter more deserving of our attention. Herewith, a modest, though obvious, proposal.[7]

The Chicken

The chicken is neither androgynous nor anadromous. It mates the good old fashioned way and travels neither upstream nor downstream: it just hangs around the farmyard. But don't be deceived by its ordinary habits. You see one chicken; you want to see another. It would never occur to anyone to display tanks of anadromous fish at the state fair, but every fair-goer is delighted to be confronted with cage after cage in row after row of chickens adorned in magnificently colored plumage. Some wear feathered pantaloons; others sport high arching tail feathers of fluorescent green and blue. True, featherwise, Mother Nature has discriminated a bit between the sexes, but the hen is a survivor in the harsh world of seventy-five cent per pound chicken and one dollar per dozen eggs. Chickens tend to be rewarded for what they are good at, not for their looks.

There is nothing more majestic than the self-confident crow of a rooster, and nothing more amazing than the "incredible, edible egg."[8] Fish farmers have to wait years for an anadromous fish to be ready for the processing plant, and then only a small fraction survive the ravages of man and nature. Chicken farmers, on the other hand, can mail order their day-old chicks, presorted by sex, and in eight weeks have every last one neatly wrapped in the freezer. Unlike anadromous fish, chickens are always in abundance. Chickens are the food of Kings and peasants; their eggs are an engineering marvel, as suited to art as to omelettes. There can be no doubt that chicken law is more deserving of our attention than is the law of those migrant, apolitical creatures which seem always to evade my hook, and therefore my fork.[9]

---

7. I am indebted to Mr. Marc Herzfeld, former Editor of *Environmental Law*, who suggested an article on this subject, and to Mr. Bruce Weyhrauch, Editor-in-Chief of *Environmental Law*, who, despite a reviewer's comment that this Article is "nothing to crow about," asserted his authority in the "pecking order" on the ground that "[r]eaders weary of fish law should be no doubt glad to cacciatore…[the] chicken article as a postscript to Volume 16:3." Letter of April 16, 1986.

8. This line is stolen from somewhere, but as with the many aphorisms quoted below, it is assumed that the saying has become part of the public domain, and that, in any event, the author of the statement would probably rather not be cited.

9. Purchase, of course, is out of the question for those who engage in the lonely life of scholarship with knowledge as their only compensation.

Laying An Egg

Given the importance of the topic, it may surprise some readers to know that chicken law scholarship is embryonic at best. The reason is regretfully obvious. Who would have the nerve to sign his name to a discourse on chicken law? As the Reverend Edmund Saul Dixon wrote in 1849: "It is possible that anyone claiming to be considered as an educated gentleman, may be thought to have done a bold thing in publishing a book on Poultry, and giving his real name on the title page."[10] Legal academics are generally striving for the respect of their peers. Breaking new ground is risky business, unless one is at the top with only oneself to impress. Having already risked my career by investing several years in a study of earthquake law,[11] I have decided to take the next logical step and pursue chicken law. My hope is that future generations will think of me in relation to chicken law the way scholars today think of Ulisse Aldrovandi in relation to the sociology of the chicken. Aldrovandi, it seems, was the first person since the Romans to write of the chicken without the prophylactic of a pseudonym.

Ulisse Aldrovandi, a sixteenth century professor of natural history at the University of Bologna, was the author of a nine volume treatise on animals, a full volume of which was devoted to the chicken. Wrote Aldrovandi:

> No proof is required, for it is clear to all, how much benefit the cock and his wives provide for the human race. They furnish food for both humans who are well and those who are ill and rally those who are almost dead. Which condition of the body, internal or external, does not obtain its remedies from the chicken?... The cock and the hen, desirous of generating offspring, make their genes eternal under the leadership of Nature.[12]

Notwithstanding its obvious importance, before Aldrovandi's revival of the classical studies "the chicken [had] dropped from the consciousness of the

---

10. Dixon went on to point out that earlier authors on the chicken had "only ventured to meet the public criticism under the shelter of an assumed title." Dixon, who published his TREATISE ON THE HISTORY AND MANAGEMENT OF ORNAMENTAL AND DOMESTIC POULTRY in 1849, is quoted in P. SMITH & C. DANIEL, THE CHICKEN BOOK 9 (1982) [hereinafter cited as SMITH & DANIEL].

11. J. HUFFMAN, GOVERNMENT LIABILITY LAW: A COMPARATIVE STUDY (1986). [Sorry about that, but sometimes one has to reach a bit in citing one's own work.]

12. Quoted in SMITH & DANIEL, *supra* note 10, at 43. Aldrovandi published the first volume in 1599 at the age of 77. He is to be forgiven for using the term "cock" to describe a male chicken, for he did not have benefit of the reforms of English puritanism which brought us the less offensive term, "rooster." Purists will argue that he did not use the word cock since he was, after all, writing in Latin and would have used the word *cucurio*. However, as Smith and Daniel point out: "In many cultures the word for the male chicken has been the same as the word for the male sexual member...." *Id.* at 51 n.

learned community in the Western world."[13] Of course, as modern chicken scholars Page Smith and Charles Daniel have observed, "its neglect by the learned and scholarly world made no difference to the chicken."[14] And so it is today and always. The chicken will care nothing of this treatise on federal chicken law. There will be no plea for the legal standing, or is it roosting, of the chicken. I can only plead on my own behalf, perhaps for the roasting of the chicken, or the right of the city dweller to husband the chicken for the other pleasures it brings."[15]

Hatching the Egg

Being first to a field of study has its difficulties, but also its advantages. Central among the advantages is the opportunity to define the boundaries and describe the organization of the topic. Herewith, a map for the future scholar, if not for this one. In the cruel world of publish or perish, it is best to avoid putting all of one's eggs in one basket. Hence, I have broken this project into several pieces.

As the title indicates, this Article is Part III of a series. Part I, which remains unwritten, might deal with the history of chicken law. It is an epic history which spans the centuries of human civilization and the continents of human settlement. Chickens are raised for meat and eggs in every corner of the world, having accompanied or preceded the European explorers to the new world.[16] Where there are chickens, there is chicken law, and nowhere is it more abundant than the United States. The history of chicken law is important in the United States because chicken rearing is "the ultimate, democratic, a-hundred-percent American calling...[which] promise[s] everything—growth and progress, nature, science, independence, and, finally, money in modest

---

13. SMITH & DANIEL, *supra* note 10, at 41.

14. *Id.* Smith and Daniel go on to observe that "[l]ike its master, the farmer, it went on year after year, decade after decade, century after century, a generation to a year, roughly speaking, for many more than a thousand generations. It went on through its own Dark Ages, laying eggs beyond counting, rewarding uncounted husbandmen generously or meagerly, according to their deserts." *Id.* at 41–42.

15. I have in mind the simple pleasures of watching the young chicks grow and listening to the pleasant chatter of the hens as they scratch for bugs and other delicacies in the dust of the farmyard, not the sort of thing which led to the expulsion from college of Dr. Samuel Gall, inventor of the gall bladder who "majored in animal husbandry, until they caught him at it one day." T. Lehrer, *In Old Mexico*, on AN EVENING WASTED WITH TOM LEHRER, side 1, no. 6 (Lehrer Records TL-202).

16. "Anthropologists have argued heatedly and rather inconclusively about whether chickens preceded Columbus to the New World...." SMITH & DANIEL, *supra* note 10, at 29.

amounts."[17] Nothing having all those attributes goes long unregulated in the United States.

Part II of the series might treat state and local chicken law. Before the twentieth century, state and local law was the meat and potatoes (chicken and dumplings?) of the practicing chicken lawyer. It continues of some importance in matters relating to land use regulation, but as with most areas of the law, the federal Leviathan has spread its wings over much of chicken law. Aside from zoning regulations designed to protect the blissful silence of urban America from the barnyard sounds of the rooster, state and local chicken law is heavily concerned with cockfighting.

Cocking, as it is known to its practitioners and followers, is "doubtless the oldest sport known to man...."[18] Its hapless regulation over the centuries stands as a monument to the futility of legislated morality. The Greeks, wise here as with so many things, legislated for annual cockfights for the citizens of Athens,[19] but ever since societies have struggled to ban the sport, although Henry VIII, not surprisingly, thought it quite good fun.[20] The Englishman Richard King denounced cockfighting as "surely one of the most barbarous [games], and a scandal to the practitioners who follow it....At the scenes of cruelty the greatest depredations are committed by the attendants thereon, the most prophane and wicked expressions are made use of, the most horrid and blasphemous oaths and curses denounced against Fortune...."[21] The English Parliament declared cockfighting illegal in 1834.[22] American reformers sought to achieve a similar national ban, but they "had much slower going than their English cousins."[23] The matter was left to the states, a few of which have rejected the hyprocrisy of seeking to ban that which they cannot.[24]

The Jurisprudential Chicken

Part IV of the subject must certainly be the jurisprudence of chicken law. The ancient proverb, "You're gluing an egg together," to warn of a futile undertaking, well describes much of the law, while the modern aphorism, "You

---

17. *Id.* at 266.
18. *Id.* at 69.
19. *Id.* at 71.
20. *Id.* at 78.
21. *Id.* at 95. Apparently, Mr. King had never seen an ice hockey game.
22. *Id.* at 96.
23. *Id.* at 105.
24. According to Smith and Daniel, cockfighting continues to be legal in Arizona, Oregon, Arkansas, and Florida. *Id.* at 106.

can't unscramble an egg," rings true to those who would deregulate our society. Long before Garrett Hardin wrote of the tragedy of the commons,[25] Thomas Fuller observed that "[i]t is no good hen that cackles in your house and lays in another's."[26] "To have both the hen and the egg" is the quest of our modern welfare state,[27] but our politicians continually remind us that "eggs and oaths are easily broken." John Florio once wrote "[t]hey are sorry houses where the hens crow and the cock holds his peace,"[28] but that was nearly 400 years before D. H. Lawrence wrote of "Cocksure Women and Henhouse Men."

Not writing Part IV straight away is as "hard as sneaking by an eager cock," however we law teachers well know that our students, for the most part, "have other eggs to fry." But even the law student will take an interest in the eternal query, "which came first, the chicken or the egg?" If the course is Constitutional Law, they know the answer is the chicken. Not even a jumbo egg outweighs the chicken. In other courses, resort will be had to a rule of greater certainty; something like cartoon figure Hugo's explanation that it was the chicken because "It works out alphabetically." Of course, we would prefer a judicial citation. Most judges have considered it a question of fact, but federal district Judge Luther Bohanon views it as an "ought," rather than an "is" question."[29]

The Roar of the Rooster, The Smell of the Guano

Consider the case of *David Rust v. Hubert Guinn*.[30] It seems the Guinns live on eighty acres in Jackson County, Indiana. Adjacent to their farm reside 495,000 chickens. The Guinns, "who are presumably persons possessed of ordinary olfactory sensibilities,"[31] arrived in 1965, the chickens in 1969. The Guinns were

---

25. Hardin, *The Tragedy of the Commons*, 162 Sci. 1243 (1968).

26. T. Fuller, Gnomologia (1732), *quoted in* Smith & Daniel, *supra* note 10, at 137.

27. Smith and Daniel wisely observe that "[i]t is a characteristic of our society that we have lived under the illusion that we could indeed 'have both hen and egg'; that we could have the egg, in short, without the cackling hen; the hen without the crowing cock; the flesh of the chicken without the unpleasant task of killing, plucking, and cleaning it. But... we must still pay the piper." Smith & Daniel, *supra* note 10, at 139.

28. J. Florio, First Frutes (1578), *quoted in* Smith & Daniel, *supra* note 10, at 143.

29. Judge Bohanon said, "I don't know which would be best—whether the egg before the chicken or the chicken before the egg...." Daiflon, Inc. v. Bohanon, 612 F.2d 1249, 1263 (1979).

30. Rust v. Guinn, 429 N.E.2d 299 (Ind. App. 1981).

31. *Id.* at 300.

subsequently visited by flies and a "redolence emanating from the [manure] la-goons [which] achieved such a state of odoriferocity" as to cause Mrs. Guinn to vomit, gag, and otherwise nauseate.[32] The court awarded the Guinns $9500 in damages. On appeal the defendant urged that a jar of chicken manure had been erroneously admitted into evidence. The Indiana Court of Appeals ruled for the plaintiffs on the ground that "[w]e cannot presume that all the jurors, or any of them, were familiar with the aromatic characteristics of chicken manure."[33]

Of course, not all judges are thus favorably disposed to chicken manure. Fed-eral district Judge Manuel Real sentenced defendant Larry Flynt to several months for contempt after Flynt called him a "chicken-shit-son-of-a-bitch"[34] and an as-sortment of other appellations which fell far short of the customary "your honor." Judge Real seems to have acted appropriately, although the Supreme Court has made it clear that the mere use of the term chicken shit "cannot constitutionally support the conviction of a criminal" where it is used to describe an alleged as-sailant rather than a judge.[35] Although obscenity is in the mind of the beholder,[36] fowl language is defined by the person to whom it is applied.

Those who speak fowl of the judge learn well the old adage that the chick-ens will come home to roost. But the judge must also be wary of the return-ing chicken, warned Lord Justice Bowen in *Cooke v. New River Co.*, not for speaking of chicken excrement, but for the expression of obiter dicta, which "like the proverbial chickens of destiny, come home to roost sooner or later in a very uncomfortable way to the Judges who have uttered them, and are a great source of embarrassment in future cases."[37]

Neither Fish Nor Fox

Judges have been much concerned about foxes in the hen house, even those of "pious countenance."[38] In the tradition of anadromous fish groupies and other environmentalists, Seventh Circuit Judge Harlington Wood dissented

---

32. *Id.*
33. *Id.* at 305.
34. United States v. Larry Flynt, No. 84-5041, slip op. (9th Cir. 1985).
35. Eaton v. City of Tulsa, 415 U.S. 697, 698 (1974).
36. "I can tell you things about Peter Pan, and the Wizard of Oz, there's a dirty old man." T. Lehrer, *Smut*, on THAT WAS THE YEAR THAT WAS, side 1, no. 6 (Reprise Records 6179).
37. 38, ch. D. 56, 71 (1888), *quoted by* Mr. Justice Reed in Darr v. Burford, 339 U.S. 200, 214 n.38 (1950).
38. Eggleston v. Chicago Journeymen Plumbers Local Union No. 130, 657 F.2d 890, 895 (1981), *cert. denied*, 455 U.S. 1017 (1982).

from Judge Richard Posner's efficient holding that a Corps of Engineers' permit was properly granted. Said Judge Wood, relying on the permittee's assessment of alternatives "is a little like consulting the fox about the best location for the chicken house."[39] The District of Columbia Circuit has objected that the Federal Energy Administration should not be permitted "to dig a den for the fox inside the chicken coop,"[40] while Third Circuit Chief Judge Aldisert urged in dissent that a deported American citizen had found "the Soviet fox to be the keeper of the chicken house."[41]

Without doubt, the most puzzling line of cases in federal chicken law is that which seeks to determine whether a particular critter is fish or fowl. Admittedly, many rules of law are ill-defined, particularly in this era of hard looking, policy making judges, but to assert that a case is neither fish nor fowl is a self-indictment for the most heinous of judicial vagaries. Anyone who has laid eyes, or better yet hands, upon a slimy anadromous fish and a beautifully feathered chicken will know the line between fish and fowl to be a clear one.

Unfortunately, the good name of the chicken has been subjected to some abuse by the criminal element of America. Fried chicken outlets seem to be a favorite meeting place for criminals, particularly those involved in drug peddling. Worse yet are those who have stooped to burying marijuana under the chicken coop,"[42] and even drying cocaine in the incubator.[43] Apparently it is thought that the aromas, of which the Jackson County Guinns complained, will serve to conceal the odor of the marijuana.[44] Perhaps this also explains the attractiveness of fried chicken outlets as drug transaction sites. Chicken farmer Stanley Philip Mack claimed to have been entrapped by authorities who discovered cocaine which he claimed was used in conditioning his cocks during fights.[45] Of course, Mack might have found some need for an expert in state and local chicken law as well.

---

39. River Road Alliance, Inc. v. Corps of Engineers, 764 F.2d 445, 458 (1985) (Wood, J., dissenting). *See also* Power, *The Fox in the Chicken Coop: The Regulatory Program of the U.S. Army Corps of Engineers*, 63 VA. L. REV. 503 (1977), *cited in* National Wildlife Fed'n v. Alexander, 613 F.2d 1054, 1064 n.20 (1979).

40. Ginsburg, Feldman & Bress v. Federal Energy Admin., 591 F.2d 717, 730 (1978), *cert. denied*, 441 U.S. 906 (1979).

41. United States v. Kowalchuk, 773 F.2d 488, 501 (1985).

42. United States v. Moccia, 681 F.2d 61 (1982).

43. United States v. Coronel, 750 F.2d 1482 (1985).

44. United States v. Pool, 660 F.2d 547 (1981).

45. United States v. Mack, 643 F.2d 1119 (1981).

The Constitutional Chicken

At the constitutional level, chicken law is pervasive. Every law student knows the "sick chicken cases," in which the Supreme Court invalidated the National Industrial Recovery Act as an unconstitutional delegation of legislative power and as beyond the scope of the federal power to regulate interstate commerce.[46] Commentators have suggested that the unanimous decision, not the chickens, was sick,[47] and in any event both bases of the decision died not long after the case was decided. Chickens came to the aid of Thomas and Tinie Causby who succeeded in persuading the Supreme Court that landing approaches by military aircraft distressed the Causby chickens which resulted in an unconstitutional taking of private property under the fifth amendment.[48] Although the decision held out some hope for the health of the takings clause, that provision has since suffered numerous relapses such that its defenders no longer seem bound by political reality in urging its interpretation.[49] Modern takings doctrine leaves chickens where dissenting Court of Claims Judge Madden would have put them. Judge Madden suggested that the chickens would just have to get used to life in the modern world, airplanes and all, just as they had been forced to adapt to "the incredible racket of the tractor starting up suddenly in the shed adjoining the chicken house."[50] Surely this is legal argument at its best.

Although the federal juggernaut has long since taken sick chickens under its wing, and today's chicken farmer has not nearly the rights of the Causbys, rights more fundamental than mere economic liberties have blossomed in the fertile field of chicken law. The modern revival of substantive due process has its roots in a conviction for the crime of stealing chickens.[51] Jack Skinner was to be sterilized under Oklahoma's Habitual Criminal Sterilization Act for having been convicted three times of crimes amounting to felonies involving moral turpitude. Although Skinner had been convicted only once of chicken theft and twice of robbery with firearms, Justice Douglas pointed out, in finding the law a violation of the fundamental right to procreation, that "[a] person who enters a chicken coop and steals chickens

---

46. Schechter Poultry Corp. v. United States, 295 U.S. 495 (1935).

47. See Stern, *The Commerce Clause and the National Economy, 1933–1946*, 59 Harv. L. Rev. 645 (1946).

48. United States v. Causby, 328 U.S. 256 (1946).

49. R. Epstein, Takings: Private Property and the Power of Eminent Domain (1985).

50. Causby v. United States, 60 F. Supp. 751, 759 (1945), *rev'd sub nom.* United States v. Causby, 328 U.S. 256 (1946).

51. Skinner v. Oklahoma, 316 U.S. 535 (1941).

commits a felony; and he may be sterilized if he is thrice convicted."[52] The law, said Douglas, "runs afoul of the equal protection clause...."[53] Although one may not be sterilized for stealing chickens, one may be disciplined under article 134 of the Uniform Code of Military Justice for engaging in sex with a chicken.[54] Although Justice Douglas urged in another case that the provisions were unconstitutionally vague,[55] Justice Blackmun said the issue was simply one of right and wrong and felt assured that "[f]undamental concepts of right and wrong are the same now as they were under the Articles of the Earl of Essex (1642)...."[56]

Do Chickens Have Roosting?

There is more that could be said about human rights, but what about the rights of the chicken? Alas, there is little to be said. No do-gooder, knee-jerk environmentalists are hounding the government about chicken rights. They are too busy agitating about the rights of snail darters, pupfish, and anadromous fish. Only the lonesome voice of young Newt Winger cries out from an appendix to *Grove v. Mead School District No. 354* as Volume 753 of Federal Reporter, 2d Series winds to a close.[57] Newt is a character in Gordon Park's *The Learning Tree*. Shortly after sitting down to their regular Sunday supper of fried chicken, the Wingers are visited by Pastor Broadnap who more than shares in the meal. Later on, Newt sets to thinking.

> He thought, "What are grasshoppers for anyway, and snakes and mosquitoes and flies and worms, wasps, potato bugs and things? Seems they ain't much good to the world, but God put 'em here. Seems they got as much rights as we have to live. If the grasshoppers didn't eat the crops, they'd starve. No worse'n us killin' hogs and chickens so we don't go hungry. Hogs and chickens and cows and rabbits and squirrels, possums and such must hate us much as we hate mosquitoes and gnats and flies. Dogs and cats and horses are 'bout the luckiest. 'Bout the only ones we don't go round killin' off all the time. The Ten Commandments say we oughtn't kill, then we come home from church and wring a chicken's neck for dinner—and Reverend Broadnap eats more'n anybody else." Newt stretched. "Too much for me to figger out," he said aloud.[58]

---

52. *Id.* at 539 (citation omitted).
53. *Id.* at 541.
54. United States v. Sanchez, 29 C.M.R. 32, 11 U.S.M.A. 216 (1960).
55. Parker v. Levy, 417 U.S. 733, 766 (1974) (Douglas, J., dissenting).
56. *Id.* at 763 (Blackmun, J., concurring).
57. 753 F.2d 1528 (1985), *cert. denied,* 106 S. Ct. 85 (1985).
58. *Id.* at 1545.

It is a good question, Newt, but don't trouble yourself too long over it. Some chickens still have setting, though we are working hard to breed it out of them, but they certainly do not have standing.

What is a Chicken?

There is yet much to be said of federal chicken law. There are the Poultry Products Inspection Act,[59] the Packers and Stockyards Act,[60] the Cattle Contagious Diseases Act,[61] and the Egg Products Inspection Act,[62] to mention only a few. But the editor's patience is, no doubt, wearing thin. Perhaps Part III must also be left for the future.

In any event, there are weightier issues to be resolved. As Judge Friendly once stated it with succinct precision: "The issue is, what is chicken?"[63] Justice Douglas found the issue troubling: "'a bred chicken and a bred turkey are similarly situated. Each has feathers and two legs."[64] Fifth Circuit Judge Politz thinks he knows the answer: "That which looks like a duck, walks like a duck, and quacks like a duck will be treated as a duck even though some would insist upon calling it a chicken."[65] But, of course, Judge Politz was asking the wrong question. The only thing we can know for certain is no self-respecting chicken will ever get involved in anadromy. It would be too high a price to pay for the attentions of this symposium. But then, the chicken has done just fine on its own.*

59. Pub. L. No. 85-172, 71 Stat. 441 (1957) (codified at 21 U.S.C. §§ 451–470 (1982)).
60. Pub. L. No. 67-51, 42 Stat. 159 (1922) (codified as amended at 21 U.S.C. §§ 601–695).
61. Pub. L. No. 57-49, 32 Stat. 791 (1903) (codified as amended at 21 U.S.C. §§ 601–645).
62. Pub. L. No. 91-597, 84 Stat. 1620 (1970) (codified at 21 U.S.C. §§ 1031–1056).
63. Frigaliment Importing Co. v. B.N.S. Int'l Sales Corp., 190 F. Supp. 116, 117 (1960).
64. United States v. Skelly Oil Co., 394 U.S. 678, 688 (1969) (Douglas, J., dissenting) (quoting L. Eisenstein, The Ideologies of Taxation 174 (1961)), reh'g denied, 395 U.S. 941 (1969).
65. Tidelands Marine Service v. Patterson, 719 F.2d 126, 128 n.3 (1983).
* [Editor's Postscript to the Postscript: "Oh flesh, flesh, how art thou fishified!" (Mercutio to Benvolio, act II, scene IV, Romeo and Juliet (W. Shakespeare)). While no chicken wittingly gets involved with anadromy, take, for instance, the chicken's unwitting participation in the artificial propagation of the salmon species. Oregon Moist Pellets, the ubiquitous food pellet given to hatchery fish, is constantly being researched to give the world a healthier, cheaper pellet. Lest the chicken feel its comeuppance, a recent study found that "poultry by-product meal" and "hydrolized feather meal" (the former consisting of a tasty blend of the carcasses "of slaughtered poultry, such as heads, feet, and intestines, exclusive of feathers") could be used as a "major source of protein if fish meal became scarce" but, it should be noted, the poultry meal's "protein quality is inferior" to those

pellets made of fish. J. Westgate, A. Hemmingsen & J. Conrad, Hatchery Biology: Columbia River Fishery Development, Annual Progress Report Fish Research Project (1979) (available from Oregon Dep't of Fish and Wildlife, Portland, Or). Perhaps, if they just included the chicken's feathers. . . .]

A Call for a New
Buffalo Law Scholarship

*Erik M. Jensen**

Some of us who have long been interested in animal law[1] are only now starting to go public. I, for one, have intended since 1979 to write the definitive article on parrot law,[2] but I have hesitated to tell my dean of this hidden desire. Sheepish proponents of other species have also been waiting anxiously to declare themselves.[3]

It was with particular pleasure, therefore, that I recently came across the *Buffalo Law Review,* a publication that competes with the *Kansas Law Review,* in the library. Buffalo law has many attractions for academic study, and I was delighted that a specialized journal devoted to such scholarship exists. We have been celebrating anniversaries of the nation's founding since 1976; what better way for us academics to honor the various bisontennials than to focus on the buffalo?

The *Buffalo Law Review* has provided an opportunity for scholars to come to terms with the world of buffalo law, but the potential has not been fulfilled.

---

* Professor of Law, Case Western Reserve University, Cleveland, Ohio. The author sees no reason why one person should take all the blame for this commentary, and he therefore wishes to thank his colleague, Jonathan Entin, for his helpfully absurd comments on an earlier draft.

1. With the species-centrism characteristic of humanity, I generally use the term "animal law" to mean the law developed by humans to control relationships with animals, rather than the internal ordering mechanisms developed by the animals themselves. However, since consistency is limiting, I may ignore my own definition. *See, e.g.,* notes 26–31 and accompanying text (discussion of buffalo family law).

2. Luckily, parrots should be able to survive until I complete the project. *See Casablanca* (Metro-Goldwyn-Mayer 1942) (Richard Blame reminding Ilsa Lund that "[w]e'll always have parrots").

3. At one time a former colleague of mine wanted to put together a law school course on "Law and the Chicken," studying the sick chicken case, eggshell plaintiffs, Henn on Corporations, and so on. That he is a *former* colleague does not reflect my institution's evaluation of the project's merits. (I must admit, however, that the institution may not have been capable of an informed judgment. *See* W. PERCY, LOVE IN THE RUINS 219–20 (Dell paperback ed. 1972) (ridiculing the linguistic abilities of "chicken**** Ohioans"). Before the idea had passed beyond the embryonic stage, he moved up (or down) the law school pecking order, becoming a dean. He took his ideas with him — poultry in motion? — leaving chicken law scholarship unhatched at this school.

In fact, I have difficulty in seeing what many of the articles within its pages have to do with buffalo law. I suppose an argument can be made that law is a seamless web and that any legal problem eventually affects the buffalo.[4] All of law can therefore be seen as buffalo law.[5] That theory has some appeal, I must admit, but it is not fully satisfying.

The *Kansas Law Review* can do better. Because the *Buffalo Law Review* editors have not filled the void, this journal must now take the lead[6] by putting buffalo law at the center of its activity. This journal is an appropriate forum for several reasons, at least one of which is based on theory. Two Rutgers University professors have recently suggested that the Great Plains states were never suitable for human habitation and that those states should, in effect, be returned to the buffalo.[7] Discounted by the Governor of Kansas as "a real buffalo pie in the sky idea,"[8] the notion nevertheless has some merit. This journal, whose sponsoring institution depends on public support, cannot afford to ignore the effects of relinquishing the state of Kansas to the tax-exempt buffalo.

I. The Shortage

That other legal journal has not lived up to expectations, but I do not question the wisdom of its editorial board. Editors cannot publish articles that are not written, and they now have few buffalo law articles from which to choose. I am aware of no law school offering a course in buffalo law.[9] Although I gather from reading advance sheets that specialists in the subject exist[10] — and I have reason to think that firms of specialists have

---

4. For example, the *Buffalo Law Review* recently published an American Indian law article, Smith, *Republicanism, Imperialism, and Sovereignty: A History of the Doctrine of Tribal Sovereignty*, 37 BUFFALO L. REV. 527 (1988–89). As numismatists know, Indians and buffalos are two sides of the same coin.

5. Or parrot law. *See supra* note 2 and accompanying text.

6. *See* Chinese Zodiac placemat, Golden Wok Restaurant, Cleveland, Ohio (meal of Oct. 16, 1989) ("Buffalo: A Leader, you are bright and cheerful. Compatible with the snake and rooster; your opposite is the goat.") (on file with the author).

7. *See Return the Great Plains to Buffalo, Planners Say,* Cleveland Plain Dealer, Oct. 10, 1989, at 11-D, col. 1.

8. *Id.*

9. Some do offer trial practice courses, which teach a form of buffaloing. *Cf.* Henry v. Farmer City State Bank, 127 F.R.D. 154, 157 (C.D. Ill. 1989) ("counsel either are trying to buffalo the court or have not done their homework") (quoting Szabo Food Serv. v. Canteen Corp., 823 F.2d 1073, 1082 (7th Cir. 1987), *cert. dismissed,* 485 U.S. 901 (1988)).

10. *See, e.g.,* United States v. McGraw-Edison Co., 718 F. Supp. 154, 159 (W.D.N.Y. 1989) ("Buffalo counsel shall attend in chambers.").

formed[11]—the academic literature is skimpy. Legal scholars have been slow to pick up on buffalos.[12] Why is there so little buffalo scholarship today?[13]

I am convinced that the primary reason is the difficulty of research. The traditional research services do not isolate buffalo law materials into a discrete category; West Publishing Company has no key number for the buffalo. The computer research services are only slightly more helpful. Put "buffalo" and its variants into the computer and you wind up with lots of cases that mention the snow-covered city on Lake Erie's shores,[14] that cite precedents with the word "buffalo" in the name,[15] or that use "buffalo" as a verb.[16] I don't want to read all that stuff,[17] and I bet others feel the same way.

Buffalo law has generated little academic excitement[18] also because of the Supreme Court's absence from buffalo jurisprudence. Areas of the law can become noteworthy simply because the Court deals with them, but nothing like that has happened with buffalo law. I suspect, but cannot prove, that the Justices are not directly to blame—that it is litigants who have kept the buffalo cases out of Washington. No self-respecting buffalo proponent relishes appearing before a body that was once called the Burger Court.[19] Chief Justice Burger may be gone, but we are tasting the aftereffects of his regime. Eventually, one hopes, litigants will muster sufficient courage, forcing the Court to play catch-up and to put buffalo law on the front burner.

---

11. *See, e.g.,* New York State Energy Resources & Dev. Auth. v. Nuclear Fuel Servs., 714 F. Supp. 71, 73 n.5 (W.D.N.Y. 1989) (referring to "Buffalo firm"). They must send out buffalo bills.

12. Picking up *after* buffalos is beyond the scope of this essay.

13. By using the term "little buffalo scholarship," I do not mean to suggest that research on miniature buffalos has priority over research on the larger variety. "Greater buffalos" do seem to have been given disproportionate consideration in the case law. *See, e.g.,* Greater Buffalo Press, Inc. v. Federal Reserve Board, 866 F.2d 38 (2d Cir.), *cert. denied,* 109 S. Ct. 3159 (1989). But reverse sizeism has no place in buffalo scholarship. *Cf. infra* note 20.

14. *See, e.g.,* A.A. Poultry Farms, Inc. v. Rose Acre Farms, Inc., 881 F.2d 1396, 1398 (7th Cir. 1989) (Indianapolis area egg dealer had "cracked markets as far away as Buffalo"). Another chicken case! *See supra* note 3.

15. *E.g.,* Buffalo Forge v. United Steelworkers of America, 428 U.S. 397 (1976). Everyone seems to cite this case—it has something to do with labor law—and it really screws up buffalo research. How does one forge a buffalo anyway?

16. *See, e.g.,* Mid-State Fertilizer Co. v. Exchange Nat'l Bank, 877 F.2d 1333, 1340 (7th Cir. 1989) ("Judges should not be buffaloed by unreasoned expert opinions.").

17. Nor do I want to do the research on parrot law, which suffers from many of the same problems. Someone is always parroting someone else. Thank goodness there's no Parrot City.

18. Big academics have remained calm.

19. The buffalos themselves may be nervous undergoing the grilling common in litigation. *See* Buffalo Shook Co. v. Barksdale, 206 Va. 45, 141 S.E.2d 738 (1965).

II. The Call

We cannot wait for the Supreme Court, however. Neither research difficulties nor Supreme Court hesitancy should prevent the development of a
scholarly field. If authority is scant—or if it is too much of a hassle to find—
we academics can proceed in the time-honored way by writing "think pieces."
I suggest we do just that: Let us bury the editors of this journal in material
that will form a new buffalo scholarship.[20]

In urging a new direction,[21] I envision something approaching a stampede
of legal academics into buffalo law. A herd mentality has been criticized in
some quarters,[22] but it should be encouraged in this special context. Think
buffalo![23]

On what should we focus our scholarship? Buffalo scholarship, like the buffalo him- or herself, should be wide-ranging, but we might begin at the beginning. The threshold requirement for buffalo law, it seems to me, is to define the field: What distinguishes the buffalo from other beings for legal
purposes? What is the essence of buffalo?[24] Should buffalo law be subsumed
by bovine law, or does it stand on its own four feet? At a minimum, we should
clarify the nature of the buffalo sufficiently so that confused judges can place
the animal in his or her proper habitat.[25]

---

20. I do not mean to distinguish new buffalos from old. Ageism has no place in buffalo scholarship. *Cf. supra* note 13. *But see* United States v. Young Buffalo, 591 F.2d 506 (9th
Cir.), *cert. denied*, 441 U.S. 950 (1979).

21. Governmental thinking about the buffalo has already taken new directions. In the
early 1980s Secretary of the Interior James Watt tried to outflank his critics by remodel-
ling the Interior Department's seal—the symbol, not the animal—so that the symbolic
buffalo faced right rather than left. The change was sometimes justified on the basis of
"artistic reasons," *see* N.Y. Times, May 7, 1981, at B12, col. 2, but a spokesman later admitted that Watt "thought the right side should have equal time." Gailey, *Watt Turns His
Buffalo to the Right*, N.Y. Times, May 21, 1982, at A18, col. 4.

When Watt left office after a turnaround in his own fortunes, "right-facing buffaloes
were [no longer] in vogue," and the buffalo returned to the orientation he or she had taken
since 1849. N.Y. Times, Jan. 24, 1984, at A13, col. 4.

22. *See, e.g.*, F. NIETZSCHE, BEYOND GOOD AND EVIL ¶ 212 (1886) (disparaging the situation "[t]oday,...when only the herd animal is honored and dispenses honors in Europe"), *reprinted in* THE PORTABLE NIETZSCHE 446 (W. Kaufmann ed. 1954).

23. Lest any reader misconstrue my approval of a herd mentality, I should emphasize
that the scholarship must be unfettered. In the best traditions of academic inquiry, we must
let the buffalo chips fall where they may.

24. *See* Mid-State Fertilizer Co. v. Exchange Nat'l Bank, 877 F.2d 1333 (7th Cir. 1989).

25. *See, e.g.*, Mississippi v. Marsh, 710 F. Supp. 1488, 1491 (S.D. Miss. 1989) (referring
to "rough fish such as catfish and buffalo"). Perhaps I am being unfair to the *Marsh* judge.
Helping the buffalo survive by creating alternative aquatic environments is a praise-wor-

Once the threshold has been passed,[26] substantive areas will demand attention. Buffalo family law holds particular promise. For example, *C.J. Tower & Sons of Buffalo, Inc. v. United States*,[27] a decision of the now-extinct Court of Customs and Patent Appeals, appears to recognize the buffalo family unit. "Sons of buffalo" has the warm ring of an earlier family-oriented era, evoking images of young buffalo bundled up for the trek to school.[28] But consider the problems needing analysis. We have developed no formalities to memorialize buffalo marriage.[29] What is the appropriate family unit? Moreover, the case law emphasis on "sons of buffalo" suggests an excessive male-orientation.[30] The emergence of buffalo-feminist (or, if you prefer, feminist-buffalo) studies[31] is necessary if buffalo daughters are not to be shortchanged.

After we open the door to feminist-buffalo law studies, critical buffalo-legal studies and buffalo law and economics will surely not be far behind.[32] One might posit the buffalo as a metaphor for subhyperbolic meta-spacial synergistic power relationships in our society. Or one might study how law has moved inexorably to an efficient allocation of buffalo.[33] The possibilities are endless, and I am sure your mind is already filling with buffalo think pieces waiting to be disgorged.

III. Conclusion

The possibilities may be endless, but this commentary is not. We are just about there. Few have heard of buffalo law, but I have suggested that the

---

thy enterprise, and if that was the judge's point, I commend him. A buffalo would indeed be one rough fish.

26. Another threshold question comes to mind: Can you imagine Mr. Buffalo carrying a new Mrs. Buffalo into their new home? *But see infra* note 29 and accompanying text (questionable marital status of buffalos).

27. 673 F.2d 1268 (C.C.P.A. 1982).

28. Education obviously remains important in the buffalo community. *See* Buffalo Teachers Fed'n v. Arthur, 467 U.S. 1259 (1984); Moore v. Buffalo Bd. of Educ., 465 U.S. 1079 (1984).

29. I am reminded of a *New Yorker* cartoon in which a distressed kitten is reassured by his elders that his status is not peculiar: all cats are bastards. *See* my memory (1989) (computer research services not yet set up for cartoons).

30. *Cf. supra* notes 13 & 20.

31. *Cf.* "Buffalo Gals, Won't You Come Out Tonight?" (cassette tape of singing author, who doesn't know how to find citation information for this item, is on file at the *Kansas Law Review*).

32. Given my research habits, I find all of these possibilities appealing. Think pieces are easiest without documents to read, and none of these schools of thought, in its non-buffalo manifestation, cares about textual analysis—of judicial opinions or anything else.

33. *I.e.*, almost none anywhere.

Kansas Law Review can change that fact. It is time to begin a new deal for buffalo law, this is the place to do it, and this commentary is a humble attempt at that beginning.

The World's Greatest Law Review Article

*Andrew J. McClurg**

I. Introduction

This[1] is[2] the[3] world's[4] greatest[5] law[6] review[7] article.[8] It[9] is a bold, brash piece, unashamed to proclaim: "Yes, I am nontraditional scholarship. What about

---

* Professor of Law, University of Arkansas at Little Rock. I would like to thank Laurence Tribe, Sandra Day O'Connor, Richard (I like to call him "Rick") Posner, Judge Lance Ito and a lot of other legal personalities with good name recognition. They didn't have anything to do with this article, but there's no law that says I can't thank them just for being them in this important space for name-dropping. Special thanks to the editors of the *Harvard Law Review* for their hard work, unless they never bothered to read my submission, in which case I hope they spend eternity lost in a Sisyphean *supra-infra* citation loop. Finally, no introduction would be complete without thanking everyone for their "helpful comments," including Lisa, the waitperson at Vino's Bar in Little Rock, who suggested I move my notebook computer before someone dumped a pitcher of beer on it.

1. "This" is a pronoun that means "the person or thing mentioned or understood." Webster's New World Dictionary 1392 (3d ed. 1988). I will be happy to find a more recent source if the editors at an elite journal think this one is too dated, because I aim to please. *See* John Lennon & Paul McCartney, "Paperback Writer" (Northern Songs Ltd. 1966) ("I can make it longer if you like the style, I can change it 'round and I want to be a [law review] writer, darrr-darrr-darrr, [law review] writer"). Along the same line, if I should *hereinafter* screw up and use *supra* when I mean *infra*, please don't say *See!* Rather, *cf.* you can find it in your hearts to forgive me. Compare it to some really horrible faux pas like USING THE WRONG TYPEFACE, and it won't seem so bad.

2. "Is" is an intransitive verb. Webster's New World Dictionary, *supra* note 1, at 715. The word has a long, tedious history that, although totally irrelevant, I will explain in elaborate detail because I don't want the time I spent researching it to have been wasted. In Middle English is is found in ... [three pages of dreadfully boring etymological history follows]. Is is sometimes used as an abbreviation for islands, but that topic is beyond the scope of this article.

3. "The" is an article used to refer to a particular person, thing or group. *Id.* at 1386.

4. Pay attention! I'm talking *GLOBAL* here, which is very hot right now. It goes without saying that my global realm is jam-packed with diversity and virtually overflowing with multiculturalism.

5. Brace yourself, law review editors! This conclusion is actually my *own, original* thought. I spent three days researching to see if anyone had thought it before, but if they

it?" Looking for a sound thesis? Hah! Child's play. Try a great plot, crammed with suspense, romance and thousands of potboiling footnotes.

And yet, perhaps the paramount beauty of the work is that, despite being light years ahead of the competition, it never strays too far from its roots. In other words, it is nontraditional but in a classic, traditional, bet-hedging sort of way. We're talking about an article that: rethinks practically on automatic pilot, drives a hundred miles an hour *toward a model*[10] of important stuff, is subject to spontaneous deconstruction, tosses the word hermeneutics around like a walk on the beach, puts *post* in front of (and sometimes behind) at least one word on every page, and, best of all, will take a thaumaturge[11] to figure out.

* * *

[Unbelievable amounts of *really* great material are omitted here.]

CLXIII. Conclusion

In conclusion, I am confident that legal academicians everywhere will agree, probably unanimously, that the only important thing lacking in The World's

---

did they didn't write it down anywhere. My mother read a draft of the article and commented on its brilliance, so I suppose you could cite to her in a pinch (with a *see* signal only since she did not actually come right out and say it was the "greatest"). In any event, I assure you this original thought was an isolated incident and will not happen again.

6. As used in this article, "law" includes any positivist, naturalist, realist, feminist, nihilist, hedonist, economic, semiotic, narcotic, psychotic, post-modern, post-millennial, post-office syndrome, or any other theory of the rules we live by. Take your pick. If I play my cards right, the finished product will be so obtuse that no one will have a clue what it means anyway, which will naturally lead to the assumption that it's a brilliant piece.

Of course, there's law and then there's *scripture*. The reader should disregard anything herein that even remotely conflicts with *The Bluebook. The Bluebook: A Uniform System of Citation* (15th ed. 1991). *The Bluebook*, widely misunderstood, was originally an English translation of the *Tao Te Ching*, a book of Eastern philosophy written 26 centuries ago. Interview with Lao-tzu, "Larry King Live" (A Dream I Had, Mar. 29, 1995). Taoism advocates a life of complete simplicity. Somewhere along the way, some Ivy League law students got hold of this great work and... well, let's just say they have at times lost sight of the original purpose.

However, even today *The Bluebook* remains a source of great, spiritual comfort in troubled times. Just recently, for example, my significant other dumped me for a professor from a higher echelon law school who regularly publishes in the better journals. I became completely distraught, to the point where, I am sad to admit, I was a danger to myself. However, *The Bluebook* proved to be my guiding light. Now, instead of contemplating jumping in front of trains, I meditate about the intricate rules for abbreviating railroads. *See The Bluebook, supra*, § 10.2.2(b), at 61 (*PLEASE!* Just see *subsection (b)*, do not even think about looking at either subsection (a) or subsection (c) because that might be construed as *seeing generally*, which would require me to add one of these annoying explanatory parentheticals).

Greatest Law Review Article[28,343] is a colon in the title, but that is only because the author is beyond caring about such things, *way beyond.*

7. I'm taking a rest here, but I promise to compensate for it by making the next foot-note extra-long and monotonous.

8. "Article" is the one and only perfect word to describe what I'm trying to accom-plish here, unless, of course, a student law review editor thinks a different word would be better, in which case I will gladly defer to his superior wisdom.

9. From now on, I will use exclusively feminine pronouns, even for inanimate objects, to show I'm really with it, or I should say, with her.

10. Pretty cool italics, huh?

11. One of the truest measures of great legal scholarship is using words that no one understands. To assure that the terminology in my article meets this high standard, I made a lot of it up.

28,343. Andrew J. McClurg, *The World's Greatest Law Review Article.* Only the first of many, many citations, I'm sure.

Fundamental Principles
of American Law[*]

Patrick M. McFadden[**]

In all types of legal writing, whether by scholars or by practitioners, it is customary to cite an authority or authorities to show support for a legal or factual proposition or argument.

—THE BLUEBOOK: A UNIFORM SYSTEM OF
CITATION 4 (16th ed. 1996)

With the cool detachment of anthropologists describing human sacrifice among the Maya, the editors of the *Bluebook* thus calmly report on that peculiar human custom of legal citation. The self-interested nature of the editors' report—providing an apology for both the 365 pages and steady royalty income that follow—makes it no less accurate. But the measured tone of the report does underplay the significance of legal citation to those who must actually do it—an importance that ranges from cultish obsession to defeated indifference. Some of us never lose the zeal of the newly converted, compulsively searching every legal text for canonical purity. Others of us become equally ardent schismatics, embracing, for example, the Maroon heresy. Still others lapse in the faith, either making a principled decision that there are better ways to spend our time or simply feigning contempt because we can't for the life of us remember if the space goes between the "F." and the "2d" or the "F." and the "Supp."

But one thing is certain: we all complain. Law review editors grouse about the mindless tedium and thanklessness of cite-checking,[1] while authors whine about the tyranny of jump cites, parentheticals, and the editorial obsession to

---

    * Copyright © 1997 California Law Review, Inc.

    ** Professor of Law, Loyola University Chicago School of Law. Several reputable scholars reviewed earlier drafts of this article. It is not in their interest to reveal who they were nor in mine to reveal their reactions. My sincere and explicit thanks, however, to Alexandra and Stanley Mamangakis, who for the past three summers have provided me a cool, quiet office in Greece. Just don't tell them I wrote this, too.

    1. *See, e.g.*, E. Joshua Rozenkranz, *Law Review's Empire*, 39 HASTINGS L.J. 859 (1988) (containing, *inter alia*, a former editor's brief tirade on footnote work, with special bonus sections on alienation and the reproduction of hierarchy). Wonder who got to Josh?

footnote *everything*.[2] I suggest that we all pipe down and approach this matter like the mature, stouthearted men and women that we most certainly are. Sure, there are problems with law review footnotes, but let's just roll up our sleeves and take care of them.[3]

This Article, for example, solves one of the biggest problems in legal scholarship: the need to find authority for statements that are obviously true or completely unsupportable.[4] What legal writer or editor has not struggled to find cites for propositions like "the world is becoming increasingly complex"[5] or "justice delayed is justice denied"?[6] Therefore, as a public service, this author and the *California Law Review* now provide (i) a soberly-titled article, (ii) in a highly regarded journal of legal opinion, (iii) that states the obvious and argues the unsupportable. No more combing through Bartlett's *Quotations*,[7] no more desperate searches through the *World Almanac and Book of Facts*,[8] or God forbid, *Corpus Juris Secundum*.[9] Everything you need

---

2. *See, e.g.,* John E. Nowak, *Woe Unto You, Law Reviews!*, 27 ARIZ. L. REV. 317 (1985) (excoriating law review scholarship and predicting little chance for improvement — persuasiveness undercut by lack of footnotes). Professorial complaints about law review style have become as common as drive-by shootings, and you can find the articles for yourself. But do not miss the "Goodbye" series, inspired by Fred Rodell: Fred Rodell, *Goodbye to Law Reviews*, 23 VA. L. REV. 38 (1936) (swearing off law reviews); Fred Rodell, *Goodbye to Law Reviews — Revisited*, 48 VA. L. REV. 279 (1962) (author caught in a lie, but unrepentant); Abner J. Mikva, *Goodbye to Footnotes*, 56 U. COLO. L. REV. 647 (1985) (swearing off footnotes in judicial opinions); Abner J. Mikva, *Goodbye to Footnotes: Relinquishing a Tradition*, TRIAL, Aug. 1986, at 46 (in case you missed it the first time); Richard A. Posner, *Goodbye to the Bluebook*, 53 U. CHI. L. REV. 1343 (1986) (swearing off the Bluebook); Charles Alan Wright, *Goodbye to Fred Rodell*, 89 YALE L.J. 1455 (1980) (confirming that what goes around comes around).

3. *Cf.* PLACES IN THE HEART (Tri-Star 1984) (former flying nun does what it takes to bring in the cotton and save the farm).

4. "The [law review] author may not assert so much as 'The sun rises in the east' without citing Copernicus." Ron Coleman, *Citing Cites That Cite Cites: Are There Any New Ideas in Legal Scholarship?*, STUDENT LAW., Feb. 1989, at 13. And if you don't believe journalist Ron Coleman, Professor Delgado fills the breach: "Essentially, each assertion of law or fact that you make in the body of your article will require a footnote." Richard Delgado, *How to Write a Law Review Article*, 20 U.S.F. L. REV. 445, 451 (1986). He's serious, though he does, in a big-hearted sort of way, make exceptions for "topic sentences, conclusions of paragraphs and sections, and passages of pure argument." *Id.*

5. *See* Patrick M. McFadden, *Fundamental Principles of American Law*, 85 CALIF. L. REV. 1749, 1752 (1997) (reporting that the law is becoming increasingly complex).

6. *See id.* (confirming that justice delayed is justice denied).

7. JOHN BARTLETT, FAMILIAR QUOTATIONS (Justin Kaplan ed., 16th ed. 1992).

8. THE WORLD ALMANAC AND BOOK OF FACTS 1997 (1996).

9. As Morris Cohen has been telling us for years, the rule for legal encyclopedias is "look, but don't touch." *See, e.g.,* MORRIS L. COHEN ET AL., HOW TO FIND THE LAW 386 (9th ed. 1989) (proclaiming that legal encyclopedias "have come to be viewed primarily as

is here,[10] and if it's not, there is something close enough for a *Cf.* cite.[11] Even if you could find the needed citations for yourself or command a sycophantic research assistant to do so, why bother? Now, for the first time ever, almost every obvious or unsupportable statement you will ever need can be found in one highly reputable place.

A simple demonstration will confirm the incalculable value of such an effort:

> The world is becoming increasingly complex.
> Justice delayed is justice denied.

Like shooting ducks in a barrel. Both propositions now have the backing of the *California Law Review.* I myself have used these propositions already, which you can confirm by returning to footnotes five[12] and six[13] and accompanying text. Best of all, this Article helps not only you, the support-starved reader, but me, the promotion-starved author.[14] You can now drag yourself

---

research tools, useful for case-finding and as introductions to research, but not as independent authority"). Woe to the scholar who cites *American Jurisprudence,* thus to suffer the steely gaze of Marjorie Rombauer. *See* MARJORIE DICK ROMBAUER, LEGAL PROBLEM SOLVING 166 (5th ed. 1991) (warning that legal encyclopedias are "never" to be cited in "scholarly material").

10. *But see* THE BEATLES, *All You Need Is Love, on* MAGICAL MYSTERY TOUR (Capitol 1967) (suggesting that love is all you need).

11. For example,

> The theory of language determines the theory of the text. The real being of literature occurs in the temporal hearing of words. The literary text is *oral speech* heard in time. As image, as print, as object of mastery, the word appears in an invidious spatial guise. But as an evanescent sound activated in and through body and mind, the literary word comes into its proper temporal being. *Cf.* Patrick M. McFadden, *Fundamental Principles of American Law,* 85 CALIF. L. REV. 1749 (1997) (discussing fundamental principles of American law).

This passage (without the cite) was selected at random and stolen from VINCENT B. LEITCH, DECONSTRUCTIVE CRITICISM 81 (1983) (containing a whole lot more where that came from). Vince, I think, could have used a little extra support.

12. *See supra* note 5 and accompanying text. Must you be told everything twice?

13. *See supra* note 6 and accompanying text; *see also supra* note 12 (incisively criticizing the reader for slavishly reading every footnote).

14. Actually, that's misleading. I've already climbed to the top of the charts. *See* Letter from James S. Wiser, Executive Vice President and Dean of Faculties, Loyola University Chicago, to Patrick M. McFadden, Associate Professor of Law, Loyola University Chicago School of Law (Feb. 28, 1996) (announcing the author's promotion to full professor) (on file with author and author's attorney); *see also* LAURENCE J. PETER & RAYMOND HULL, THE PETER PRINCIPLE (1969) (explaining my promotion and a great deal more about my law school; yours, too, I imagine). Despite its uselessness on the promotion front, frequent citation to this Article can't hurt when my Dean (Nina S. Appel, an extraordinarily perceptive and, may I add, hardworking and underappreciated administrator) ladles out the annual pool of merit raises. But I digress.

out of any scholarly hole you dig, and I get to grab for the brass ring in Fred Shapiro's next update of "The Most-Cited Law Review Articles"[15] in America. The *California Law Review* cleans up, too.[16]

The next section of this Article has several important features. First, an introductory paragraph provides some nauseatingly pretentious and thoroughly vapid claptrap about the foundations of American law. But that's what the title of this Article promises, and that's what I intend to deliver. Second, the same paragraph provides a couple of long footnotes, quite out of character with the rest of the piece. These footnotes will look like strings of completely unrelated, randomly selected cases from federal and state courts. This is because they are strings of completely unrelated, randomly selected cases from federal and state courts. They are designed to provide weighty citations in your future work. You can give the appearance of having struggled with a group of difficult cases, or at least bask in the reflected glow of *my* hard work, by dropping a footnote that reads: *"See, e.g.,* Patrick M. McFadden, *Fundamental Principles of American Law*, 85 CALIF. L. REV. 1749, 1754 n.1 and cases cited therein." There are two such footnotes ahead, in case you need to show balance: *"But see id.* n.2 (citing further cases)." Third — and this is the heart of the piece — you will find a series of high-minded phrases and patently obvious facts. These passages are arranged in roughly the order you will need them in any future article, beginning with your topic's importance to the life of the nation and concluding with profound reflections on law and society. As could be expected, these high-minded phrases and patently obvious facts often run at cross-purposes, and frequently contradict each other entirely. You will, therefore, need to make substantial use of ellipses when you lift your quotes.

Now listen. If our little plan here is going to work, we all have to pretend that we didn't see the first part of this Article. We have to pretend, from now on, that I have written a carefully conceived, thoroughly researched article that seeks to plumb the very foundations of American law. It is therefore crucial that you *razor out everything in this Article between the title* (leave my name) *and the end of this paragraph.* The editors and I have even taken the precaution of beginning the next paragraph with footnote number one ("1"),[17] so we are pretty certain that the subterfuge will work. Now dig

---

15. Fred R. Shapiro, *The Most-Cited Law Review Articles,* 73 CALIF. L. REV. 1540 (1985).

16. Which explains its apparent lapse in judgment in accepting this piece: everyone has a price. *Cf.* Johann Wolfgang von Goethe, FAUST (Barker Fairley trans., Univ. Toronto Press 1970) (1808) (recounting German citizen's regrets over bad deal).

17. *See infra* note 1 (a law review first).

around for that razor from your first year of law school and get to work. Do it now.

* * *

American law is founded on a series of factual premises, political axioms, and juridical principles that are seldom stated explicitly but that infuse and inform our legal discourse.[1] In this Article, I will canvass those premises, axioms, and principles[2] and, by collecting them all in one place, lay the groundwork for later studies. Such studies, crucial to our understanding of American law, will not only map the hermeneutical and epistemological relations between the premises, axioms, and principles, but will subject them, both individually and collectively, to internal as well as external critique.

I

There is nothing so important, nothing so worthy of serious study, as the law's treatment of the family. There is nothing so important, nothing so worthy of serious study, as the law's treatment of commerce. There is nothing so important, nothing so worthy of serious study, as the law's treatment of public wrongs, private wrongs, public power, private power, private property, international relations, race relations, gender relations, and the stewardship of natural resources.

---

1. *See, e.g.,* Barenblatt v. United States, 360 U.S. 109, 134 (1959) (holding that Congressional witness could properly be convicted of contempt for refusing to answer questions about his affiliations with Communist Party); Partee v. San Diego Chargers Football Co., 668 P.2d 674, 675–76 (Cal. 1984) (determining that state antitrust law does not apply to interstate activities of professional football team); Wieser v. Missouri Pac. R.R. Co., 456 N.E.2d 98, 104-05 (Ill. 1983) (reversing lower court's refusal to grant defendant's *forum non conveniens* motion); State v. Galloway, 708 P.2d 508, 513 (Kan. 1985) (deciding that criminal defendant was given a speedy trial); Miller v. Catholic Diocese, 728 P.2d 794, 797 (Mont. 1986) (affirming dismissal of teacher's wrongful discharge complaint against operator of parochial school); People v. Rodriguez, 424 N.Y.S.2d 600, 608 (Sup. Ct. 1979) (granting lawyer-priest's motion for permission to wear clerical garb while defending client in court).

2. *See, e.g.,* The Paquete Habana, 175 U.S. 677, 700 (1900) (declaring that international law is part of United States law); The Fairisle, 76 F. Supp. 27, 31 (D. Md. 1947) (determining amount and distribution of salvage award for refloating of ship), *aff'd sub. nom* Waterman S.S. Corp. v. Dean, 171 F.2d 408 (4th Cir. 1948); Wakefield v. Little Light, 347 A.2d 228, 237–38 (Md. 1975) (upholding lower court judgment refusing jurisdiction over custody of Native American child found domiciled on reservation in Montana); Clechale & Polles, Inc. v. Smith, 295 So. 2d 275, 277 (Miss. 1974) (holding that landlord's election to treat holdover tenant as trespasser could not later be changed to treat holdover as tenant for new term); McBride v. Clayton, 166 S.W.2d 125, 130 (Tex. Comm'n App. 1942) (deciding that dissolved corporation had lost insurable interest in decedent executive before executive's death and that former shareholders were not permitted to share in insurance proceeds).

II

This study is important because the law of torts, property, contracts, decedents' estates, and commercial enterprise, as well as civil procedure, criminal procedure, and our revenue laws, say something important about us as a society. The message is clouded, however, because the law of torts, property, contracts, decedents' estates, and commercial enterprise, as well as civil procedure, criminal procedure, and our revenue laws, have been buffeted by the winds of change.

III

Our society has grown increasingly diverse. Our society has grown increasingly complex. Our lives have grown increasingly complex. The rate of social and political change has escalated dramatically. The world is getting smaller. Income disparities between rich and poor grow ever-wider. Western hegemony is fast disappearing. The end is near.

IV

The law, however, has not adapted. The law has adapted more slowly than we might have wished. The law wisely resists every transitory change in the social wind.

V

Yet the law must always adapt to new conditions or be rendered irrelevant or worse. At the same time, men and women arrange their affairs on the basis of the laws as they stand, even those of dubious wisdom, and such laws cannot be changed without overturning well-settled expectations and disrupting important legal relations.

VI

In the final analysis, the law must be fair. Our efforts to ensure the law's clarity and predictability can never justify unfairness in the individual case. In the final analysis, the law must be clear and predictable, even at the expense of individual litigants. Without clarity and predictability, the law becomes corrosively unfair to us all.

VII

The ordinary meaning of a word or phrase must be given effect. To do otherwise risks interpretive chaos and impermissibly shifts law-making authority from the statehouse to the courthouse. The surest way to misread a law is to read it literally.

VIII

Overturning precedent destabilizes long-settled expectations and cuts against the rule of law. Blind adherence to precedent can never be justified.

IX

All law is politics. In one sense, of course, all law is politics, but they are not exactly the same. Law and politics, while related, are different fields of human endeavor. Despite the reductionist impulse to collapse law into politics, they have little to do with each other. The law stands on its own, as it must.

X

American law has been disfigured by endemic racism, sexism, ethnocentrism, xenophobia, homophobia, and the imperialistic demands of mature capitalism. "Systemic" critiques of American law are based on a category mistake: particular laws, but not all law, can be characterized as racist, sexist, ethnocentric, xenophobic, homophobic, or imperialistic. We have come a long way. We still have a long way to go.

XI

The law has stunted economic growth and hampered free exchange. Economically inefficient laws are bad laws. Economic concerns are important, but not decisive. Economic concerns are relevant, but they are always trumped by non-economic values. Economic analysis is simply irrelevant.

XII

The sun rises in the east and sets in the west. It's always several hours later in Europe. Tomorrow is another day.

* * *

Now get back to work, and worry about something more important.

VI. Bibliography

A Compendium of Clever and Amusing Law Review Writings: An Idiosyncratic Bibliography of Miscellany with in Kind Annotations Intended As a Humorous Diversion for the Gentle Reader[*]

Thomas E. Baker[**]

TABLE OF CONTENTS

[*] Copyright © 2002 by Thomas E. Baker. All rights reserved.
[**] Professor and member of the founding faculty, Florida International University College of Law; former James Madison Chair in Constitutional Law and former Director, Constitutional Law Center, Drake University Law School (1998–2002); B.S. 1974 Florida State University; J.D. 1977 University of Florida; thomas.baker@fiu.edu. The author thanks Todd E. Chelf, John P. Danos, William J. Miller, and Lindsey A. Moore for their research assistance.

I. Introduction

A few explanatory comments are in order to introduce this Compendium. The world of the American law review resembles Middle Earth for all its strange inhabitants, secret rituals, and foreboding folklore.[1] Perhaps the only thing to rival its alternate reality is the virtual reality of the Internet.[2] The depth and breadth of law review literature defies facile characterization, but it can be stated without fear of contradiction that the truly clever or amusing law review article is the quintessential *rara avis*. Law review articles—and the people who write them and the people who read them—are serious to a fault.[3] Indeed, whenever a judge, a lawyer, a law professor, or a law student writes something truly funny he or she runs the risk of waking up days later, in restraints and sedated in a little room with a fellow in a white coat holding a clipboard.[4] Their day-to-day livelihood simply is not too lively, either in style or content. I believe this professional reality makes the occasional humorous article that much more of a treasure to behold. My purpose here is to collect and display these writings first, so that my reader might simply enjoy them and second, so that their authors might receive some deserved recognition.

Compiling a list of clever and amusing law review writings is not an easy task, certainly not one that can be accomplished logically or linearly. My criteria cannot be articulated with any specificity or precision. I could claim that I searched for writings that fit my title; in fact, I settled on my title after my search was completed. These articles *are* clever or amusing to me and, I hope

---

1. Russell Korobkin, *Ranking Journals: Some Thoughts on Theory and Methodology*, 26 Fla. St. U. L. Rev. 851 (1999); William R. Slomanson, *Legal Scholarship Blueprint*, 50 J. Legal Educ. 431 (2000); Reinhard Zimmerman, *Law Reviews: A Foray Through a Strange World*, 47 Emory L. J. 659 (1998); Nathan H. Saunders, Note, *Student-Edited Law Reviews: Reflections and Responses of an Inmate*, 49 Duke L.J. 1663 (2000).

2. *Compare* Bernard J. Hibbits, *Last Writes? Reassessing the Law Review in the Age of Cyberspace*, 71 N.Y.U. L. Rev. 615 (1996) (finding that the use of online services and electronic law journals correct some of the problems of traditional law reviews, but leave most of the criticisms unaddressed), *with* Aside, *Challenging Law Review Dominance*, 149 U. Pa. L. Rev. 1601 (2001) (discussing the modern trend of the Internet replacing law reviews as the medium for legal discourse). *See generally Constitutional Law Symposium*, 49 Drake L. Rev. 391 (2001) (discussing various constitutional law issues surrounding Internet usage).

3. *See* Thomas E. Baker, *Tyrannous Lex*, 82 Iowa L. Rev. 689, 712 (1997) ("[L]aw reviews are to law what masturbation is to sex"); Kenneth Lasson, *Scholarship Run Amok: Excesses in the Pursuit of Truth and Tenure*, 103 Harv. L. Rev. 926, 928 (1990) ("The system is askew. The academy has a problem.").

4. *But see* Thomas E. Baker, *A Review of Corpus Juris Humorous*, 24 Tex. Tech L. Rev. 869 (1993) (discussing Thomas E. Baker's Top Ten List of the Most Clever Judicial Opinions).

and trust, most people will find something here that is funny. If not, I respectfully submit my reader may be a likely occupant of that little room with the white-coated fellow with his clipboard. Certainly, *he* would not laugh at anything here.

To call my bibliographical techniques a research strategy would be an exaggeration.[5] My research assistants and I worked over the usual suspects. The *Index to Legal Periodicals* includes the topic "Legal Humor," although entries often are few and far between.[6] We minded previously-published bibliographies[7] and law review symposia.[8] We mined the footnotes of articles on the subject of legal humor.[9] We performed various and sundry online searches too numerous to recount, using Westlaw and LEXIS-NEXIS. We walked up and down the law review stacks in the library, thumbing through selected journals and law reviews, like the *American Bar Journal, The Journal of Legal Education*, and *Green Bag 2d*, searching for the proverbial needles. We ran down leads that were posted in response to our queries on Discussion List Serves by participants who did not have anything better to do.[10] We launched our Internet browsers determinedly and indeterminately, leaving postings along the way to mark the return path back here.[11] We tried our best to search out clever and amusing articles anywhere and everywhere we could think to look. It does say something about legal education and the legal profession, however, that there is no such thing as the *Journal of Legal Humor*.[12]

This was a diversion, to be sure, but a challenging diversion, most certainly, and I hope in turn it will be a diversion that my gentle reader will find en-

---

5. *See generally* Mary Beth Beazley & Linda H. Edwards, *The Process and the Product: A Bibliography of Scholarship About Legal Scholarship*, 49 Mercer L. Rev. 741 (1998).

6. *See, e.g.*, 39 Index to Legal Periodicals & Books 830 (Richard A. Dorfman ed., 2000).

7. *See, e.g.*, Edward J. Bander, *A Survey of Legal Humor Books*, 19 Suffolk U. L. Rev. 1065 (1985); Edward J. Bander, *Legal Humor Dissected*, 75 Law Libr. J. 289 (1982); James D. Gordon III, *A Bibliography of Humor and the Law*, 1992 BYU L. Rev. 427.

8. *See, e.g.*, Symposium, *Nova [Humor in the] Law Review*, 17 Nova L. Rev. 661 (1993); *Symposium on Humor and the Law*, 1992 BYU L. Rev. 313.

9. *See, e.g.*, J.T. Knight, *Humor and the Law*, 1993 Wis. L. Rev. 897.

10. The author thanks several unnamed members of the LawProf discussion list-serv for their nominations.

11. *See McClurg's Legal Humor Headquarters at* http://www.lawhaha.com.

12. *See* Tracey E. George & Chris Guthrie, *An Empirical Evaluation of Specialized Law Reviews*, 26 Fla. St. U. L. Rev. 813 (1999) (discussing the specialization of law reviews and journals and listing the areas of specialization, of which, humor is not included). *But see* Ronald L. Brown, *Rave Reviews: The Top Ten Law Journals of the 1990s*, 12 Legal Reference Servs. Q. 121 (1992) (predicting, humorously, that the top ten law journals of the 1990s will be highly specialized).

joyable and entertaining and perhaps even useful. This definitely is a keeper. Put a copy in your "Humor File." If you do not have such a file, start one. Everyone, especially someone like you who reads law reviews, needs a "Humor File" to pull out and enjoy from time to time. For ready reference, the entries are loosely categorized under ten headings: Biography; Book Reviews; Case Studies; Constitutional Law; Contracts; Law Practice; Legal Education; Legal Humor; Legal Scholarship; and Miscellany. Each entry appears only once.

This bibliography is incomplete, of course, and penultimately I offer my sincere apology to any authors whose clever or amusing writings were overlooked. Finally, I also offer my insincere apology to any authors whose writings are included here but who were not in fact trying to be clever or amusing.

II. Biography

William D. Araiza et al., *The Jurisprudence of Yogi Berra*, 46 EMORY L.J. 697 (1997): Compiles the wit and wisdom of Yogi Berra, Hall of Fame Major League Baseball player and coach; applies Berra's quotes to various areas of the law including, for example, "If you ask me anything I don't know, I'm not going to answer" as it applies to the doctrine of judicial abstention, "If people don't want to come to the ballpark, nobody's going to stop them" as a maxim for civil rights jurisprudence, and "It gets late early out there" as an illustration of the midnight deadline rule for collecting banks.

Edward J. Bander, *Holmespun Humor*, 10 VILL. L. REV. 92, 503 (1964–1965): Collects numerous humorous anecdotes about Supreme Court Justice Oliver Wendell Holmes, Jr.; Holmes was the kind of person who laughed at others far more easily than he laughed at himself.

Ronald Collins, *Gilmore's Grant: Or the Life & Afterlife of Grant Gilmore & His Death*, 90 Nw. U. L. REV. 7 (1995): Provides a historical account of Grant Gilmore's contributions to the law with a comedic emphasis on his book *Death of Contract*; now *that* is an inherently funny subject.

David Currie, *The Most Insignificant Justices: A Preliminary Inquiry*, 50 U. CHI. L. REV. 466 (1983): Launches an examination of the factors that distinguish significant from insignificant members of the Supreme Court, and speculates about which Justice might be the least significant or most insignificant, singling out Justice Duvall for special honors; a study about the most insignificant law professor, however, would have to be book-length.

Frank H. Easterbrook, *The Most Insignificant Justice: Further Evidence*, 50 U. CHI. L. REV. 481 (1983): Extends Professor Currie's study of the insignificant Justices of the Supreme Court through statistical analysis; recognizes default winner — Justice Thomas Todd with fourteen opinions and an otherwise modest judicial tenure; Charles Alan Wright once repeated the story that a judge-friend of his had compared being appointed to the Supreme Court to being invited to spend the night on Cleopatra's barge — anticipation would quickly give way to anxiety/insecurity and eventually end in disappointment because one's imagination always exceeds reality in such matters.

Daniel A. Farber, *"Terminator 2 1/2": The Constitution in an Alternate World*, 9 CONST. COMMENT. 59 (1992): Describes an alternative constitutional reality as if James Madison died before he could author the Bill of Rights; counterfactual history is interesting, and it reminds us that writing history has more in common with writing a novel than we usually realize or historians care to admit.

Roy B. Herron, *The Best of Justices Joe Henry and John Wilkes: Supreme Humor*, 31 TENN. B.J. 26 (Mar./Apr. 1995): Reviews the works of two of Tennessee's most humorous state supreme court justices; one wonders just how many others there were; go Vols.

Alex Kozinski, *My Pizza with Ninó*, 12 CARDOZO L. REV. 1583 (1991): Recounts eating pizza with Supreme Court Justice Antonin Scalia; analogizes Scalia's approach to pizza with his "plain meaning" approach to the Constitution; and predicts Scalia will be remembered as one of the greatest Justices to serve on the Supreme Court; ordering a large ego with anchovies.

David Mellinkoff, *Who Is "John Doe?,"* 12 UCLA L. REV. 79 (1964): Speculates about the origin of John Doe as a fictitious name; offers several possibilities from a survey of the etymology of the word "doe"; everyone who is old enough, or who watches old movies on cable television, knows that Gary Cooper is the real John Doe.

Ronald Rychlak, *The Lighter Side of the Green Movement: The Three Stooges as Early Environmentalists*, 48 OKLA. L. REV. 35 (1995): Provides the definitive legal work on the Three Stooges, including their efforts to bring environmental concerns to society's attention; to a deconstructionist this is a critique of the illegitimate hierarchy of the tripartite system of separation of powers; "Whoop, whoop, whoop...Ouch!"

Adam Winkler & Joshua Davis, *Postmodernism and Dworkin: The View from Half-Court*, 17 NOVA L. REV. 799 (1993): Examines interpretive legal theories of Ronald Dworkin and postmodernists by applying them to the half-court rule of basketball; fans of basketball should call for a technical foul.

III. Book Reviews

Benjamin C. Bair, *Law School: A Survivor's Guide by James D. Gordon III*, 93 MICH. L. REV. 1261 (1995) (reviewing JAMES D. GORDON III, LAW SCHOOL: A SURVIVOR'S GUIDE (1994)): Styled after the book it reviews as a survivor's guide to book reviews; pokes fun at book reviewers; congratulates Professor Gordon on his humorous, but not disrespectful, look at law school and the legal profession; why should law school be treated better than Rodney Dangerfield?

Thomas E. Baker, *The Supreme Nonet*, 18 CONST. COMMENT. 291 (2001) (reviewing BARBARA A. PERRY, "THE SUPREMES:" ESSAYS ON THE CURRENT JUSTICES OF THE SUPREME COURT OF THE UNITED STATES (1999)): A rhymed review of a book of biographical essays about the nine Justices; there is nothing amusing about them, of course, the Justices and the essays; the review does manage to poke a little fun at them, but only good-naturedly and meaning no disrespect; still, leave this one off the resume; note to self—send reprints only to other smart-ass professors—this Article is strike *one*.

Thomas E. Baker, *A Review of Corpus Juris Humorous*, 24 TEX. TECH L. REV. 869 (1993) (reviewing JOHN B. MCCLAY & WENDY L. MATTHEWS, CORPUS JURIS HUMOROUS (1991)): Reviews a compilation of humorous opinions and related legal materials; debunks the dichotomy between serious and humorous writing; provides a Top Ten List of the Most Clever Judicial Opinions; this Article is strike *two*.

Ronald L. Brown, *Rave Reviews: The Top Ten Law Journals of the 1990s*, 12 LEGAL REFERENCE SERVS. Q. 121 (1992): Publishes an address delivered at the 1991 Conference of Law Reviews; predicts the rise of permanent jobs for law review editors in the 1990s; correspondingly projects the Top Ten Law Journals for the decade; includes *The Journal of Legal Acronyms, The Journal of the Jurisprudence of Fruit, The Joys of Jewish Cooking and the Law Journal, The Lyrical Law Review, The Journal of Original Manuscripts, The Journal of Legal Lingerie, Journal of Star-Paging, Journal of Law Au Naturel, Journal of Legal Repetition*, and *The Journal of Twilight Zoning*; remarkably overlooks *The Journal of Law Review Humor*.

Jim Chen, *Something Old, Something New, Something Borrowed, Something Blue*, 58 U. CHI. L. REV. 1527 (1991) (reviewing THE BLUEBOOK: A UNIFORM

System of Citation (15th ed. 1991)): Offers a good-humored but pointed critique of the 15th edition of *The Bluebook*; includes a review of new *Bluebook* rules, *Bluebook* history, and *Bluebook* politics; hey, dude, *ALWD* rules!

James D. Gordon III, *Oh No! A New Bluebook!*, 90 Mich. L. Rev. 1698 (1992) (reviewing The Bluebook: A Uniform System of Citation (15th ed. 1991)): Gives an in-depth look into the path-breaking citation styles featured in the 15th edition of *The Bluebook*; this is not about the useful *Bluebook*, the one that lists the value of used cars.

Erik M. Jensen, *The Empire Strikes Back: Outsiders and the Struggle Over Legal Education*, 52 Okla. L. Rev. 515 (1999) (reviewing Arthur Austin, The Empire Strikes Back: Outsiders and the Struggle Over Legal Education (1998)): Begins with the disclaimer that the reviewer is a colleague of the book's author and that he likes him, but is quick to point out that he is one of very few people who do; the book and the review are about the passing of the guard in legal education; different generations looking at each other over a great divide; the book subscribes to the empirically sound theory that most new ideas are bad; the review emphasizes that there is no particular reason to buy the book because the reader can simply check it out of the library — so much for the reviewer's claim to like the author.

Erik M. Jensen, *A Survivor's Guide to Law School*, 96 W. Va. L. Rev. 1191 (1994) (reviewing James D. Gordon III, Law School: A Survivors Guide (1994)): Asks and answers that question from time immemorial, "Aw, come on. What could a law professor at Brigham Young University — for chrissakes — say that is funny about law school (or about anything else, for that matter)?"

Erik M. Jensen, *The Heroic Nature of Tax Lawyers*, 140 U. Pa. L. Rev. 367 (1991) (reviewing John Grisham, The Firm (1991)): Applauds Grisham for giving tax lawyers an identity — any identity — but criticizes him for misrepresenting the life of a tax lawyer; in fact, most tax lawyers need to get a life.

Arthur Allen Leff, *Memorandum*, 29 Stan. L. Rev. 879 (1977) (reviewing Roberto Mangabeira Unger, Knowledge and Politics (1975)): Written in the form of a memorandum to Roberto Mangabeira Unger from the Devil; Unger ended the book being reviewed with the entreaty "Speak, God"; the review concludes, "If He exists, Me too"; this is further proof that God does not read law reviews, as if any further proof was needed.

James A. Lindgren, *Fear of Writing*, 78 Cal. L. Rev. 1677 (1990): Compares the *Texas Law Review Manual on Usage & Style* (6th ed. 1990) and Merriam-Webster's *New Dictionary of English Usage* (1989); concludes that it is disturbing to see how far Texans will go to avoid writing naturally and advises that "if you are just trying to write better English, don't buy the Texas Manual"; in the abstract, "Texas style" seems to qualify as an oxymoron.

Richard A. Posner, *Goodbye to the Bluebook*, 53 U. Chi. L. Rev. 1343 (1986) (reviewing The Bluebook: A Uniform System of Citation (14th ed. 1986)): Provides a scathing critique of *The Bluebook* and its rules; labels it a hypertrophy to legal citation; provides ample examples of excessive insistence on uniformity and, inter alia, "useless elaboration of citation form"; who is more likely to show up in DSM-IV under compulsive-neurotic—the editors of *The Bluebook* or reviewers of *The Bluebook*?; trick question.

Richard Weisberg, *How Judges Speak: Some Lessons on Adjudication in* Billy Budd, Sailor *with Application to Justice Rehnquist*, 57 N.Y.U. L. Rev. 1 (1982) (reviewing Herman Melville, Billy Budd, Sailor (1962)): Discusses the relevance of works of fiction to the law; examines the story of *Billy Budd, Sailor* for its legal lessons and cultural themes; applies these lessons and the concept of "considerate communication" to one of then-Justice Rehnquist's opinions; it is uncertain whether this Article made a big difference to the current Chief Justice who served in the Army as a weather observer and who eventually awarded himself gold stripes on the sleeves of his robe.

IV. Case Studies

Aside, *Don't Cry Over Filled Milk: The Neglected Footnote Three to* Carolene Products, 136 U. Pa. L. Rev. 1553 (1988): Focuses on a footnote other than the famous footnote four from *United States v. Carolene Products Co.*, 304 U.S. 144 (1938), as a springboard to a sarcastic and pun-filled look at the excessive use of footnotes; examines dairy jurisprudence as a part of bovine law (the *Carolene* case dealt with milk products); and speculates as to the extraterrestrial origin of *The Bluebook*; to attribute *The Bluebook* to extraterrestrials is to deny the existence of intelligent life in the universe; to admire *The Bluebook* is to deny the existence of intelligent life on Earth.

Allan Axelrod, *Was* Shylock v. Antonio *Properly Decided?*, 39 Rutgers L. Rev. 143 (1986): A dazzling display of microeconomic theory as it applies to the rule for imprisonment and starvation of debtors and the creditor's right to seize the debtor's corpse; concludes such practices are not good public policy; in his day, Shakespeare did not need to pick on lawyers; he had plenty of other villains to pick from among English royalty; things change as much as they stay the same.

David Gray Carlson, *Tales of the Unforeseen*, 27 HASTINGS L.J. 776 (1976): Cartoon panels depict the facts and reasoning in the famous *Palsgraf v. Long Island Railroad Co.*, 162 N.E. 99 (N.Y. 1928), case in torts; proximately humorous.

Do We Have to Know This for the Exam?, 7 CONST. COMMENT. 223 (1990): Borrowing a page from Andy Warhol's postmodern depictions of soup cans, this is a reproduction of the actual combinations of which Justices authored, joined, and dissented from which of the nine parts of the Supreme Court's opinion in *Georgia v. South Carolina*, 497 U.S. 376 (1990), a state boundary dispute case, no less and no more, in the Court's original jurisdiction.

Jared Tobin Finkelstein, Comment, *In re Brett: The Sticky Problem of Statutory Construction*, 52 FORDHAM L. REV. 430 (1983): Discusses the principles of statutory interpretation as applied to the official baseball rules; specifically, considers whether the American League President properly applied the rules in overturning the umpire's decision to disallow a home run because the batter's bat was covered with too much pine tar; the MLB rulebook resembles *The Bluebook* on many levels.

Lon Fuller, *The Case of the Speluncean Explorers*, 62 HARV. L. REV. 616 (1949): Publishes a decision by the Supreme Court of Newgarth in the year 4300; strictly speaking this classic Article is not law review humor, but it is so creative and clever and has become so famous that it is included here; *see, e.g.,* Stephen L. Pepper, *The Case of the Human Sacrifice*, 23 ARIZ. L. REV. 897 (1981); Ira P. Robbins, *Jurisprudence "Under-Mind"?: The Case of the Atheistic Solipsist*, 28 BUFF. L. REV. 143 (1979).

James D. Gordon III, *Free Exercise on the Mountaintop*, 79 CAL. L. REV. 91 (1991): Criticizes the decision in *Employment Division v. Smith*, 494 U.S. 872 (1990), through the author's favored technique of a dialogue, this time between a student and his spiritual teacher; seriously critiques what the author regards as the Court's emasculation of the Free Exercise Clause, but along the way has a lot of fun with the footnotes, replete with famous quotations, asides, and amusing digressions; should we say a prayer that the Justices will overrule themselves?

James D. Gordon III, *Interplanetary Intelligence About Promissory Notes as Securities*, 69 TEX. L. REV. 383 (1990): Comments on the Supreme Court decision in *Reves v. Ernst & Young*, 494 U.S. 56 (1990); outlines how to determine whether a promissory note is a security; analyzes the issue from the perspective of interplanetary aliens (Zoron and Monset); concludes that the Justices are indeed from another planet; according to the Constitution only the President has to be a natural-born citizen, so aliens can serve on the High Court; some have, but the government is not telling us which ones.

David Eccles Hardy, *Great Cases in Utopian Law*, 6 J. CONTEMP. L. 227 (1979): Presents the opinion of the Utopian High Court in *Rumplestilskin v. Beautiful Princess* (1691); next the handsome Prince will have business cards printed up to pass out instead of kisses.

Humor Guide, *The* Syufy *Rosetta Stone*, 1992 BYU. L. REV. 457: Gives the answer key to the over two hundred movie titles which Ninth Circuit Judge Alex Kozinski managed to work into the opinion in *United States v. Syufy Enterprises*, 903 F.2d 659 (9th Cir. 1990); this is truly an amazing feat; most federal judges do not even go to the movies.

Wayne R. LaFave, Mapp *Revisited: Shakespeare, J., and Other Fourth Amendment Poets*, 47 STAN. L. REV. 261 (1995): A leading expert on the Fourth Amendment analyzes the Supreme Court's famous decision in *Mapp v. Ohio*, 367 U.S. 643 (1961), in a series of opinions written as parodies in the style of famous poets, including William Shakespeare and Dr. Seuss; "Give me a P... Give me an R...Give me an I...Give me a V...Give me an A...Give me a C...Give me a Y...What's it spell?...Exclusionary Rule."

Kenneth Lasson, Rummel v. Estelle: *Mockingbirds Among the Brethren*, 18 AM. CRIM. L. REV. 441 (1981): Discusses the Supreme Court's Eighth Amendment decision in *Rummel v. Estelle*, 445 U.S. 263 (1980), through a poetic memorandum; describes the stresses and strains and frustration of the Justice who had to cast the deciding vote in the style of Edgar Allen Poe's poem *The Raven*; nevermore.

Jasper Bogus McClod & Pepe Le Peu, Note, *Legislative and Judicial Dynamism in Arkansas:* Poisson v. d'Avril, 22 ARK. L. REV. 724 (1969): Written as a spoof note on the imagined opinion of *Poisson v. d'Avril*; describes the Arkansas Court in a majority decision of 1–5 upholding a hypothetical statute which purported to repeal "all laws and parts of laws"; imagines the court interpreting the Act to repeal all Arkansas statutory laws and not *the* common law because of the use of the plural "laws" rather than the singular "law" in the Act; extols some specific side effects such as abolishing the statute making it a crime to drive blindfolded cattle.

Note, Regina v. Ojibway, 8 CRIM. L. QTRLY. 137 (1966): Parodies common law reasoning in matters of statutory interpretations to answer the issue whether a pony with feathers on its back is a small bird under the relevant statute; actually cited and relied on in *Stevens v. City of Louisville*, 511 S.W.2d 228, 230 (Ky. Ct. App. 1974); a classic that once was funny, i.e., on first reading back in law school.

Michael L. Richmond, *The Annotated* Cordas, 17 Nova L. Rev. 899 (1993): Offers a witty annotation to *Cordas v. Peerless Transportation Co.*, 27 N.Y.S.2d 198 (N.Y. City Ct. 1941); highlights the ironic disparity between the scholarly attention given to the decision in the contracts casebooks and the scant use of the case by courts in resolving real live disputes; one should be more concerned about lawyers who practice law from their law school class notes.

Ridgely Schlockverse III, *Mad Dogs and Englishmen:* Pierson v. Post *[A Ditty Dedicated to Freshman Law Students, Confused on the Merits]*, 17 Nova L. Rev. 857 (1993): Writing under a pen name, Professor Kenneth Lasson provides a legal and lyrical adaptation of Noel Coward's *Mad Dogs and Englishmen*; focuses on the real property case of *Pierson v. Post*, 3 Cai. R. 175 (N.Y. Sup. Ct. 1805); the poem is replete with witty footnotes.

Scott M. Solkoff, *If the Law is a Jealous Mistress, What Ever Happened to Pay Toilets? A Digest of the Legally Profound*, 17 Nova L. Rev. 715 (1993): Discusses off-the-wall legal theories from actual cases; includes attempts at suing the devil, complaints that female prison guards do not wear enough clothing, and claims that a prisoner had been injected with an electric beam causing him to receive voices inside his head; concludes with a commentary on the demise of the pay toilet.

Special Feature, *We Stoop to Comment, 367 F. Supp. 373 (E.D. Pa. 1973)*, 12 Duq. L. Rev. 717 (1974): Provides a poetic comment on the decision and the reporting of *Mackensworth v. American Trading Transportation Co.*, 367 F. Supp. 373 (E.D. Pa. 1973), in which the District Judge and the West Keynote writer rhymed their work; someone has a lot of time on their hands; perhaps, they should try their hand at compiling a bibliography of humorous law review articles.

Three Theorems on Judicial Review, 2 Const. Comment. 5 (1985): Satisfies the author's yearning for the precision of formal logic by using provable and disprovable theorems for "the first truly elegant proof that *Marbury* [*v. Madison*, 5 U.S. 137 (1803)] was right"; thus, exorcising the ghost of Justice John Bannister Gibson of the Pennsylvania Supreme Court whose critical but never read opinion, is cited in every Con Law casebook ever written, Eakin v. Raub, 12 Sargeant & Rawle 330 (Pa. 1825); at his confirmation hearing before the Senate Judiciary Committee, Antonin Scalia refused to discuss *Mar-*

bury v. Madison in case the issue of judicial review comes before him in the future; it makes you wonder just what an originalist would do if an originalist had it all to do over again; just what was the original intent of original intent?

V. Constitutional Law

Aside, *The Common Law Origins of the Infield Fly Rule*, 123 U. Pa. L. Rev. 1474 (1975): Analogizes the development and application of baseball's infield fly rule with the development and application of the common law through time immemorial; identifies four factors involved in the development; hypothesizes that both share significant elements; a classic parody of the entire genre of the law review note.

Arthur Austin, *The Dark Side of the Second Amendment*, 4 Green Bag 2d 229 (2001): Begins with the observation that "true eccentrics alternate between irascible foolishness and profound revelation"; the rest of the Article—and the Second Amendment—is somewhere in-between.

Boris I. Bittker, *The Bicentennial of the Jurisprudence of Original Intent: The Recent Past*, 77 Cal. L. Rev. 235 (1989): Gives a "futuristic" look to 1996, the bicentennial of original intent; outlines famous "cases" since the bicentennial, e.g., the *Corporate Due Process* case in which the Fifth Amendment's guarantee of Due Process was limited to the framers' original intent that it did not apply to corporations; explains that since these cases had been decided, litigation regarding precedential decisions brought into question by these new cases has dramatically increased forcing the need to decide what materials can be relied upon to determine the framers' intent and what principles should govern whether the now questionable precedents should stand; ends with the historical stand-off between the Special Master appointed in the case going unpaid until the Supreme Court advises on the reconciliation of the *Legal Tender* cases with the doctrine of original intent, and the Supreme Court declining to render an advisory opinion until the Special Master decides whether the Supreme Court can render advisory opinions.

David P. Bryden, *The Devil's Casebook*, 3 Const. Comment. 313 (1986): Provides an essay on cynicism; lists constitutional law cases and concepts annotated in the manner of cynic Ambrose Bierce's *Devil's Dictionary* (1911); each entry contains one or more irreverent one-liners, e.g., "*United States v. Ballard*—If you talk to God, you are praying; if God talks to you, you have schizophrenia. Thomas Szasz."

Jim Chen, *Rock 'N' Roll Law School*, 12 CONST. COMMENT. 315 (1995): Connects themes found in Supreme Court jurisprudence with messages found in rock 'n' roll lyrics; if you read this Article backwards, it says "Rehnquist is Satan"; no, wait, that is another recent article read forwards.

Jim Chen, *The Constitutional Law Songbook*, 11 CONST. COMMENT. 263 (1994): A collection of songs covering important constitutional issues such as political speech, separation of powers, due process, and strict interpretation; provides whimsical lyrics to be sung to familiar tunes; the only problem is that most con law profs are tone deaf.

John P. Elwood, *What Were They Thinking: The Supreme Court in Revue, October Term 1999*, 4 GREEN BAG 2D 27 (2000): A critical analysis of a term that pundits analyzed and discussed *ad naseum*; but according to the author at some level it was an "unexceptional term"; humorous analysis of each Justices' performances and opinions, except for Justice Kennedy who "neither wrote nor did anything that could make him the object of fun"; always remember that there are nine Justices but there were only three stooges.

Jesse I. Etelson, State v. Raskolnikov, 42 N.Y.U. L. REV. 223 (1967): Imagines a hypothetical opinion of the Supreme Court of the state of South Nikita; applies the *Miranda v. Arizona*, 384 U.S. 436 (1966), analysis to a murder and robbery where the facts of the crime are those told by Dostoyevsky in the famous *Crime and Punishment*; the hypothetical names of the hypothetical justices writing the opinions phonetically recreate the author's last name; rumor has it that the author had to have his name legally changed to make the Article work but it was his tenure piece.

Daniel A. Farber, *An Economic Analysis of Abortion*, 3 CONST. COMMENT. 1 (1986): Carries Richard A. Posner's suggestion of market for babies one step farther (retroactively) by applying Law and Economics to abortion; hypothesizes that a representative could be appointed on behalf of a fetus to bid against its parents in their decision to abort; explains that an economic approach to abortion is the only approach to give full weight to both the interests of both the parents and the fetus.

York Moody Faulkner, Comment, *A Negative Incentive Based Proposal for Campaign Finance Reform: Lessons from Nottingham*, 1992 BYU L. REV. 493: Provides a tongue-in-cheek reminder of the difficulty of obtaining needed political reform; proposes a campaign finance method with the key element being a tax on gross campaign receipts that curbs excessive fund raising and also creates a fund to assist the poorer candidates; "Hey, Buddy, can you spare a few million?"

Richard H. Field, Comment, *Frankfurter, J., Concurring...*, 71 HARV. L. REV. 77 (1957): Details a poetic exercise of Justice Frankfurter's famous Plimsoll line of due process in *Fikes v. Alabama*, 352 U.S. 191, 199 (1957) (Frankfurter, J., concurring); Frankfurter made fun of his colleagues in his diary knowing it would be published posthumously although he did not have much of a sense of humor about himself; perhaps he was right that there was nothing funny about him.

John J. Flynn, *A Comment on "The Common Law Origins of the Infield Fly Rule,"* 4 J. CONTEMP. L. 241 (1978): A response to Aside, *The Common Law Origins of the Infield Fly Rule*, 123 U. PA. L. REV. 1474 (1975); critiques the Aside's approach and develops several alternative interdisciplinary approaches to the subject of the infield-fly rule; both the Aside and this response were written in the off season when the authors did not have anything better to do.

James D. Gordon III, *An Unofficial Guide to the Bill of Rights*, 1992 BYU L. REV. 371: Explains the first ten amendments through everyday application; e.g., Establishment Clause prohibits religious displays by government unless accompanied by Rudolph the Red-Nosed Reindeer; although not as breathless, this version is better than Melanie Griffith's version in the remake of the movie *Born Yesterday*.

Jack Achiezer Guggenheim, *The Evolution of Chutzpah as a Legal Term: The Chutzpah Championship, Chutzpah Award, Chutzpah Doctrine, and Now the Supreme Court*, 87 KY. L.J. 417 (1999): Tracks the use of the Yiddish word "chutzpah" in judicial opinion writing and legal doctrine; comments on the history of Yiddish and Jewish American lawyers in the practice of law; marks Justice Scalia's ground breaking use of "chutzpah" in *National Endowment for the Arts v. Finley*, 524 U.S. 569, 597 (1998) (Scalia, J., concurring), as the first employment of the word in the official reporter of the High Court; this also is the title of *one* of Alan "the-'M'-does-not-stand-for-'Modest'" Dershowitz's autobiographies.

Erik S. Jaffe, *"She's Got Bette Davis['s] Eyes": Assessing the Nonconsensual Removal of Cadaver Organs Under the Takings and Due Process Clauses*, 90 COLUM. L. REV. 528 (1990): Nothing funny about this Article or its subject, certainly; but the title merits inclusion here; *hear generally* J. DESHANNON & D. WEISS, BETTE DAVIS EYES (EMI Records 1981).

Erik M. Jensen, *16th Century 19th Amendment Jurisprudence*, 4 GREEN BAG 2D 465 (2001): *Cf.* next entry.

Erik M. Jensen, *19th Century 16th Amendment Jurisprudence*, 3 Green Bag 2d 241 (2000): *Cf.* previous entry.

Maurice Kelman, *Is the Constitution Worth Legal Writing Credit?*, 44 J. Legal Educ. 267 (1994): Purportedly discovered in the archives at the College of William & Mary; a memorandum to George Wythe; there is no record that James Madison or Gouverneur Morris were given academic credit for their efforts at framing the Constitution; does not shed any light on why it takes two witnesses to convict for treason.

Andrew J. McClurg, *A Day in the Life of Justice Antonin Scalia*, ATLA Docket (Ark. Trial Lawyers Ass'n), Spring 1997, at 7: Presumably an unauthorized account of Justice Scalia careening through his day and other people; reveals a tongue-in-cheek portrait of this most colorful Justice; the Justice himself, of course, would prefer a color-blind portrait.

Michael Stokes Paulsen, *Is Bill Clinton Unconstitutional? The Case for President Strom Thurmond*, 13 Const. Comment. 217 (1996): Applies the premise of a "living constitution" to the minimum age qualification for the presidency; argues that the constitutional provision should be understood to have evolved with advancements in medicine and longer life spans, resulting in a contemporary minimum qualification of approximately fifty-nine years of age; applies that age minimum to the line of succession to conclude that Senator Strom Thurmond was the lawful President at the time of the writing; that makes sense because James Madison liked Thurmond when he was a kid.

Norman Redlich, *A Black-Harlan Dialogue on Due Process and Equal Protection: Overheard in Heaven and Dedicated to Robert B. McKay*, 50 N.Y.U. L. Rev. 20 (1975): Details a dialogue between Justices Black and Harlan in heaven; imagines the former extolling the virtues of and defending his strict constructionist/absolutist view of the Constitution, and the latter advocating a due process approach to deciding constitutional issues; illustrates the two Justices' respective views by discussing many of the Court's significant decisions, including some decided after their deaths, e.g., Roe v. Wade, 410 U.S. 959 (1973); Furman v. Georgia, 409 U.S. 902 (1972).

Norman Redlich, *The Supreme Court—1833 Term—Foreword: The Constitution—"A Rule for the Government of Courts, as Well as of the Legislature,"* 40 N.Y.U. L. Rev. 1 (1965): Parodies the *Harvard Law Review*'s annual "Foreword" by critiquing the important decisions of the Marshall Court and its excesses in enhancing its own importance and expanding federal powers; mocks academic hubris by concluding that the Marshall court and its Chief Justice would pass into "the judicial obscurity which they so richly deserve"; can a foreword be too forward?

Aviam Soifer, *Confronting Deep Strictures: Robinson, Rickey, and Racism*, 6 CARDOZO L. REV. 865 (1985): Offers a deconstructionist view of the integration of Major League Baseball by the first African-American player, an event which may not have been as beneficial for his race as conventional wisdom would suggest; relies on baseball imagery to present baseball as a metaphor for life; for some fans life is a metaphor for baseball.

VI. Contracts

Douglass G. Boshkoff, *Selected Poems on the Law of Contracts*, 66 N.Y.U. L. REV. 1533 (1991): Provides twenty-nine limericks based on contract cases, the original manuscript of which was allegedly found in and is currently on file with the mythical Raintree County Memorial Library; these are the kind of limericks one expects to find in a law review, as opposed to a public restroom.

Jean Braucher, *The Afterlife of Contract*, 90 NW. U. L. REV. 49 (1995): Continues Grant Gilmore's *The Death of Contract* (1995); apparently there is life of contract after the death of contract; has nothing to do with the living Constitution.

James D. Gordon III, *Consideration and the Commercial-Gift Dichotomy*, 44 VAND. L. REV. 283 (1991): Critiques and predicts the eventual death of the doctrine of consideration in a sequel to his Article *A Dialogue About the Doctrine of Consideration*; continues the discussion of the doctrine of consideration; client proposes replacing the doctrine in the context of commercial promises with a theory of promises related to exchange of values; affords a great deal of consideration to consideration.

James D. Gordon III, *A Dialogue About the Doctrine of Consideration*, 75 CORNELL L. REV. 987 (1990): Imagines a dialogue between a hypothetical lawyer and a client president of a coal company who wants the lawyer to draft an amendment to a contract for the sale of coal; ends with the client suggesting the doctrine of consideration has little utility in the business world; the real issue is whether a lump of coal is equal to a peppercorn.

Marianne M. Jennings, *Does Secured Transaction Mean I Have a Lien? Thoughts on Chattel Mortgages (What?) and Other Complexities of Article IX*, 17 NOVA L. REV. 689 (1993): Cleverly takes the reader step-by-step through the process of creating a lien under UCC Article IX; offers commentary on the intricacies, complexities, and inanities of Article IX; provides a list of rules for surviving Article IX, including: Rely on counter help, never read Article IX, and never try to figure out where to file—just file everywhere and often.

Marianne M. Jennings, *I Want to Know What Bearer Paper Is and I Want to Meet a Holder in Due Course: Reflections on Instructions in UCC Articles Three and Four*, 1992 BYU L. REV. 385: Proposes Articles 3 and 4 of the UCC can be interesting material for law students; gives examples for law professors to give to their students; provides suggested ways for students to exercise their new knowledge and irritate/confuse/stump bank tellers; do not try this at an airport or else you will never clear security.

VII. Law Practice

Louis Auchincloss, *The Senior Partner's Ghosts*, 50 VA. L. REV. 195 (1964): Tells a fictional tale about the firm of de Grasse & Prime; Prime attempts to write a biography exposing the evil ways of his former partner and mentor de Grasse, Prime discovers that now it is he that has become the man that he so despises; happier endings apparently require more billable hours.

Thomas E. Baker, *2020 Year-End Report on the Judiciary by the Chief Justice of the United States*, 24 PEPP. L. REV. 859 (1997): Imagines the future of the U.S. Courts of Appeals in a future when caseload has undone all familiar procedures; includes the Coin Toss Calendar of the Court of Appeals for Las Vegas and the Scratch-an-Appeal cards from the Court of Appeals for Atlantic City; the author needs to get a life; *three* strikes and he is *out*.

Boris I. Bittker, *Tax Shelters for the Poor?*, 51 TAXES 68 (1973): A series of interoffice memoranda and I.R.S. filings and rulings by the fictitious Wall Street law firm trying to do *pro bono* tax planning for the poor, including taking an exemption for losses to coin-operated machines; making fun of lawyers, not the poor, although both will always be with us; indeed, if there are so many poor because God so loves them, then what could possibly explain why there are so many lawyers?

Neal Boortz, *Open Season on Lawyers*, 17 NOVA L. REV. 985 (1993): The complete text of a bill before the Georgia legislature to amend the general statutes to regulate the hunting of lawyers; this type of state legislation would be preempted by a proposed federal statute that would adjust the reciprocal trade quotas between Japan and the United States to offset imported Japanese automobiles with exported American lawyers.

Jess M. Brallier, *Life, Lawyers, and Book Royalties*, 17 Nova L. Rev. 767 (1993): Provides a short essay by the author of *Lawyers and Other Reptiles* (1992); recounts the author's observations about lawyers throughout life including the moment when the realization struck that life with lawyers is far worse than life without; records a high level of bemusement at having received hundreds of letters submitting lawyer jokes for a second edition of the book from self-effacing attorneys; the author did not hear back from any lawyers who effaced others.

Joe Butler et al., *Dedication to the South Dakota Lawyer: A Collection of Essays*, 40 S.D. L. Rev. 238 (1995): Addresses legal topics including legal civility, office workloads, mentoring, competency reviews, and the nature and history of the practice of law in South Dakota; does not address the effect on South Dakota if North Dakota does change its name.

Paul L. Caron, *Tax Myopia or Mamas Don't Let Your Babies Grow Up to Be Tax Lawyers*, 13 Va. Tax Rev. 517 (1994): Comments on the disparagement and misperception of tax attorneys in both popular and legal culture; observes the segregation of tax law as a detriment to the field; notes that initial exposure to the Internal Revenue Code causes students either to become completely enamored with tax or to avoid all tax issues for the rest of their careers; the former are the rarer, if not the more interesting cases.

David Cohn, Comment, *Snakes, Bananas and Buried Treasure: The Case for Practical Jokes*, 17 Nova L. Rev. 883 (1993): Tracks the jurisprudence of litigation over practical jokes that someone found less than funny; argues for a "theory of practical joke jurisprudence" in which the dispositive question is whether a "discerning viewer would find the joke funny?"; a truly discerning person understands that practical jokes separate the joker from the jokee.

Jay Dushoff, *Opening Statements and Final Arguments*, C975 ALI-ABA 363 (1995): Provides a humorous checklist designed to aid litigators with their opening and closing statements; more enjoyable than staying at a Holiday Inn Express to gain the same level of confidence and expertise.

Major Thomas Keith Emswiler, *Defying Precedent: The Army Writing Style*, 143 Mil. L. Rev. 224 (1994): Examines the state of poor legal writing; discusses how principles from the *Army Writing Style* can make for better writing in any context; "Ten-hut! Give me ten tight paragraphs."

Arthur Garwin, *When on Mars*, 17 Nova L. Rev. 941 (1993): Describes a fantastic version of the Martian rules of professional conduct for lawyers; includes standards like "a lawyer shall give a client at least as much timely information as the lawyer would hope to receive from a used car salesperson," and for expediting litigation "a lawyer shall treat every case as if the lawyer represents the plaintiff"; someone should write a book about how plaintiff lawyers are from Venus and defense lawyers are from Mars.

Marianne M. Jennings, *Buying Property from the Adams Family*, 22 REAL EST. L.J. 43 (1993): Humorously details issues of real property history; considers property histories involving deaths, criminal behavior, and communicable diseases; closes with "Jennings's Psychological Questions for Buyers Concerned About Prior Property Use and History" which includes such items as "[w]hy do neighborhood children with garlic around their necks race by this house screaming?" and "[w]hy have seventeen families lived in this house in the past eighteen months?"; why, indeed.

Erik M. Jensen, *A Monologue on the Taxation of Business Gifts*, 1992 BYU L. REV. 397: Provides a comic monologue discussing tax lawyers and business gifts; argues business gifts should not continue to have effect for federal income tax purposes; this will never appear on the Comedy Channel.

Arnold B. Kanter, *Ugly as SIN*, 17 NOVA L. REV. 763 (1992): Provides an excerpt from a special subcommittee of a law firm executive committee convened to address the lack of women employed with the firm; the all-male committee designates itself SIN, the Subcommittee on Institutional Non-discrimination; recounts the chauvinism of the members by recounting suggestions like women will have to leave trials to give birth, and this problem could be avoided by hiring only less attractive women; it is very self-revealing to have left out any and all discussion of the professional possibilities for less attractive men.

Alex Kozinski, *Trademarks Unplugged*, 68 N.Y.U. L. REV. 960 (1993): Criticizes trademark law by comparing our current system to "unplugged" music; almost disqualified from this bibliography for actually being about law.

Alex Kozinski, *The Wrong Stuff*, 1992 BYU L. REV. 325: Offers some finer points on how to lose an appeal; examples include: Cheating on the page limit of the brief with creative font and margin sizes, burying winning arguments, attacking the district judge, failing to attach or quote relevant statutory language, stonewalling the judges during oral arguments and interrupting their questions; when he turned down a seat on the Supreme Court, John G. Johnson, one of the great appellate lawyers of the 19th century, said, "I would rather talk to the damned fools than have to listen to them." Michael J. Hirrel, Book Review, 46 FED. COMM. L.J. 289 (1994).

Kenneth Lasson, *To Kill a Mockingbird: Stare Decisis and* M'Naghten *in Maryland*, 26 MD. L. REV. 143 (1966): Discusses how the *M'Naghten* test for insanity is an entrenched "pillar of jurisprudence" despite new formulations and modifications; the rule is likely to persist and survive; acknowledges the dilemma a Maryland judge may encounter in trying to decide whether to continue to uphold the use of the test through a clever poem modeled after Poe's "The Raven"; portrays the raven as a mockingbird imploring an appellate Justice to continue the use of the *M'Naghten* test; Boo Radley was not from Maryland, besides he was not the crazy one.

Paul A. LeBel, *The Bases Are Loaded and It's Time to Get a Restraining Order: The Confounding Conflation of America's Two National Pastimes*, 17 NOVA L. REV. 813 (1993): Examines the similarities between litigation and baseball all the way down to the sharing of pinstripes; imagines a news report from a not-too-distant future when litigiousness might run amok in baseball; but the sports pages today read like advance sheets already.

Peter Lushing, *The Exclusionary Rule: A Disputation*, 7 CARDOZO L. REV. 713 (1986): Details a hypothetical scene at a tavern during "decompression" hour after court in which an earnest young prosecutor and a die-hard defense attorney engage in a dialogue regarding the exclusionary rule; concludes with the prosecutor advocating the abolition of the rule and the defense attorney telling the prosecutor his problem is with the Fourth Amendment itself, not the exclusionary rule; both have been blacklisted from happy hour.

Maurice H. Merrill, *The Prophet's Mistake*, 11 OKLA. L. REV. 166 (1958): Provides a poem in which a judge locks up a man falsely claiming to be a prophet sent by God to influence the judge's decision in a criminal case; reasons that if the man had actually been sent by God, he would have known the correct trial procedures; reproduces the story originally told by Lord Campbell in *Lives of the Chief Justices of England* (1876); Pontius Pilate would say, "Been there. Done that."

Elmer M. Million, *Wills: Witty, Witless, and Wicked*, 7 WAYNE L. REV. 335 (1960): Reviews humorous wills including poetic wills, phonographic wills, and unusual bequests; another installment testators were dying to write.

Elmer M. Million, *Humor in or of Wills*, 11 VAND. L. REV. 737 (1958): Discusses humorous clauses in wills throughout history; none of the testators died laughing.

Myron Moskovitz, *The O.J. Inquisition: A United States Encounter with Continental Criminal Justice*, 28 VAND. J. TRANSNAT'L L. 1121 (1995): A play script comparing the United States and the civil-law European criminal justice system using the O.J. Simpson fact scenario; potential sponsors include Isotoner Gloves and Ginsu Knives.

Don Musser, *An Exposition on the Preparation and Use of Expert Testimony—A Satire*, 42 NEB. L. REV. 396 (1962): Provides a transcript of Judge Musser's comments to the Nebraska State Bar Association; questions the objectiveness of expert testimony; uses examples of experts in the fields of medicine, real estate, and S.O.B.'s; most judges can take judicial notice of S.O.B.'s, however.

Thomas W. Overton, *Lawyers, Light Bulbs, and Dead Snakes: The Lawyer Joke as Societal Text*, 42 UCLA L. REV. 1069 (1995): Analyzes the state of the legal profession in the United States; looks behind lawyer jokes to consider the problems that contribute to cynicism about the legal system; it can be said about lawyers that they are persons of average morality who deal with above-average temptations; philosophically speaking, however, there is so much cynicism in the world one has to wonder whether it will be enough.

Antonin Scalia, *Judicial Conference—Federal Circuit*, 128 F.R.D. 409, 452 (1989): Provides pointers on how to write an effective Supreme Court brief; includes a good many Ninograms; wait for his book *How to Write an Effective Dissent and Still Be Friends* (very forthcoming).

Antonin Scalia, *Judicial Proceeding—D.C. Circuit*, 124 F.R.D. 241, 283–88 (1989): Outlines the most and least admirable characteristics of appellate counsel to the D.C. Circuit; still waiting for the sequel about appellate judges.

Charles M. Sevilla, *Great Fractured Moments in Courtroom History*, 17 NOVA L. REV. 669 (1992): Provides twenty-four samples from the author's larger compilation of humorous, ridiculous, and absurd quotes from the courtroom, *Disorder in the Court* (1987); the fact that you can fool some of the people all of the time and all of the people some of the time is the foundational principle of the jury system.

Kathie J. Sullivan, *The Librarian as Archaeologist*, 89 LAW LIBR. J. 222 (1997): Recounts a day in the life of a law firm librarian; details the adventures of cleaning out files from years past; do not wait for the movie.

Frank G. Swain, *The Therapy of Humor in the Practice of Law*, 50 LAW LIBR. J. 200 (1957): Collects poems that are intended to remind both judges and lawyers that humor is important in the practice of law; lawyers in fact invented "happy hour" so that they could get it over with and get back to billing hours.

Erasmus Van Pasento (Robert S. Ryan), *The Dajongi Experience: A Comparative Study in Federal Jurisdiction*, 18 STAN. L. REV. 451 (1966): Traces the development of unsophisticated and pragmatic jurisdictional rules in the fictitious Dajong Republic; describes how the introduction of Western legal thought threatens a "cure" to the aberrant approach of this misguided nation; Grasshopper and Cricket go to law school.

Ralph Warner & Toni Ihara, *Becoming a Partner*, 17 NOVA L. REV. 951 (1993): Offers humorous tips on becoming a partner in a law firm; includes such tips as "plan to be born white, male and Protestant," "learn to order lunch in Italian," and finally, "save your money"; written after the authors went out on their own but, of course, it was a mutual decision between them and the firm.

D. Robert White, *Recruiting Letters*, 17 NOVA L. REV. 709 (1992): Offers help with interpreting what law firms really mean by recruitment letters they send; provides pairs of sample letters with each pair containing one letter reflecting what the firm actually wrote and the other explaining what was really meant; reading between the lines allows one to save face.

Charles Yablon, *Suing the Devil: A Guide for Practitioners*, 86 VA. L. REV. 103 (2000): Posits that litigation against Satan is "an idea whose time has come"; provides a legal history of Satan from the trial of Job to *The Devil and Daniel Webster* (Townsend Ludington ed., 1937); analyzes the Devil's weaknesses including his vulnerability in equity as the source of all evil; suggests fraud as a plausible cause of action against the Devil as he is the deceiver who "makes us all believe that we can be happy"; next, "the Devil made me do it" will be an allowable criminal defense.

VIII. Legal Education

Roger I. Abrams, *Law and the Chicken: An Eggs-Agerated Curriculum Proposal*, 17 NOVA L. REV. 771 (1993): Proposes building the first-year law curriculum in each subject around famous "chicken" cases, e.g., *Frigaliment Importing Co. v. B.N.S. International Sales Corp.*, 190 F. Supp. 116 (S.D.N.Y. 1960), in which Judge Friendly asks that seminal—or is it ovular—question, "what is chicken?"

Aside, *Challenging Law Review Dominance*, 149 U. PA. L. REV. 1601 (2001): Examines the societal shift from paper to server to argue that websites that seek to replace law reviews by publishing scholarly articles on the Internet "tend to suck"; Beavis and Butthead are elected to the Board of Editors of the law review.

Arthur Austin, *Law Professor Salaries*, 2 Green Bag 2d 243 (1999): Expresses a profound concern about the threat to higher salaries being posed by the de-objectification of legal scholarship by tenured radicals; law professors should dance with the scholarship that brought them to the academic dance in the first place; pass the doctrine and pour me another martini.

Arthur Austin, *The Alchemy of Promotion and Tenure*, 75 Denv. U. L. Rev. 1 (1997): This story illustrates in all its infamy the law school gamesmanship practiced by faculty members over promotion and tenure; read it to find out how it turns out.

Arthur Austin, *Scoff Law School Debates Whether a Male Can Teach a Course in Feminist Jurisprudence*, 18 J. Legal Prof. 203 (1993): Explores the Byzantine politics of law school faculties through a fictional account; prudently does not address the critical question of whether a law professor—of either sex/gender—has to be a jurisprude to teach jurisprudence.

Daniel H. Benson, *The You Bet Metaphorical Reconstructionalist School*, 37 J. Legal Educ. 210 (1987): Boldly, at the time, deconstructs and mocks critical legal studies; what is a little jargonized, illegitimate, hierarchical hegemony among friends?

Paul Bergman, *2010: A Clinical Odyssey*, 1992 BYU L. Rev. 349: Describes a hypothetical faculty meeting; details a dialogue (set to the tune of various songs) of debate over clinical teaching versus case method between those arch-protagonists Roberto Unger and Carl Rogers; Roger Miller would never go near a law school.

C. Steven Bradford, *Random Questions About Law School and the Law: The World's First Socratic Law Review Article*, 78 Neb. L. Rev. 587 (1999): Once reserved for the classroom, the Socratic method reaches out from the pages of a law review; includes topical questions with the answers provided in footnotes; "Why isn't the corporation a parent corporation owns called a child corporation?" Answer: "Is it because we consider children subsidiary?"; this is reminiscent of the stand-up comedy style of Stephen Wright ("What is another word for *Thesaurus*?").

C. Steven Bradford, *Ten Reasons to Attend Law School*, 1993 BYU L. Rev. 921: The tenth reason to attend law school is to support law professors "who, because of their various personality disorders and sartorial problems, are otherwise unemployable"; indeed, in cities with more than one law school, polyesters are endangered species.

C. Steven Bradford, *The Gettysburg Address as Written by Law Students Taking an Exam*, 86 Nw. U. L. Rev. 1094 (1992): Illustrates various exam-writing inadequacies of law students through hypothetical "answers" to a hypothetical exam question asking students to write the opening line of *The Gettysburg Address*; concludes that even more people could be insulted in text and footnote if the author had taken more time, but also admits that law professors deserve little credit for writing exam questions that elicit such answers; this Article was written when the author should have been grading blue books.

Art Buchwald, *Commencement Day Address*, 27 Cath. U. L. Rev. 1 (1977): Reprints the commencement speech of this noted humorist who concludes that he could have said something profound, but his audience would have forgotten it in ten minutes; therefore, he decided to give a speech that made them laugh before it was time to go home.

Anthony D'Amato, *Minutes of the Faculty Meeting*, 1992 BYU L. Rev. 359: Creates the hypothetical (or perhaps typical) minutes of a law school faculty meeting in which absolutely nothing is accomplished; the Marx Brothers get tenure.

Wylie H. Davis, *That Balky Law Curriculum*, 21 J. Legal Educ. 300 (1969): Considers the law school politics and difficulty of curriculum reform; proposes an entire curriculum of Mule Law, Mule Law I through Mule Law XXIX, with every course covering only cases which deal with mules, i.e., tort cases about mules, criminal law cases about mules, contract cases about mules, et cetera; if this Article were written today, it would suggest a web-based course on mules; as an aside, any veteran of academic wars will tell you that reforming the law school curriculum is as easy — and as satisfying — as moving a graveyard.

Daniel A. Farber, *The Jurisprudential Cab Ride: A Socratic Dialogue*, 1992 BYU L. Rev. 363: Describes a dialogue between a tired law professor and a cab driver who looks and sounds suspiciously like Socrates; begins when the cabbie asks the professor if he should obey the law just because he might get caught breaking it; ends with the professor admitting his theory of legal obligation is defective but that he is willing to walk the rest of the way home, through the snow, rather than suffer another question on the meter; surprisingly, the author is a law professor without any experience driving a taxi.

James D. Gordon III, *Humor in Legal Education and Scholarship*, 1992 BYU L. Rev. 313: Extols the virtues of humor to legal teaching and scholarship while acknowledging its risks; gives examples, and provides helpful and informative footnotes, e.g., "'[c]ondescending' means talking down to people." *Id.* at 314 n.10.

James D. Gordon III, *How Not to Succeed in Law School*, 100 YALE L. J. 1679 (1991): Offers an insider's insights on the law school experience; takes a somewhat jaundiced view of such topics as admissions, the first year, faculty, curriculum, exams, interviewing, and graduation; this Article actually is in the real *Yale Law Journal*.

Michael A. Heller, *The Cutting Edge of Poster Law*, 49 J. LEGAL EDUC. 467 (1999): Anyone who walks around a law school will recognize the art form of the law school poster; explores the law of posters and posters about the law; it is only a matter of time before someone founds the Britney Spears Law Student Association just for the poster.

Robert M. Jarvis, *If Law Professors Had to Turn in Time Sheets*, 86 CAL. L. REV. 613 (1998): A glimpse into the academic life gained from this fictitious daily log of a law professor's professional activities on the East Overshoe State Law School faculty; thirteen hours worth of incites (pun intended).

Erik M. Jensen, *Critical Theory and the Loneliness of the Tax Prof*, 76 N.C. L. REV. 1753 (1998): "Tax professors are the air-fresheners of the American law school"; "If a tax prof tries to talk about serious tax research with a bunch of law school generalists, the room clears out instantly"; this Article is critical of critical theory, in theory and in fact.

Erik M. Jensen, *Tough on Scholarship*, 39 WAYNE L. REV. 1285 (1993): Offers an account of hiring strategies and promotion and tenure standards at Sloth School of Law; given the fact that it was the first law school with a gardening clinic, "[t]here is mulch to be proud of at Sloth."

Ron Lansing, *Faculty Meetings: "A Quorum Plus Cramshaw,"* 17 NOVA L. REV. 817 (1992): Recounts the minutes from a faculty meeting as recorded by Head Faculty Secretary Cramshaw; this no-nonsense, old-fashioned secretary records the meeting with great care and parliamentary detail; the *minutia* of the minutes provide their own commentary on the typical dysfunctionality of faculty meetings; it is a little-known fact that the bromide "the whole does not equal the sum of its parts" was first said about a law school faculty meeting; it is a well-known fact that it applies to every faculty and all faculty meetings.

Paul A. LeBel, *The Law School Expansion Draft*, 43 J. LEGAL EDUC. 606 (1993): Imagines five hypothetical news articles reporting: First, President Clinton's intent to fulfill a campaign pledge of a law school in every state; second, Alaska's failed bid to buy and move a law school to the state; third, announcement of the Association of American Law Schools' plan for an expansion draft modeled after Major League Baseball's to staff newly established law schools; fourth, a riot at a law school precipitated by publication of the list of faculty to be protected in the upcoming draft; and fifth, law school dean and faculty's punditry about the fact that "mistakes were made"; *see supra* note ** (noting author's affiliation).

Paul A. LeBel, *Legal Education and the Theatre of the Absurd: "Can't Anybody Play This Here Game?,"* 1992 BYU L. REV. 413: Reveals the author's thoughts on legal education through a Socratic dialogue where indoctrination into the military is similar to beginning law school; illustrates the inertia of legal education through the fable "The Emperor with No Clothes"; the author later served as a dean for a short time and presumably got it out of his system.

Paul A. LeBel, *Law Professor Trading Cards—"Has Anyone Got a Monaghan for a Tribe?,"* 38 J. LEGAL EDUC. 365 (1988): "[G]ot 'em…got 'em…got 'em… need 'em…got 'em"; but one really has to wonder out loud whether anyone would be willing to trade a LeBel for a Baker in the first place?

James B. Levy, *Escape to Alcatraz: What Self-Guided Museum Tours Can Show Us About Teaching Legal Research,* 44 N.Y.L. SCH. L. REV. 387 (2001): Discusses the challenges of teaching legal research; suggests using an "Alcatraz" approach to teaching legal research which emulates prerecorded self-guided museum tours; argues that the "Alcatraz" method will excite and create interest in law students much like the Alcatraz prison tour does with non-felons; there is nothing funny about solitary confinement or *The Bluebook.*

Andrew J. McClurg, *Dear Employer…,* 47 J. LEGAL EDUC. 267 (1997): A letter of reference that sets up the student being referenced; the introduction to a letter a law professor would write for a student like Forrest Gump or Ted Bundy; the reader must fill-in the body of the letter.

Andrew J. McClurg, *Poetry in Commotion:* Katko v. Briney *and the Bards of First-Year Torts,* 74 OR. L. REV. 823 (1995): Uses the infamous *Katko v. Briney,* 197 N.W.2d 351 (Iowa 1972), spring gun case from Iowa to examine the stifling effect legal education and the Socratic method has on creativity; shares examples of his students' poems about the case; the author assigns his students to write poems about tort cases; what rhymes with course evaluations?

Sandra Craig McKenzie, *Law School: Preparation for Parenthood,* 37 J. LEGAL EDUC. 367 (1987): Provides a short dialogue between the author and her preschool children; demonstrates how parents can use legal analysis in relating to their children; one cannot imagine why *Parents Magazine* turned down the Article.

Robert W. Millar, *The Shade of Sir Edward Coke Reports the Baseball Game Played Between the Law School Faculty of Northwestern University and the Law Review Editorial Board on Tuesday, the 9th Day of May, 1939*, 54 Nw. U. L. Rev. 153 (1959): Reprints a description of the 1939 faculty-law review baseball game at Northwestern as it might have been codified by Sir Edward Coke; by the way, he mispronounced his own name "Cook."

James E. Moliterno, *On the Future of Integration Between Skills and Ethics Teaching: Clinical Legal Education in the Year 2010*, 46 J. Legal Educ. 67 (1996): Takes a prophetic look at clinical legal education in 2010; observes the virtual demise of in-house clinics and their replacement by externships and simulation along with the almost complete shift of professional responsibility teaching into skills courses; the author's primary prognostication error was not to choose a date far enough in the future so that he will not be alive then.

Howard L. Oleck, *The Pompous Professions*, 18 Clev.-Marshall L. Rev. 276 (1969): Discusses pomposity in the learned professions; focuses on the pompousness of law faculty and deans such as the professor who has actually published a book rather than a "mere" law review article; concludes that a professor who is pompous and arrogant cannot be all bad if the students study hard; does not reach the question of whether it is pompous *per se* to write an article about pomposity.

William L. Prosser, *Needlemann on Mortgages*, 9 J. Legal Educ. 489 (1957): Tells the tale of a library prank when some work-study students made up a fictitious book about a law school course that was giving students fits; they started some word-of-mouth that the book was the answer to a student's prayers and then faked the record that the only copy was checked out and not returned; all hell breaks loose around the law school; anyone who has spent any time at a law school will have a hard time believing that this was not based on a true story; if it is not true, it should be.

Gail Levin Richmond & Carol A. Roehrenbeck, *From Tedious to Trendy: A Tax Teacher's Triumph*, 17 Nova L. Rev. 739 (1993): A script of a play that tells the story of two third year law students planning to graduate and improve the quality of education at their law school by making the faculty and instruction less boring; portrays the students creating a new syllabus for Income Tax entitled "Tax Styles of the Rich and Famous"; the denouement is that the boring professor receives tenure based on outstanding teacher evaluations as a result of the changes recommended by the third year students; never happen — on many levels.

Michael L. Richmond & Robert M. Jarvis, *An Exemplar for Peer Evaluation*, 14 J. LEGAL PROF. 21 (1989): Reproduces a report to the faculty recommending a colleague still be awarded tenure, although the candidate died in the interim, a fact the report concludes might affect his future scholarship but not his teaching; gives new meaning to the problem of academic deadwood.

Marc Rohr, *Socrates' Class: A One-Act Play*, 17 NOVA L. REV. 839 (1993): A one-act play in which a student on his way to law school is transported via tornado to ancient Greece where he finds himself in Socrates' "Greek Jur." class and strikes up a conversation with classmates Plato, Aquarius, and Zorba; after much questioning by Socrates about how to solve the riddle of the mysterious law student, the scene concludes with the law student choosing to remain in Athens to assume the role of a god; in real life he would want to become an Article III judge.

Harold See, *Criteria for the Evaluation of Law School Examination Papers*, 38 J. LEGAL EDUC. 361 (1988): Outlines fair grading criteria from the student's point of view; suggests that legal analysis should receive a half point and writing "I enjoyed the class" at the end of the blue book examination should increase the final grade a full letter grade; the flaw in this Article may well be that it reasons from a false premise that grading has any criteria, real or imagined.

Marshall S. Shapo, *Propositions of Opposition: A Guide for Faculty Members Engaged in the Assessment of Prospective and Present Colleagues*, 37 J. LEGAL EDUC. 364 (1987): Reduces the commitment of time and energy in such matters to an absolute minimum; provides a checklist of humanity, at least the subcategory of humanity that populates law school faculties; provides pairs of moves and countermoves for all candidates and all circumstances; a labor-saving device for the overwrought law professor; most law professors, however, are underwrought.

Kevin H. Smith, *How to Become a Law Professor Without Really Trying: A Critical, Heuristic, Deconstructionist, and Hermeneutical Exploration of Avoiding the Drudgery Associated with Actually Working as an Attorney*, 47 U. KAN. L. REV. 139 (1998): Provides a vantage on the decision-making and dedication that goes into an academic career; provides the reader with a self-testing quiz on "should you become a law professor?"; discusses the qualifications for gaining employment; details the application and interview process; explains that achieving tenure, inter alia, "requires that you prove yourself adept enough at the Byzantine politics of academia to still have a sufficient number of faculty members willing to vote for you after five to seven years"; regrettably, the Article was undone by the asterisk footnote disclaimers that colleagues not hold this Article against the author and that being a law professor "is the greatest job in the world."

Grant M. Sumsion, Comment, *Reflections of a 3L—A Thought Piece*, 1992 BYU L. Rev. 549: Attempts to dispel the "miserable myth" that law school is a miserable experience by explaining year-by-year the events and situations encountered in law school; argues we should understand law school for what it is, something beyond our control that is "annoying, frustrating, and at times downright heartbreaking"; the glass *is* half-empty *and* half-full; it does not take an Einstein to understand that if $E=MC^2$, then just as surely $C=JD$.

Oren S. Tasini, *Concise Guide to Surviving the First Year of Law School*, 17 Nova L. Rev. 849 (1993): Provides a week-by-week guide to new law students for making it through the first semester; includes tips like pick the right people for your study group or your life may become a living hell, avoid dating a fellow first-year law student so as to avoid having pillow talk about federal diversity jurisdiction, and realize that the light at the end of the tunnel is a freight train called finals.

Gerald F. Uelmen, *Id.*, 1992 BYU L. Rev. 335: Analyzes the decline in technique of the art of invective by lawyers; proposes to increase civility in name-calling by lawyers through a course taught in law school which would increase the students' vocabulary; includes sample final exam in this great tradition of the American bar, i.e., the legal profession, not saloons and taverns.

Eugene Volokh, *Hum a Few Bar Exam*, 2 Green Bag 2d 125 (1998): Sets out a new, more melodious version of the bar exam; a sample question in environmental law would be: "Big wheel keeps on turning; Proud Mary keeps on burning (or "boining"). What is the maximum level of particulate emissions Proud Mary may put out?"; postmodernism meets the bar examiners; the bar examiners meet postmodernism.

D. Robert White, *Getting into the Right Law School ("My Roommate the Moonie Scored in the 98th Percentile on the LSAT and Got into Harvard. Why Didn't I?")*, 17 Nova L. Rev. 979 (1993): Provides commentary on the vaunted LSAT; offers strategies for success such as be familiar with the style of questions and bring a good supply of anti-diuretics; poses mock exam questions to mock the exam questions.

Uncle Zeb, *The Best of Zeb 1995–1998*, Craig Broscow ed., THE GREEN BAG (1999), *available at* http://www.greenbag.org/Zeb.pdf: Compiles witty advice column responses to letters from law students on topics such as "romance," "current events," "jobs," "fighting the law school blues," and "the inexplicable and random"; responds to a question on how to know if one hates law school enough to drop out by opining: "You have been fooled into accepting the premise that unless you can prove otherwise you should stay in law school. The premise is the other way around. Why would any rational person stay here?"

Timothy R. Zinnecker, *"Dear Diary" Moments in the Semester of a UCC Law Professor*, 50 MERCER L. REV. 603 (1999): Diary entries divulge a semester's worth of high points, for example, writing the perfect final exam; as well as the low points, for example, the faculty approving a measure to exclude UCC-related articles from the definition of "scholarship" for the purposes of promotion, tenure, and retention; the last entry that describes comments on course evaluations are probably made up; probably.

IX. Legal Humor

Edward J. Bander, *A Survey of Legal Humor Books*, 19 SUFFOLK U. L. REV. 1065 (1985): Encourages law and literature professors to include humor in their courses; provides examples of legal humor through a survey of humorous legal pieces; the Godfather of law review humor.

Edward J. Bander, *Legal Humor Dissected*, 75 LAW LIBR. J. 289 (1982): Analyzes the types of legal humor; sources of legal humor; bibliography of works the author considers humorous; deserves part of the credit — or part of the blame — for inspiring this annotated bibliography.

Robert F. Blomquist, *Playing on Words: Judge Richard A. Posner's Appellate Opinions, 1981–82 — Ruminations on Sexy Judicial Opinion Style During an Extraordinary Rookie Season*, 68 U. CIN. L. REV. 651 (2000): Examines appellate judicial opinion writing styles; examines the method by which Judge Posner adds humor in his opinions; highlights several of the Judge's more humorous *bon mots*; cannot tell if the author was one of his law clerks or just has a lot of appeals in the Seventh Circuit; Judge Posner has written more books than some of us have read, but he is not exactly Jerry Seinfeld, or even Woody Allen.

Richard Delgado & Jean Stefancic, *Scorn*, 35 WM. & MARY L. REV. 1061 (1994): Analyzes the use of scornful humor by the Supreme Court both in opinions and oral arguments; argues that this type of humor is inappropriate for the Supreme Court and brings it to the verge of becoming an illegitimate institution; one could say the authors scorn scorn but they are seriously serious.

Patricia Ewick & Susan S. Sibley, *No Laughing Matter: Humor and Contradictions in Stories of Law*, 50 DePaul L. Rev. 559 (2000): Discusses and speculates on the meaning of humor and law by examining the stories people tell about law; shares highlights from interviews with over four hundred people; concludes that while people find the law funny, people rarely find humor in their first-hand experiences with the law; but legal humor is a laughing matter for a bibliographer of legal humor.

David A. Golden, Comment, *Humor, the Law, and Judge Kozinski's Greatest Hits*, 1992 BYU L. Rev. 507: Offers excerpts from some of Judge Alex Kozinski's opinions as an illustration that legal opinions can be witty and humorous while still articulating complex points of law; responds to critics who are labeled the "humor-impaired."

James D. Gordon III, *A Bibliography of Humor and the Law*, 1992 BYU L. Rev. 427: A complete bibliography of articles that are humorous and articles about legal humor; another worthy benefactor of this annotated bibliography.

Kenny Hegland, *Humor as the Enemy of Death, or Is It "Humor as the Enemy of Depth"?*, 1992 BYU L. Rev. 375: Responds to a request to write a humorous piece dealing with law and humor; proposes that serious/humorous dualism is a false dichotomy because each can communicate important matters, though they communicate differently; makes a passionate plea for more humor in legal writing that generally has gone unanswered; certainly it is beyond peradventure that law reviews are a laughing matter.

Adalberto Jordan, *Imagery, Humor, and the Judicial Opinion*, 41 U. Miami L. Rev. 693 (1987): Favors the discreet use of imagery and humor in judicial opinions as a means of demystifying the law and making opinions more readable; defends creative judicial writing at least in theory; collects what the author regards as the best examples of judicial writing, focusing on the opinions of two contemporaries of humor on the United States Court of Appeals for the Fifth Circuit, Judge Irving Goldberg and Chief Judge John Brown; have quip and quill, will rue and rule.

J. Richard Neville, Comment, *Humorous Anecdotes of the Georgia Judiciary, 1884–1920*, 41 Mercer L. Rev. 655 (1990): Examines the Georgia Bar's practice of exchanging humorous stories at their bar meetings during the period 1884–1920; provides several examples of the many stories recorded at that time; focuses on the Georgia judiciary; relates a particularly interesting tale of a Georgia judge who stops court proceedings in order to flee from revenue officers; insists that humor is indispensable to the profession of law; good old…humor.

Elton B. Richey, Jr., Comment, *The Court Jesters*, 41 Mercer L. Rev. 663 (1990): Comments on how humor about the legal system and lawyer jokes help both the general public and those within the legal profession cope with too little or too much "justice" in "the system"; recognizes that most people's negative attitude about lawyers stems from the fact that "the law" prevents them from getting what they want; concludes that humor is necessary for both lawyers and nonlawyers—or laypersons—to deal with the ambiguous and complex nature of the legal system; maybe the profession should step back and realize that lawyer jokes are just jokes, not hate speech; if you cannot take a joke, if you have no sense of humor, then you should have gone to medical school.

Fred Rodell, *Goodbye to Law Reviews—Revisited*, 48 Va. L. Rev. 279 (1962): Again, explains why legal writing is "pretentious poppycock" on the 25th anniversary of the writing of *Goodbye to Law Reviews*; narrows the attack on the language used in legal writing; condemns the utilization of pretentious polysyllabic verbiage or, as he would prefer, the use of big fancy words; urges the use of plain and simple language in legal writing so that any legal piece could be published in a popular magazine; violates a solemn vow not ever to write in law reviews again.

Fred Rodell, *Goodbye to Law Reviews*, 23 Va. L. Rev. 38 (1936): Classic Article critiques legal writing, particularly law review writing; summarizes the problem with almost all legal writing to be its content and its style; criticizes overabundance of footnotes, lack of humor or creativity, and boring topics; comments on book review sections as the only redeeming part of the law reviews; ultimately labels law reviews "spinach" to invoke the classic cartoon from *The New Yorker*; makes a solemn vow not ever to write in law reviews again.

Marshall Rudolph, Note, *Judicial Humor: A Laughing Matter*, 41 Hastings L.J. 175 (1989): Disapproves of judicial humor in the courtroom and in judicial opinions; agrees with the decision in *In re Rome*, 542 P.2d 676 (Kan. 1975), censuring a judge's misguided attempts at humor as judicial misconduct; maintains that judicial humor is neither judicial nor humorous; concludes with a proposed amendment to the *ABA Code of Judicial Conduct* that would make judicial humor subjecting litigants to ridicule a violation; a serious article about a very serious subject—humor.

George Rose Smith, *A Critique of Judicial Humor*, 43 ARK. L. REV. 1 (1990): Considers when humor might be appropriate in judicial decisions; suggests that humor be brief and relevant to the occasion; reminds readers that poetry, puns, and subtitles may not be funny in the first place, and may well be inappropriate in some places; one wonders what the author would say about this annotated bibliography.

X. Legal Scholarship

Arthur Austin, *The Top Ten Politically Correct Law Reviews*, 1994 UTAH L. REV. 1319: Ranks the Top Ten Politically Correct Law Reviews based on criteria including dedication to critical race theory, feminism, critical legal studies, and deconstruction; tracks the development of political correctness at several major law reviews including as Numero Uno the *Cardozo Law Review*, and finishing off the top ten, the *Harvard Law Review*; identifies politically correct scholarship to be based upon "empathy, emotions, and life experiences"; written by a Case Western Reserve professor and published in the *Utah Law Review* without empathy, emotions, or experience at being PC.

Arthur D. Austin, *Why Haven't the Crits Deconstructed Footnotes?*, 17 NOVA L. REV. 725 (1993): Posits that footnotes, like crits, women, minorities, and the homeless, are oppressed; applies the deconstructionist technique to challenge the privilege of the text and the marginalization of footnotes; compares the patriarchal nature of the text with the nurturing and empathic qualities of footnotes; recommends a Jacques Derrida double-column presentation so that the text and the footnotes would appear and be viewed side-by-side; Jacques Derrida is funnier than Jacques Cousteau, but then, the French think Jerry Lewis is funny.

Arthur D. Austin, *Footnote Skulduggery and Other Bad Habits*, 44 U. MIAMI L. REV. 1009 (1990): Offers advice to forlorn student editors of law reviews on the nuances and tactics of footnoting; remarks that "discerning, intelligent—or unethical—manipulation of footnotes can be a significant factor in achieving promotion, tenure, and status"; remarks on the importance of quantity and density in footnote writing; describes several types of footnotes including the titillating note, the non-verifiable note, the ideological note, and self-citation; waits until footnote two to cite to the author's own previous work.

Arthur D. Austin, *The "Custom of Vetting" as a Substitute for Peer Review*, 32 ARIZ. L. REV. 1 (1990): Discusses and critiques the practice of publicly vetting law review articles (sharing them with colleagues and crediting the reviewers); explores the dichotomy between academics and vocationalists; refers to the role of student editors in screening faculty publications as legal education's "family skeleton"; advocates private vetting among close associates rather than the now-too-common asterisk footnote listing and thanking every fancy professor at every fancy law school, living and dead.

Arthur D. Austin, *Footnotes as Product Differentiation*, 40 VAND. L. REV. 1131 (1987): Describes a strategy for using footnotes to "grease the path to promotion and tenure"; includes commentary on how to craft footnotes to differentiate an article for the competition; covers types, styles, and trends in footnoting; contains a respectable footnote count of 107 notes spread over twenty-four pages.

Randy T. Austin, Comment, *Better Off with the Reasonable Man Dead or the Reasonable Man Did the Darndest Things*, 1992 BYU L. REV. 479: Discusses the replacement of the Reasonable Man by the Reasonable Person in order to have gender-neutral language; chronicles what the Reasonable Person knows or should know and what the Reasonable Person has done and has not done, all through footnoted cites to cases.

Thomas E. Baker, *Tyrannous Lex*, 82 IOWA L. REV. 689 (1997): The author attempts to measure the amount of law the United States produces in one year, the Gross Legal Product or GLP; the measurements of legal scholarship observe that "law reviews are to law what masturbation is to sex"; obviously could only be written by a well-published and thrice-tenured professor; absolutely the last humorous entry by this author, until this annotated bibliography eventually is published.

J.M. Balkin & Sanford Levinson, *How to Win Cites and Influence People*, 71 CHI.-KENT L. REV. 843 (1996): Provides a cynical commentary regarding Fred Shapiro's *The Most-Cited Law Review Articles*, 73 CAL. L. REV. 1540 (1985); offers advice on how to become one of the most-cited members of the legal community in the form of ten maxims; the maxims include such career advice as: Make sure you attend Harvard, Yale, or the University of Chicago law schools, publish all of your articles in the law reviews from these schools, and then get a tenure-track appointment at one of these schools; encourages writing articles on the ubiquitous Fourteenth Amendment as well as on subjects that students will want to cite; tentatively suggests that Shapiro's work has connections to "garbology"; we are all waiting for the sequel about law professors who love non-elite law reviews too much.

C. Steven Bradford, *As I Lay Writing: How to Write Law Review Articles for Fun and Profit*, 44 J. LEGAL EDUC. 13 (1994): Provides advice for faculty on how to publish a law review article; gives a step-by-step process for achieving publishing success; includes pointers on satisfying the critical legal studies movement, the law and economics crowd, and the radical feminists; encourages self-citation, the use of quality footnotes, and the use of complex jargon to sufficiently confuse and impress the audience; offers strategies for the submission and editing processes; the topic of how to write law review articles is not preempted by this Article.

John F. Bramfeld, *Love Those Law Reviews*, 5 SCRIBES J. LEGAL WRITING 101 (1994–1995): Reproduces a pointed and humorous letter critiquing articles in a law review; remarks on the poor writing and editing of three articles; sarcastically expresses dismay that the third article actually cited a case; law reviews do not give money-back guarantees.

Craig Brownlie, Note, *Marxism and Critical Legal Theory: Why Groucho?*, 17 NOVA L. REV. 921 (1993): Reveals the relationship between the Critical Legal Studies proponents, "the Critters," and the legal theory of Groucho Marx; examines Marx's thoughts on trial work, contracts, and the practice of law; recounts uses of Marx's quips in legal opinions and writings; Marxism never had it so good.

Richard B. Cappalli, *The 1990 Rose Awards: The Good, the Bad, and the Ugly — Titles for Law Review Articles*, 41 J. LEGAL EDUC. 485 (1991): Recognizes the best titles of law review articles; the "I Can't Wait to Curl Up With This Award" goes to Robert A. King, *The Tax Treatment of Boot Distributions in Corporate Reorganizations Under Section 356(a)(2) — Commissioner v. Clark, the Latest or the Last Word?*, 11 WHITTIER L. REV. 723 (1990); the NCAA's Bowl Championship Series replaced this one-time annual award.

W. Lawrence Church, *A Plea for Readable Law Review Articles*, 1989 WIS. L. REV. 739: Bemoans the current state of law review writing; observes the detrimental effects of increasingly numerous and complex footnotes; remarks that "the expression of ideas is a joy that attracts many to the academic world. Larding up the product with several hundred footnotes is usually less thrilling"; suggests possible reforms; sadly for this author, the thrill is gone from the pages of law reviews, the thrill is gone.

Anthony D'Amato, *Brave New Scholarship*, 49 J. LEGAL EDUC. 143 (1999): Replicates the online template at lawarticle.com which allows a user to set parameters (whatever those are) for an article mill to ghostwrite the article for a fee; use the secure credit card payment option; double-click on plagiarism.

Anthony D'Amato, *As Gregor Samsa Awoke One Morning from Uneasy Dreams He Found Himself Transformed into an Economic Analyst of Law*, 83 Nw. U. L. REV. 1012 (1989): Tells a whimsical fable in which a law professor wakes up one morning as an "enormous Economic Analyst of the Law," closets himself in his bedroom where he churns out a book a day on Economics and a different law topic for his breakfast, makes his family rich, and then gets appointed a federal judge; this Article speaks to that profound existentialist question: "[W]as he then a law clerk thinking he was a judge or is he now a judge thinking he is a law clerk?"

Richard Delgado & John Kidwell, *Recent Developments in Legal Theory: How to Compare Apples and Oranges*, 7 CONST. COMMENT. 209 (1990): Proposes that new advances in legal thinking will aid in the age-old problem of comparing two dissimilar things, e.g., that of apples and oranges; outlines four approaches: Law and Economics—assign a value to each fruit; Feminism—no fair comparison until elimination of patriarchy; Critical Legal Studies—comprised of sub-schools like the irrationalist (no "core" value to fruit); and Law and Literature—approach the comparison through great texts, e.g., the Bible where the use of the apple by the Serpent may reflect that apples are more tempting than oranges.

Lance Dickson, *Forewords and Afterwords*, 5 SCRIBES J. LEGAL WRITING 141 (1994–1995): Describes humorous misspellings of "foreword" in various publications; recounts actual misuses of the words "forward" and "foreward" in place of the proper "foreword"; looking forward to the next foreword from this author.

Robert A. Emery, *The Albany Law School Journal: The Only Surviving Copy*, 89 LAW LIBR. J. 463 (1997): Excerpts from the first student-edited law review in 1875; provides insight into the life of a 19th century law school student; this just may be fictional law office history.

Daniel A. Farber, *The Deconstructed Grocery List*, 7 CONST. COMMENT. 213 (1990): Describes a law professor working on his tenure piece as being so immersed in theories of constitutional interpretation that he cannot fill a simple late night grocery shopping list; applying the various theories to the task of shopping so confuses the professor that he cannot decide whether a tomato is really a tomato or whether he should buy pasta as a substitute for tuna; unlike law professors, shoppers should take themselves and how they shop quite seriously.

Daniel A. Farber, *Brilliance Revisited*, 72 MINN. L. REV. 367 (1987): Adopts a somewhat more serious tone than the self-described "elliptical, humorous style" of the article on "brilliance" that is the subject of Farber's *The Case Against Brilliance*, 70 MINN. L. REV. 917 (1986); responds to criticisms of that earlier essay; conveys the message that legal scholars take themselves and what they do way too seriously; no way; way.

Daniel A. Farber, *Post-Modern Dental Studies*, 4 CONST. COMMENT. 219 (1987): Provides a sarcastic commentary on the evolution of the different legal schools of thought; analogizes legal schools of thought to dental schools of thought; examples include: Dental Formalism, Dentistry and Economics, Critical Dental Studies, and Dentistry and Literature; concludes with the thought that the future for dental scholars is bright, but fortunately fluoridation has greatly reduced the need for dentists; lawyer jokes have greatly reduced the desire for lawyers, as well.

Daniel A. Farber, *The Case Against Brilliance*, 70 MINN. L. REV. 917 (1986): Develops the thesis that in law and economics a brilliant theory (novel and unconventional) is invalid because it is brilliant; posits that in economics, a true theory would already have been discovered, while an undiscovered (and thus brilliant) theory is likely false for that very reason; argues that in law, a brilliant theory is suspect because it never would have occurred to the author of the judicial opinion on which it is based; in constitutional law, which is based on the consent of the governed, for example, what does it suggest about a theory of the Constitution of 1787 that it first occurred to a fancy law professor at a fancy law school in the 21st century?

Peter Gabel & Duncan Kennedy, *Roll Over Beethoven*, 36 STAN. L. REV. 1 (1984): Details the dialogue between Harvard Professor Duncan Kennedy and New College of California School of Law Professor Peter Gabel; presents the discussion of concepts such as "interstitial character," "unalienated relatedness," "phenomenological description," and "intersubjective zap"; this Article must be deconstructed as being humorous in order to be included in this bibliography, but the ultimate meaning and humor of a text is in the reader — not the text — or something.

Gresham's Law of Legal Scholarship, 3 CONST. COMMENT. 307 (1986): Uses the law and the theory of adverse selection to explain the lack of thoughtful and sensible articles published in law reviews; we can all take heart in the observation that the law professorate could not possibly be as silly as reading the law review literature might suggest.

Erik M. Jensen, *The Shortest Article in Law Review History*, 50 J. LEGAL EDUC. 156 (2000): Purports to be the shortest law review piece in history; consists entirely of the words "This is it."; justifies its length by claiming no less substantive content than any other law review article; discourages competitors in brevity by heralding the drafting of an "Abridged Version."

Erik M. Jensen, *Dean Breck*, 2 GREEN BAG 2D 395 (1999): Tells a tragic tale of the aftermath of publishing a humorous law review article; chronicles a professor's quixotic quest to become a dean; fails to answer the question why anyone would want to be a dean; seriously—or humorously—why would anyone want to be a dean?

Erik M. Jensen, *The Unwritten Article*, 17 NOVA L. REV. 785 (1993): "[*sic*]."

Erik M. Jensen, *A Call for a New Buffalo Law Scholarship*, 38 U. KAN. L. REV. 433 (1990): Offers a pun-filled dissertation on buffalo law; reveals the author's dismay at finding no articles treating buffalo law in the *Buffalo Law Review*, and his attempt to "fill the void" with this piece; uses innumerable plays on words, proposes to form a "new buffalo scholarship" replete with buffalo schools of thought, e.g., feminist buffalo studies and critical buffalo legal studies; wherever Dorothy and Toto are now, this Article will always be in Kansas.

Cameron Johnston & Moses Torts, *A Twenty-Fifth Anniversary Special: The Law from Moses Forward*, 25 S.D. L. REV. 208 (1980): Collects eight legal fables that tell the story of a diverse but familiar group of attorneys; includes moral lessons; Aesop, Esq.

Herma Hill Kay, *In Defense of Footnotes*, 32 ARIZ. L. REV. 419 (1990): Defends footnotes in the new era of "citation analysts" as the really important part of law review articles where citation of one's work (in someone else's article, not one's own) is a measure of one's worth as a scholar; boldly provides an article of footnotes followed by an article of the accompanying text; includes an article with nine suppressed footnotes; something definitely is being suppressed here.

J.T. Knight, *Humor and the Law*, 1993 WIS. L. REV. 897: Discusses the dearth of humor in law review articles as compared to other areas of law where humor abounds; argues that law and humor are not mutually exclusive; concludes that the benefits of using humor in law review articles outweigh the risks; this author favors funnier law review writing, not funnier law review reading, mind you.

Alex Kozinski & Eugene Volokh, *Lawsuit Shmawsuit*, 103 YALE L.J. 463 (1993): Chronicles the increasing use of Yiddish in legal writing; how do you spell "*chutzpah*"?

Wayne R. LaFave, *Surfing and Scholarship: The Emerging Critical Cyberspace Studies Movement*, 84 GEO. L.J. 521 (1996): Presents a mundane analysis of the exclusionary rule and the protections of the Fourth Amendment as shown in *Mapp v. Ohio*, 367 U.S. 643 (1961); accompanies the text with a witty array of footnotes referencing sites and sources on the Internet; includes references to Internet resources for insights on traveling in Ohio, learning more information about Cosmo Kramer, finding the Constitution online, and locating Snoopy's homepage; provides a humorous critique of the Internet in legal research by a distinguished scholar who is old enough to know better.

Ronald B. Lansing, *The Creative Bridge Between Authors and Editors*, 45 MD. L. REV. 241 (1986): Urges the National Conference of Law Reviews to encourage creative writing and innovative style; offers a law review version of the nursery rhyme "Humpty Dumpty" with accompanying footnotes; expresses grateful gratitude that Shakespeare did not use footnotes; "'To be (see generally Aristotle's Metaphysica) or not to be (see generally Nietzsche's Nihilism); that is the question (for examples of questions see LSAT or Multi-State Bar Exam).'"

Kenneth Lasson, *Scholarship Amok: Excesses in the Pursuit of Truth and Tenure*, 103 HARV. L. REV. 926 (1990): Provides pointed commentary on the system of legal scholarship; suggests that the system of legal education is profoundly askew to value publication for tenure over classroom teaching and public service; critiques the current state of legal research, analysis, and writing; suggests that scholarship is often "inalterably bound up in politics."

Andrew J. McClurg, *The World's Greatest Law Review Article for Anyone Taking Life Too Seriously*, 81 OCT. A.B.A. J. 84 (1995): Written for anyone who lives by *The Bluebook*; an over-the-top piece of satire of a law review article that begins: "This [FN1] is [FN2] the [FN3] world's [FN4] greatest [FN5] law [FN6] review [FN7] article. [FN8]."

Patrick M. McFadden, *Fundamental Principles of American Law*, 85 CAL. L. REV. 1749 (1997): Undertakes the task of providing authority for "statements that are obviously true or completely unsupportable"; attempts to include almost every such statement within the text of a single article to alleviate the difficulty of searching for authority for the obvious; lists twelve obviously true and completely unsupportable statements about the world and the law, concluding with "[t]he sun rises in the east and sets in the west. It's always several hours later in Europe. Tomorrow is another day." Subsequently (as lawyers say when they mean "from now on"), anyone need only cite to this Article for these propositions; singing the blues, but following *The Bluebook*.

Maurice H. Merrill, *The Arkansawyer's Lament*, 10 Okla. L. Rev. 167 (1957): Poetically complains of the American Law Institute's unwillingness to draft Restatements that support real improvements in the law; proves there is a good reason there is no *Restatement of Poetry*.

Abner J. Mikva, *Goodbye to Footnotes*, 56 U. Colo. L. Rev. 647 (1985): Condemns the overuse of the footnote; eloquently makes the point that footnotes in judicial opinions have taken on a life of their own; e.g., footnote four in *United States v. Carolene Products Co.*, 304 U.S. 144, 152 (1938), when Justice Stone slipped a sea change into constitutional law beneath the line and in a case about skim milk; extols the elimination of footnotes or at the very least, the sparse use of them for citation to authority only; concludes, tongue-in-cheek, with a footnote-in-your-face.

Robert J. Morris, *The New (Legal) Devil's Dictionary*, 6 J. Contemp. L. 231 (1979): Lists over eighty legal terms and their definitions which the author suggests should be added to Ambrose Bierce's *The Devil's Dictionary*; for example, "Strict scrutiny, n. Voyeurism of a suspect class."

Cheryl B. Preston, *It Moves, Even If We Don't: A Reply to Arthur Austin, The Top Ten Politically Correct Law Reviews*, 63 Tenn. L. Rev. 735 (1996): Replies to Professor Austin's ranking of the "political correctness" of law reviews, which is annotated *supra*; criticizes Austin's ranking methods and traditional "white, male, and western" approach; as a result, the PC rating of the *Tennessee Law Review* increased dramatically; what are those orange and white checkerboarded end zones all about, anyway?

William L. Prosser, *Der Gegenverkehr des Wasserniedersinkens in der Nordlichen und der Sudlichen Hemisphare*, 51 Minn. L. Rev. 899 (1967): Describes frustration at the difficulty of acquiring modest amounts of requested grant monies to study worthwhile issues; proposes a grandiose project no foundation could refuse in which the noted Professor Prosser and twenty-five other distinguished law professors would charter a yacht to sail around the world to study the rotation and revolution of various bodies; e.g., the draining of water, the coiling of snakes, the movement of cocktail parties, the corkscrewing of pigs' tails, et cetera; but then what would Congress have left to do?

Ronald D. Rotunda, *Law Reviews—the Extreme Centrist Position*, 62 IND. L.J. 1 (1986): Provides commentary and critique on the state of law reviews; gives advice to student editors; remarks that new editors "become drunk with power" and encourages them "not to become too drunk"; does not reach the issue of drunk driving, which is a difficult question—do you drink and not drive or do you drive and not drink—the prudent answer must be a law professor's "it depends."

Robert E. Scott, *Twenty-Five Years Through the Virginia Law Review (with Gun and Camera)*, 87 VA. L. REV. 577 (2001): An amusing reminisce of the influence that a dean has over a law school's law review; replete with a three-act play; the received wisdom is that the best candidate for a deanship is someone who does not want to be a dean; that says it all about deans and deaning without saying anything about ships.

David L. Shapiro, *The Death of the Up-Down Distinction*, 36 STAN. L. REV. 465 (1984): Briefly deconstructs the up-down distinction; jabs a not-so-subtle barb at the pretentiousness of the Critical Legal Studies movement; it turns out that there is no "up" or "down," there is only there there; there there.

Patric M. Verrone, *Notes and Comments: A Law Review Article*, 17 NOVA L. REV. 733 (1993): Provides a generic law review article; mocks law review articles; has a good beat and easy to dance to, give it a "10."

J. Tim Willette, Note, *Memo of Masochism (Reflections on Legal Writing)*, 17 NOVA L. REV. 869 (1993): Provides insight and advice into the process of legal writing for first-year law students; focuses on writing the open memo; tracks the process from research to writing to waiting for the grade; offers humorous quotes on writing and the law throughout the piece; the student who spent all year writing a note about secured transactions that did not get published did not find this Note terribly amusing.

XI. Miscellany

Dave Barry, *Traffic Infraction, He Wrote*, 17 NOVA L. REV. 665 (1993): Humorously extols the virtues of the American system of justice in which "every accused person unless he has a name like 'Nicholas 'Nicky the Squid' Calamari' is considered innocent until such a time as his name is printed in the newspaper"; recounts the author's day in court following receipt of a traffic citation; includes the author's intended legal strategy—groveling.

Paul Finkelman, *Baseball and the Rule of Law*, 46 Clev. St. L. Rev. 239 (1998): Makes many connections between the game of baseball and the legal system; "Play ball!" meets "Sue the Bastards!"; one wonders if the author wishes he were a ballplayer rather than a law professor; one does not wonder if any ballplayer ever wishes he were a law professor.

Glen Freyer, *The Nebbish Letter*, 17 Nova L. Rev. 685 (1993): Imagines a letter of application from one Frank Nebbish to Ignatious Linkletter III, Jr., the hiring partner for a Washington, D.C. law firm; begins with Nebbish identifying himself as a twenty-second year associate; recounts Nebbish's experiences as an unwitting bankruptcy lawyer, "legal counsel for the maritally challenged" (divorce lawyer), a small claims court specialist, a civil litigator relegated to eighth chair at trials, as a public defender, and as a legal writing instructor; encourages Linkletter to seek references from his former clients by writing the prison directly; offers to pay for lunch in order to meet with the firm; enclosures listed are a resume and "naked pictures of your wife."

Hendrik Hartog, *Pigs and Positivism*, 1985 Wis. L. Rev. 899: Examines the law regarding swine in 18th century New York City; provides lessons on legal positivism and social custom while tracing the case of a pig-owning family and the mayor of the city; it turns out that George Orwell was wrong, pigs actually favor pluralism.

Paul D. Healey, *De Minimis Curat Lex: A Compendium of Legal Trivia*, 89 Law Libr. J. 55 (1997): Discusses sources for legal trivia; compiles 466 amusing legal trivia questions; divides trivia into categories such as "Famous Cases," "Lawyers and the Legal Profession," and "Literature and Entertainment"; poses such timeless interrogatories as, inter alia, "What current talk show host has a J.D.? Answer: Geraldo Rivera"; an excellent source of some sure-winning bar bets.

Paul Horowitz et. al., *The Law of Prime Numbers*, 68 N.Y.U. L. Rev. 185 (1993): Reveals the influential role mathematical prime numbers have had in the study and practice of law; matches prime numbers to many well-known cases and accompanying doctrines; "2 was the number of weeks turn-of-the-century Britons were required to use the Carbolic Smoke Ball in order to ward off influenza," "29 was the chapter of the Magna Carta from which was derived the concept of 'due process of law'"; the list goes on and on and on—that makes three "on's"—another prime number; Laurence Tribe was a mathematician before he went to law school.

James L. Huffman, *Chicken Law in an Eggshell: Part III — A Dissenting Note*, 16 ENVTL. L. 761 (1986): Discusses the field of chicken law and all its nuances; notes that fried chicken outlets seem to be the favored meeting place for criminals; examines several of the more notable chicken cases including *United States v. Causby*, 328 U.S. 256 (1946), the famous chicken takings case; strikes several blows, fair and fowl, for the chicken.

Robert M. Jarvis, *Legal Tales from Gilligan's Island*, 39 SANTA CLARA L. REV. 185 (1998): Provides the long-awaited definitive account of the jurisprudence of the television situation comedy to conclude that what the castaways really needed on the island was a good lawyer; "okay, now hypothesize a rubber raft."

Kenneth Karst, *Federal Jurisdiction Haiku*, 32 STAN. L. REV. 229 (1979): This UCLA law professor sponsors a haiku festival each year in his federal jurisdiction class; "with apologies to Basho, Buson, and Issa"; none of the poems answers the age-old question "is this going to be on the final exam?"

Legal Humor and Oddities, available at http://lawschool.westlaw.com/shared/marketInfoDisplay.asp?id=66&code=MI&site=site: lawschool.westlaw.com weekly series of humorous miscellany; proves that huge publishing monopolies *can* have a sense of humor.

Andrew J. McClurg, *Rungful Suits*, 83 JUNE A.B.A. J. 98 (1997): Discusses the ever-expanding area of product liability by examining ladder litigation; includes top ten common ladder mistakes, e.g., "there is no such thing as safe sex on a ladder"; reprints of this Article are packed and shipped with all ladders manufactured and sold by the Acme Company, which was the supplier of props for the Roadrunner cartoons.

M.C. Mirow & Bruce A. McGovern, *An Obituary of the Federal Estate Tax*, 43 ARIZ. L. REV. 625 (2001): Provides an account of the life and times — and the demise — of the Federal Estate Tax; ... *Requiescat in Tax.*

Paul Morris, *Dear Paul: Language Tips Questions and Answers*, 17 NOVA L. REV. 729 (1993): Recounts several question and answer exchanges regarding the use of the English language; includes questions on what does "plethora" mean, how should we pronounce all those French words that pop up in the law, and what does it mean to "pole" the jury; in response to the latter, the author replies that unless what was meant was "poll" the jury, then there were likely some very surprised jury members.

Gretchen Craft Rubin & Jamie G. Heller, *Restatement of Love (Tentative Draft)*, 104 YALE L.J. 707 (1994): Argues for a codification of the principles of love "premised on the view that love, like all other aspects of human interaction, can be subjected profitably to legal analysis"; includes a survey of the three principal models under which relationships begin—the blind date model, the informal acquaintance model, or the aggravating circumstances model; includes none-too-realistic illustrations; the authors are looking for love in all the wrong places, or else they have never attended a meeting of the American Law Institute.

Louis J. Sirico, Jr., *Future Interest Haiku*, 67 N.C. L. Rev. 171 (1988): Presents haiku from famous cases such as *Shelley's Case*, 76 Eng. Rep. 206 (1551); but can there be an English-speaking haiku?; what sound does it make?; just how much future interest will there be in future interest haiku?; why do law schools teach property law as medieval real estate transactions anyway?

Louis J. Sirico, Jr., *Supreme Court Haiku*, 61 N.Y.U. L. Rev. 1224 (1986): Demonstrates how Supreme Court opinions evoke haiku moments; transcribes six Supreme Court opinions into haikus that seek to transcend the intellect; but nothing rhymes with Nino.

Gerald F. Uelmen, *The Care and Feeding of TV Court Critics*, 17 Nova L. Rev. 825 (1993): Collects amusing comments on the history of critics of the courts from Mark Twain to modern Court TV; speculates on the advances in presentation and strategy that will be demanded by playing to both juries and TV audiences; provides examples of rhymes and lyrics that judges and attorneys alike might employ on Court TV; inquiring minds want to know.

Alexander Volokh, *n Guilty Men*, 146 U. Pa. L. Rev. 173 (1997): Examines the "Blackstone ratio" that it is better that ten guilty persons escape, than that one innocent person suffer; remarks that *n*, the number of guilty persons, changes often; traces the history of *n*; just *who* is *n*—and even better for *whom*?

Charles M. Yablon, *Judicial Drag: An Essay on Wigs, Robes and Judicial Change*, 1995 Wis. L. Rev. 1129: Analyzes the legal system by using legal fashion as a looking glass; traces the history of wigs and robes in the legal system and offers conjecture to explain their continued usage; concludes that both "English judges and Batman use their costumes to hide their 'secret identity,' which is, in fact, their ordinary everyday identity"; the Lord Chancellor in Gilbert & Sullivan's operetta *Iolanthe* has nothing on Chief Justice Rehnquist.

About the Compilers

Robert M. Jarvis (jarvisb@nsu.law.nova.edu) is a member of the faculty at Nova Southeastern University Law Center in Fort Lauderdale, where he teaches Admiralty, Florida Constitutional Law, and Gaming Law. When not pursuing more serious projects, Professor Jarvis keeps busy chronicling the goings-on at East Overshoe State University, a dysfunctional institution that bears an uncanny resemblance to a number of actual law schools. His most recent account is *East Overshoe State at the Trading Deadline*, 27 Legal Studies Forum 369 (2003).

Thomas E. Baker (thomas.baker@fiu.edu) is a member of the founding faculty at the Florida International University College of Law in Miami, where he teaches Constitutional Law (Honors Section), Federal Courts, and First Amendment. He previously held the James Madison Chair in Constitutional Law at Drake University. As his bibliography in this volume amply demonstrates, Professor Baker takes himself very seriously but likes to make fun of others. This is his first—and last—book on legal humor.

Andrew J. McClurg (andrew.mcclurg@fiu.edu) is a member of the founding faculty at the Florida International University College of Law in Miami, where he teaches Intellectual Property, Products Liability, and Torts. He previously was the Nadine H. Baum Distinguished Professor of Law at the University of Arkansas at Little Rock. Professor McClurg is the former humor columnist for the *American Bar Association Journal*, creator of the award-winning legal humor web site lawhaha.com, and regularly performs "stand-up" for lawyer groups.